# Digital Revolution for the Vulnerable

Pranab Kumar Panday
A. H. M. Kamrul Ahsan

# Digital Revolution for the Vulnerable

## The Untold Story of Bangladesh's Social Safety Net Transformation

palgrave
macmillan

Pranab Kumar Panday
Department of Public Administration
University of Rajshahi
Rajshahi, Bangladesh

A. H. M. Kamrul Ahsan
Department of Public Administration
University of Rajshahi
Rajshahi, Bangladesh

ISBN 978-981-95-7979-2 ISBN 978-981-95-7980-8 (eBook)
https://doi.org/10.1007/978-981-95-7980-8



This Palgrave Macmillan imprint is published by the registered company Springer Nature Singapore Pte Ltd.
The registered company address is: 152 Beach Road, #21-01/04 Gateway East, Singapore 189721, Singapore

# Preface

We stand at an interesting and sometimes annoying point where technology and people meet. Countries worldwide are seeking to harness digital transformation to address some of the world's most significant and pressing problems. There are few areas as important or complicated as social security. It is where the promises of efficiency, openness, and inclusion meet the harsh facts of poverty, ignorance, and institutional inertia. The idea for this book, ***Digital Revolution for the Vulnerable: The Untold Story of Bangladesh's Social Safety Net Transformation***, stemmed from a strong desire to learn more about a groundbreaking experiment that is still ongoing in Bangladesh and to document it as soon as possible. At its core, it is a story about brave government change that challenges the decades-old practice of manual, paper-based, and often-hacked systems by giving the most vulnerable citizens direct access to the transformative power of digital cash transfers.

Bangladesh is a notable example of this phenomenon occurring globally, characterised by a large population, extensive bureaucracy, and an ambitious National Social Security Strategy (NSSS). Its move to digitise its huge Social Safety Net (SSN) programs is more than just a change in how things are run; it is a deep political and social statement about fairness, power, and government. A slow, paper-based, and middleman-driven method for sending essential funds for survival is replaced with a fast, trackable Government-to-Person (G2P) mobile money platform. This changes the whole environment of power, corruption, and trust. This is the first time that there is a straight line of responsibility between the state and the recipient. This book provides an in-depth examination of the consequences of this change: did it meet the promises of openness and efficiency? Most importantly, has it really helped those who need it the most get access to money and financial freedom?

It was not an easy decision for the government of Bangladesh to initiate this massive project. For decades, the SSN systems, which were crucial, had persistent problems. Leaks, shifting of funds, high overhead costs, and the infamous "middlemen"—local power brokers who often charged illegal fees, slowed down payments, and took advantage of recipients—harmed public trust and made poverty reduction efforts less effective. Digitalisation was seen as the answer: it would eliminate these middlemen, ensure payments were made on time, and establish a clear audit trail. Our study began with this hopeful idea, and we aimed to discover not only how the technology was utilised, but also how it impacted the lives of the people it was intended to help. We sought to determine whether the technology could truly dismantle the entrenched structures of patronage and corruption that had long hindered aid delivery—a question of immense weight for development practitioners globally. The quantitative data we gathered—showing that 97% of beneficiaries reported a decrease in access issues and 64% were "totally" free of intermediaries—confirm the system's ability to eliminate rent-seeking behaviour, thereby validating a core argument for digital transformation and aligning with the principles of efficient **governance**.

Yet, as with all true revolutions, the progress is not linear, and the full story is not purely one of technological triumph. While the achievement of greater efficiency and reduced leakage is undeniable, the narrative remains incomplete. How does a government ensure the benefits of digitalisation truly reach the **elderly, the illiterate, and women** in remote areas who may not own a mobile phone, lack reliable internet, or have the requisite digital skills to navigate an app? This is the **"untold story"** the title alludes to. It is the story beyond the clean data points and the aspirational policy documents. It is the human narrative of the **52% of recipients** who still rate their digital literacy as "very poor," and the plight of women whose newfound financial autonomy is complicated by deeply entrenched socio-cultural norms that force them to rely on a male relative to access their payments, thereby compromising their hard-won agency. The digital divide, we argue, is not merely an infrastructure gap; it is a profound chasm in *capability* and *empowerment* that technical fixes alone cannot solve. Understanding this chasm and proposing practical ways to bridge it is the central intellectual challenge of this book.

To navigate this complex reality, this book is structured as a comprehensive seven-chapter journey, moving logically from foundational theory to practical, evidence-based policy. **Chapter One: Introduction** serves as the vital starting point, framing the core research issue—the digitalisation of cash transfers—and clearly articulating our research questions, goals, and the relevance of this work within the broader worldwide movement towards digital social protection systems. It performs a critical analysis of the current literature, identifies existing empirical and theoretical gaps that justify this investigation, and meticulously outlines the **mixed-methods methodology** employed. This includes detailing the fusion of large-scale survey data from recipients and Union Parishad officials with rich qualitative interviews, ensuring that our findings are both statistically robust and contextually deep.

**Chapter Two: Framing the Digital Shift** is the intellectual core, dedicating itself to establishing the conceptual scaffolding for the entire investigation. Here, we present and develop three fundamental theoretical lenses. We employ Sen's Capability Approach to shift the focus from simple income transfer to the growth of individual freedoms and agency, arguing that true inclusion entails expanding recipients' *choices* over their financial resources. This is complemented by the **World Bank's Good Governance Framework**, which is used to anchor our analysis of transparency, accountability, and administrative efficiency—the key to the system's institutional success. Finally, we incorporate technology adoption theories, such as the Technology Acceptance Model (TAM) and the Diffusion of Innovations, to explain user behaviour, acceptance, and resistance to new digital interfaces. By clearly defining and operationalising key ideas such as financial inclusion and e-governance, this chapter ensures our empirical findings are interpreted through a robust, multidimensional framework, anchoring the entire study in established social and economic theory.

We then transition into the operational reality. **Chapter Three: Digital Cash Transfer Systems in Bangladesh's Social Safety Net Programs: An Overview** is a historical and institutional overview. This chapter meticulously charts the development and present landscape of digital cash transfer systems, examining the government's rationale for digitalisation and detailing the key projects, such as G2P payment systems and biometric authentication. Its main argument is that the success of the digital shift depends not just on software or hardware, but on the capacity and coordinated functions of a complex institutional framework involving ministries, banks, Mobile Financial Services (MFS) providers, and local government agencies. It specifically highlights early-stage issues related to digital infrastructure disparities and the inherent risks of exclusion in a fragmented regulatory environment.

The core empirical evaluation is presented in the subsequent two chapters. **Chapter Four: Measuring success** employs quantitative survey results and administrative data to evaluate the system's effectiveness on two critical axes: the beneficiaries' experience and administrative efficiency. Its central argument is that while digital transfers have significantly boosted *administrative efficiency* (as seen in lowered transaction costs and reduced scams, aligning with the Good Governance model), the success at the recipient *level* is more nuanced, complicated by disparities in ease of use, speed, and trust in the complaint mechanisms. We find that the ability to track payments in real-time bolsters confidence, but inconsistent internet access undermines dependability. By comparing Bangladesh's performance with systems in India and Brazil, we establish a global perspective on its achievements and shortcomings.

Building on these performance metrics, **Chapter Five: Enablers and Challenges** proceeds to a more in-depth diagnostic analysis. Its main argument is that the variance in implementation success is determined by four key environmental factors: **technological infrastructure** (e.g., uneven internet access and platform interoperability), **digital literacy** (e.g., low skills among older and female recipients), **governance methods** (e.g., institutional inertia and regulatory gaps), and the **socio-economic context** (e.g., gender dynamics and rural/urban divide). Our data, which revealed that only 33% of recipients own a mobile phone and that 40% of UP officials cite regional differences as a challenge, vividly illustrates how these factors either facilitate or fundamentally limit the application and ultimate impact of digital cash transfers, stressing that technological solutions must be accompanied by targeted social policy.

The intellectual convergence occurs in **Chapter Six: Discussion,** where findings are integrated with **theoretical perspectives**. This crucial chapter synthesises the practical lessons from the empirical chapters (Three to Five) using the theoretical tools developed earlier. Its core argument is a critical one: while digitalisation broadly supports the goals of **Good Governance** (transparency, accountability) by creating an audit trail, the realisation of **Capability Approach** goals (autonomy, empowerment) remains severely constrained by persistent challenges, such as the digital divide and low digital literacy. This chapter addresses unintended consequences, examining the tension between technocratic efficiency and the democratic ideal of inclusion, and cautions against the notion that technology alone can resolve political and social problems, instead urging stakeholders to prioritise institutional and human capacity gaps.

Finally, **Chapter Seven: Bridging the Gap** brings the entire investigation to a close. Its main argument is forward-looking: sustainable success requires a holistic strategy that combines technological refinement with targeted social interventions. The chapter synthesises the major findings—the notable reduction in corruption and timely access, countered by persistent digital illiteracy and infrastructure gaps—into a concrete, evidence-based roadmap. We offer practical policy suggestions for every stakeholder, from government agencies seeking to improve cross-agency coordination to development partners requiring targeted investments in digital infrastructure and literacy training. It concludes by positioning Bangladesh's experience as a vital case study, offering a practical yet critical guide for policymakers seeking to establish robust, inclusive digital safety nets across the Global South.

This research, both in its initial conceptualisation and in the demanding process of data collection across diverse geographical areas, benefited immeasurably from institutional support. The journey from a compelling hypothesis to a rigorous, published work requires not only dedication from the author but also strategic backing from institutions committed to generating real-world knowledge. My ability to conduct the essential initial fieldwork, engage with beneficiaries and officials, and undertake the preliminary data analysis was made possible through crucial financial assistance. I must, in closing, extend my deepest gratitude to the **Faculty of Social Science, University of Rajshahi, Bangladesh**, for providing the essential financial assistance that enabled the initial fieldwork and data analysis. Their unwavering commitment to supporting relevant, context-specific research on governance and development was instrumental in bringing this untold story to light, ensuring that the voices of the vulnerable in Bangladesh could be heard and analysed on the global stage.

Rajshahi, Bangladesh — Pranab Kumar Panday
Rajshahi, Bangladesh — A. H. M. Kamrul Ahsan

*Competing Interests* The authors have no competing interests to declare that are relevant to the content of this manuscript.

*Ethics Approval*: We took informed consent from all participants—explaining the study in plain language and making sure they knew they could withdraw any time before any interviews or focus group discussions.

# Contents

# Abbreviations and Acronyms

| | |
|---|---|
| ABD | Asian Development Bank |
| AI | Artificial Intelligence |
| BDT | Bangladeshi Currency |
| BISP | Benazir Income Support Program |
| BTRC | Bangladesh Telecommunication Regulatory Commission |
| DBT | Direct Benefit Transfer |
| DDLG | Deputy Director of Local Governance |
| DIT | Diffusion of Innovations Theory |
| EFT | Electronic Fund Transfer |
| EGPP | Employment Generation Program for the Poorest |
| FFW | Food for Work |
| G2P | Government-to-Person |
| GIS | Geographic Information Systems |
| GSMA | Global System for Mobile Communications |
| ICTs | Information and Communication Technologies |
| IFC | International Finance Corporation |
| IT | Information Technology |
| KIIs | Key Informant Interviews |
| MAP | Maternity Allowance Program |
| MFS | Mobile Financial Services |
| NGO | Non-governmental Organisation |
| NID | National Identification Document |
| NSSS | National Social Security Strategy |
| OAA | Old Age Allowance |
| PESP | Primary Education Stipend Program |
| PRSP | Poverty Reduction Strategy Papers |
| SDG | Sustainable Development Goal |

| | |
|---|---|
| SDGs | Sustainable Development Goals |
| SSN | Social Safety Net |
| TAM | Technology Acceptance Model |
| UNDP | United Nations Development Program |
| UNO | Upazila Nirbahi Officers |
| UP | Union Parishad(s) |
| US | United States |
| USSD | Unstructured Supplementary Service Data |
| UTAUT | Unified Theory of Acceptance and Use of Technology |
| VGD | Vulnerable Group Development |
| WHO | World Health Organisation |

# List of Tables

**Enablers and Challenges: Key Determinants Shaping Digital Cash Transfers in Bangladesh's Social Safety Net Programs**

# Introduction

**Abstract** By presenting the main emphasis of the research—digital cash transfers in Bangladesh's Social Safety Net (SSN) programs—this chapter sets the foundation for the book. Beginning with a background on the change from conventional to digital cash transfer systems, it emphasises the urgent need for more efficient, transparent, and inclusive welfare delivery systems. The chapter states the research goals, scope, and justification, stressing how digitisation fits with more general development concerns in Bangladesh, including the government's Digital Bangladesh agenda and international obligations to financial inclusion and poverty reduction. The chapter synthesises important national and worldwide literature, highlighting notable knowledge gaps on the efficacy and scalability of digital transfer systems in low-resource settings. It emphasises both the possibilities and limits of digital transitions in social protection, employing a critical analysis of international experiences set against Bangladesh's policy environment. This lays the groundwork for a more in-depth investigation of the operational, technological, and socio-political aspects of digital cash transfers. End with a thorough description of the book's qualitative approach—including its case study design, data collecting instruments (in-depth interviews, key informant interviews, and documentary analysis), and sampling strategy in Gaibandha District. Apart from setting the analytical path of the book, the chapter offers the intellectual and pragmatic rationale for investigating digital innovation in welfare delivery. Establishing



P. K. Panday, A. H. M. K. Ahsan, *Digital Revolution for the Vulnerable*, https://doi.org/10.1007/978-981-95-7980-8_1

the book's foundations enables this chapter to explore, read, and critique the effects and consequences of digitised SSN programs in Bangladesh in later chapters.

**Keywords** Digital cash transfers • Social Safety Net • Bangladesh • Digitisation • Welfare delivery • Financial inclusion

## 1 Introduction

Throughout the developing world, the digitalisation of cash transfers in Social Safety Net (SSN) initiatives has surfaced as a tool for poverty reduction, state-citizen interaction, and financial inclusion. In recent years, governments and development agencies have increasingly looked to digital technology as an efficiency tool and a strategic tool to reshape the interface between people and the state. At the core of this change is a fundamental promise: that technology can lower human discretion, minimise corruption, improve accountability, and make the welfare state more accessible and responsive to the needs of its most vulnerable citizens. Long-standing structural and operational inefficiencies in traditional Social safety net (SSN) delivery systems—from high administrative costs (often between 15% and 30% of total programme expenditures) to endemic leakages caused by corruption, political interference, and weak accountability mechanisms have historically undermined the effectiveness of poverty alleviation efforts (World Bank 2022). These constraints have had significant effects. For millions living on the fringes of society, errors in beneficiary lists, arbitrary exclusions, and payment delays have strengthened rather than broken cycles of poverty. In many cases, what was supposed to be a safety net turned into a new source of stress and neediness.

Acknowledging these systematic shortcomings, more and more nations—including Kenya, India, Nigeria, and the Philippines—have adopted digital payment systems, such as mobile money services and biometric authentication, to simplify delivery, enhance transparency, and lower transaction costs (GSMA 2022; Aker et al. 2016). These platforms have enabled more timely and secure payments and transparent doors for marginalised communities to access a larger range of formal financial services. By doing this, they have expanded the boundaries of what social protection can achieve in a digital government era. Having long been dedicated to social protection and poverty reduction, Bangladesh has become a remarkable example of this worldwide change. Running one of the most extensive SSN programs in the Global South, the Government of

Bangladesh covers roughly 35% of its population via more than 100 initiatives, including allowances for the elderly, widows, and people with disabilities; student stipends; and employment guarantee programs (Government of Bangladesh 2021). Digital payment systems—including bKash, Nagad, and Rocket—have been integrated into existing systems and have been crucial in reengineering how these programmes operate in recent years. Recent statistics show that digital transfers have lowered leakages from an estimated 20% in manual systems to under 5% while also speeding the speed of fund disbursement and lowering reliance on intermediary actors (Bangladesh Bank 2022).

However, despite these remarkable improvements, the road to a completely inclusive and accountable digital SSN system is far from finished. The fast technological change has highlighted and sometimes aggravated pre-existing inequalities. Digital literacy remains low in rural and peri-urban areas, where mobile and internet access are patchy, and infrastructure shortcomings persist. Lack of identification papers, mobile devices, or confidence in using digital tools creates significant obstacles for vulnerable groups—especially older women, people with disabilities, and ethnic minorities—in accessing mobile banking services (Aziz and Naima 2021a; Chowdhury et al. 2022a). Research indicates that about 35% of rural homes have consistent internet access; even fewer know how to interact meaningfully with digital platforms (BTRC 2023). These differences highlight fundamental issues regarding digital justice and the unintended consequences of rapid techno-managerial changes in vulnerable welfare settings. A timely contribution to this fast-changing policy and academic scene, *Digital Revolution for the Vulnerable: The Untold Story of Bangladesh's Social Safety Net Transformation*, this book aims to question the promises, contradictions, and effects of digitalising SSN delivery systems throughout Bangladesh. Although digital reforms have been widely praised, there is still a notable lack of grounded, context-sensitive, and empirically rich narratives highlighting the voices and experiences of those most impacted by these changes. This book fills that void.

The book's primary objective is to explain the structural and operational changes that digital technology has brought to SSN administration in Bangladesh. It aims to provide a thorough knowledge of how digitalisation has changed bureaucratic practices at both the national and local levels, altered fund distribution systems, and lowered transaction inefficiencies. The book's second goal is to investigate the socio-political, infrastructural, and institutional limits hindering the efficient use of digital delivery systems. It interacts with a critical question by stressing problems, including the digital divide, gendered barriers to technology, exclusion errors, and bureaucratic inertia: Can digital systems be inclusive in settings characterised by deep-rooted social inequality, political patronage, and institutional fragility?

Third, the book emphasises the lived experiences of SSN recipients. It highlights the voices of local officials, elderly pensioners, underprivileged ethnic groups, and rural women as they negotiate the digital environment. These stories seek to humanise what is sometimes regarded as a technical policy concern, thereby seizing digital welfare transformation's emotional, symbolic, and relational aspects. The book critically examines the governance and accountability structures supporting digital SSNs. Although technology might lower some kinds of corruption, it does not guarantee transparency or automatically eliminate rent-seeking. The book examines whether digitalisation can alter welfare governance without broader institutional changes by exploring the intersections of politics, technology, and administration. Ultimately, the book offers a series of forward-looking, empirically grounded policy suggestions. These are aimed at national and international audiences—governments, multilateral organisations, development practitioners, and academics—for those interested in creating fairer, user-centric, resilient welfare systems. The book contributes to a larger global discussion on the digital future of social protection, drawing on Bangladesh's experience and insights from other developing nations. ***Digital Revolution for the Vulnerable*** helps to clarify how technology is changing the welfare structure in the Global South by combining policy analysis, field insights, and personal testimonies. It contends that although digitalisation has great promise, one should approach it with humility, caution, and an unrelenting dedication to fairness. This book is about Bangladesh, but it is also useful for people globally. It gives both critical and positive recommendations for a time when governments all over the world are rethinking their social bonds in the age of technology.

## 2 From Cash to Code: Tracing the Digital Turn in Bangladesh's Social Safety Net

Bangladesh has undergone significant development over the last decade. For instance, the country has developed new ways to utilise digital technology to keep people secure. A key policy goal of this reform is to support the most vulnerable individuals in society and reduce poverty. In the past, social safety net (SSN) initiatives have cut down on systemic hazards, promoted social fairness, and directly aided poor people by giving them money. These programs are at the centre of Bangladesh's goal to cut down on poverty. It has been exceedingly difficult to obtain SSNs in the past due to bureaucratic hurdles, high administrative fees, financial mismanagement, and a lack of transparency and accountability (Rahman et al. 2011). These continuous structural flaws have made well-meaning attempts less successful, which has undermined people's faith in the government. The Bangladeshi government is slowly moving to digital tools to make it easier to transmit money since they know that old channels have problems. For assistance payments, systems like bKash, Nagad, and Rocket manage mobile banking, digital wallets, and electronic fund transfers (GoB 2015; Hossain 2022). These are new ways for the government to get connected to its people. These platforms offer numerous benefits, including reduced need for intermediaries, fewer instances of corruption, faster payment procedures, and greater accountability in general (Aziz 2020). The road to full automation is still full of obstacles, even with these reforms. People who live in rural areas still have huge challenges, such as not having enough computers and other digital tools, and not knowing how to utilise them correctly. It is extremely tough to utilise digital SSN systems well when there are problems with the infrastructure and the government is not paying close attention, especially in rural or disadvantaged areas (Gentilini 2022).

Digital cash transfer has changed the way social safety operates in countries like Kenya and India. People all around the globe have commended India's Direct Benefit Transfer (DBT) system, which is based on the Aadhaar biometric platform, for making service delivery better and cutting down on leaks (Bold et al. 2012). M-Pesa has made it possible for people with low incomes in Kenya to get cheap, clear financial services (Jack and Suri 2014). These case studies from around the world demonstrate the importance of addressing social, economic, and structural inequalities to ensure that everyone can access digital services. Bangladesh has achieved positive results from pilot experiments, such as the "Amar Account" plan and other digital testing within larger SSN systems. They have made it simpler for persons who are poor or on the outside to access benefits and have promoted financial inclusion (Siddiquee et al. 2022). The wider picture is still hard to understand because of problems with systemic governance, such as political favouritism, corruption, and a lack of resources in functioning agencies (Alam and Hossain 2016). If robust institutional protections and transparent monitoring mechanisms are not put in place, these elements might make the advantages of digitisation less meaningful.

In light of this, the purpose of this book is to offer a thorough and fact-based evaluation of the digital change in Bangladesh's SSN setting. Studies nowadays are mostly about the practical or technical sides of digital transfers. However, not as much has been said about the daily lives of the people who get the benefits, as well as the social and political variables that determine how programs are operated and what they do. This study fills that gap by taking a close look at how well and how efficiently digital cash transfer systems work in Bangladesh, as well as how inclusive, scalable, and long-lasting they are. The book adds to the growing discussion about digital financial inclusion and reforming social protection by focusing on the views of those who receive welfare and looking into both the pros and cons of digitalising welfare services. The goal is to provide foreign development actors, practitioners, and policymakers with valuable insights for enhancing digital governance in Bangladesh and the broader developing world, making it more equitable, resilient, and focused on the people.

## 3 Contextualising the Discourse

During the past two decades, Social Safety Net (SSN) programs have become the primary policy tools for poverty alleviation and inclusive development across the Global South. Digital technologies are being increasingly integrated into social protection systems as governments work to shield the most vulnerable people from economic shocks and systemic inequities. These developments promise to reconfigure service delivery—streamlining payment systems, lowering leakages, and extending state welfare to underprivileged areas. The roads to effective execution, however, are still uneven, and context is quite important. Around the world, countries like Kenya and India have come to represent digital transformation in SSN delivery. Kenya's M-Pesa system changed mobile money by making it possible to send money quickly, safely, and from anywhere, even in remote areas. This made it much easier for impoverished people in rural areas to get access to financial services. India's Direct Benefit Transfer (DBT) system, which is linked to the Aadhaar biometric identity database, has also reduced leakage and made it easier to hold individuals accountable for the distribution of benefits (Khera 2017). These examples show how digital

SSNs might make things more open, efficient, and inclusive, especially if there is strong political intent and good digital infrastructure.

The world has grown, but it has also proven that there are huge challenges that make it impossible for everyone to benefit from digital advantages. Studies in Sub-Saharan Africa indicate that insufficient internet connection, limited digital literacy, and socio-economic marginalisation often marginalise the individuals whom SSNs want to empower (Aker et al. 2016). Though programs like Bolsa Família and Prospera have changed in conditional cash transfers, their digitisation has run into issues, including bureaucratic bottlenecks and corruption in Latin America (Banerji and Gentilini 2013). Furthermore, the World Bank (2020a) underlined that although digital platforms can provide doors to larger financial ecosystems—thereby allowing access to credit, insurance, and savings—successful implementation relies on whether these technologies are socially inclusive and contextually adapted.

Historically, SSN initiatives have been quite important in poverty reduction in Bangladesh. Programs like the Old Age Allowance, the Allowances for the Widow, the Allowances for Deserted and Destitute Women, and Vulnerable Group Development (VGD) have been very helpful to marginalised groups. Still, these traditional programs have had problems with inefficiency for a long time, with things like wrong targeting, late payments, and problems with administration and leadership. These problems are especially pronounced in rural areas, where political favouritism, lack of control, and weak institutions hinder the distribution of resources fairly and effectively. To fix these problems, Bangladesh has started using digital methods to send and receive cash as part of its bigger G2P (Government-to-Person) project. Mobile banking apps like BKash, Nagad, and Rocket have made a big difference in how aid is delivered. With these tools, individuals who are supposed to receive money can do so directly, eliminating the need for middlemen and reducing the risk of fraud. According to Bangladesh Bank (2022), automation efforts have cut costs and sped up payments. Still, some people do not want the change to happen. Haider and Mahamud (2017) say that rural recipients, who are often poor, old, and not very good with technology, have a hard time getting to these services. Digital infrastructure gaps, inadequate mobile network coverage, and a lack of access to smartphones or ID documentation further marginalise those already on the edge.

Furthermore, problems with structural governance remain. According to Alam and Hossain (2016), the transformative potential of digital SSNs remains compromised by systematic corruption and inadequate public accountability tools. Although digitisation might theoretically improve transparency, the lack of efficient grievance redress mechanisms and restricted citizen control erodes confidence and diminishes influence. Ali and Savoia (2023) contend that local political interference and weak institutional monitoring often link exclusion errors—such as the omission of eligible beneficiaries—particularly in Union Parishads, the lowest administrative level in Bangladesh. In terms of academic research, although international studies have thoroughly investigated the consequences of digitalisation in SSNs, work in Bangladesh, in particular, remains young. Most of the current studies concentrate on logistical challenges and governance systems; little emphasis is given to the actual experiences of beneficiaries. For example, how do digital cash transfer recipients view the changes in delivery systems? Are these systems empowering or alienating for low-income populations in rural and semi-urban areas? Do digital interfaces create new kinds of exclusion or enhance financial inclusion?

This chapter seeks to close these knowledge gaps by examining the digitisation of SSN programs in Bangladesh via a multidimensional perspective. The book examines the possibilities and limitations of digital cash transfers by situating the country's experience within the broader global context. It examines the interplay of technological, institutional, and socio-political aspects that affect outcomes, ultimately yielding a substantiated study of effective and ineffective elements, along with their underlying reasons. The findings are particularly important because they will help influence national policy and international conversations about digital inclusion, financial access, and the future of social safety systems in the Global South.

## 4 Importance of the Book

This book talks about one of the most important issues in development policy today. How to set up and run SSN programs that work, are transparent to everyone, and are accountable in the digital era. In Bangladesh and other areas where millions of people still live in poverty, injustice, and terror, SSN programs are more than simply tools for politicians; they are lifelines for the most vulnerable individuals in society. Still, these programs have not been able to fulfil their full potential for a long time since they have trouble with targeting, expenditure, and management. In this case, the fact that more and more systems that give out SSNs are going digital is a very crucial turning point. Digital cash transfer systems might change social safety by lowering the number of leaks in the system, speeding up payments, and making everything clearer. Countries like Kenya, which has the M-Pesa mobile payment system, and India, which has the DBT system linked to Aadhaar, demonstrate how technology can be leveraged to enhance government assistance, reduce corruption, and empower individuals. However, they also bring up an important question: How can these kinds of systems be changed to work with the institutions and economies of places like Bangladesh? These examples from around the world are promising.

This book addresses that problem directly. It looks into Bangladesh's ongoing experiments with digital money transfer methods and rates their pros and cons. Unlike earlier studies that have concentrated mainly on system architecture, financial consequences, or rollout logistics, this work investigates the lived experiences of beneficiaries, many of whom live in rural areas with limited access to infrastructure, low levels of digital literacy, and limited interactions with state institutions. The book presents a grounded, people-centred view of technological innovation in social protection, emphasising the challenges these communities face in navigating digital systems. Furthermore, this book is significant since it interacts with the political economy of digital welfare rather than just technical evaluations. The delivery of public services in Bangladesh is deeply entrenched in problems, including patron-client relationships, local-level political interference, bureaucratic inertia, and inadequate accountability systems. Therefore, any change, including digitalisation, must struggle with this institutional and governance reality. The book thus views digital tools as part of a larger process of systematic reform that has to be inclusive, participatory, and contextually customised rather than as magic bullets.

Policymakers, international development partners, digital technology providers, and researchers will find the results and insights of this book very relevant. It gives lawmakers, especially those in rural and poor areas, evidence-based ideas for how to improve the planning and implementation of SSN programs. It gives practitioners useful tips on how to deal with application problems in places with limited resources and government rules. Scholars can use this book to add to the growing amount of work on digital inclusion, welfare reform, and the use of information and communication technologies (ICTs) in development. This book also shows that Bangladesh is still dedicated to reaching the Sustainable Development Goals (SDGs), mainly SDG 1 (No Poverty), SDG 10

(Reduced Inequality), and SDG 16 (Peace, Justice, and Strong Institutions). It takes a critical, forward-looking look at how technology can help lower poverty by making services better and encouraging more social accountability and trust between citizens and the government. Ultimately, the book is more useful because it advocates for a more nuanced, equitable, and locally grounded approach to digital transformation in social policy. This book emphasises the need to maintain equity, access, and governance at the centre of the discussion as many Global South nations embrace digitalisation as part of their development agenda. It hopes to influence a more inclusive and careful discussion on the future of digital social protection in Bangladesh and beyond by doing this.

## 5 Methodological Issues

Following Yin's (1994) model, this book employed a qualitative case study method, which is well-suited for examining complex social events in real-life settings. Five Union Parishads (UPs) in Gaibandha District were picked on purpose to show a range of contextual detail and differences in how well they run their businesses, how they use technology, and how their customers feel about them. The five chosen instances provided a varied and illustrative spectrum of conditions and practices, facilitating rich comparative insights. Examined within its socio-political environment, each UP functioned as a separate unit of study. However, beyond comparable rural settings in Bangladesh, this intentional sampling might restrict the generalisability of results. Nevertheless, the book prioritised analytical rather than statistical generalisation to produce practical and politically relevant knowledge.

Another problem with the method was accessing the data and identifying respondents, especially UP members who were not present or did not want to participate due to the tense political situation. Even so, a strong multi-stakeholder sampling method with 137 respondents (local government officials, beneficiaries, administrative officers, and industry experts) made the book stronger. Secondary sources help with triangulation, and key informant interviews (KIIs) and semi-structured interviews provides an opportunity to learn more about how people think and how institutions work. It may still be hard to hear the views of the poorest people, who are not always featured in these kinds of studies. Furthermore, even if strict ethical criteria, including informed consent and confidentiality, were upheld, self-reported data could cause response bias. Therefore, the research's credibility is enhanced by combining thematic analysis and triangulated data sources, providing a grounded knowledge of the practical reality of digital cash transfer systems in rural Bangladesh.

## 6 Chapter Plan

Seven related chapters make up this book. Every chapter advances the reader from basic ideas and contextual insights to empirical analysis, theoretical synthesis, and forward-looking policy suggestions by building on the prior one.

### *6.1 Chapter One: Introduction*

The first chapter presents the fundamental research issue—the digitalisation of cash transfers in Bangladesh's social safety net programs and its consequences for governance, efficiency, and inclusion. It outlines the research questions, goals, and relevance of the book within the larger worldwide movement towards digital financial systems in social protection, and clarifies the reasons behind the work. The chapter critically analyses the current literature on digital financial inclusion, governance innovations, and social protection systems, drawing on national and international sources. The chapter places this work as a relevant and contextually based intervention employing empirical and theoretical gap identification. A thorough explanation of the research methodology, including qualitative and quantitative approaches, case selection justification, data sources, ethical issues, and analytical tools, closes the chapter. This thorough prologue guarantees conceptual and methodological clarity for the following chapters.

### *6.2 Chapter Two: Framing the Digital Shift: Theoretical Lenses and Conceptual Foundations*

By showing and linking pertinent theoretical frameworks, Chapter Two offers the conceptual scaffolding for the book. It presents and develops three fundamental bodies of theory: (1) Sen's Capability Approach, which emphasises the growth of individual freedoms through digital access; (2) the World Bank's Good Governance Framework, which addresses transparency, accountability, and service delivery; and (3) technology adoption theories including the Technology Acceptance Model (TAM) and Diffusion of Innovations, which help clarify user behaviour concerning digital interfaces. Key ideas—such as digital cash transfers, financial inclusion, e-governance, and service efficiency—are defined and operationalised in this chapter, rendering them measurable for empirical investigation. It also presents the dependent and independent variables of the book and clarifies their conceptualisation and relationship to the general research goals. This chapter enables a richer interpretation and synthesis of the results by anchoring the empirical chapters in a multidimensional theoretical framework.

### 6.3 Chapter Three: Digital Cash Transfer Systems in Social Safety Net Programs in Bangladesh: An Overview

This chapter charts the development and present scene of digital cash transfer systems in Bangladesh's SSN initiatives. Beginning with a summary of the National Social Security Strategy (NSSS), it investigates the government's rationale for digitalisation. The key government and donor-supported projects—such as G2P (Government-to-Person) payment systems, mobile money disbursements, and biometric authentication systems—are discussed in detail. Emphasising the functions of ministries, banks, mobile operators, and local government agencies, the chapter assesses the institutional framework supporting these systems. It discusses issues such as disparities in digital infrastructure, challenges in collaboration among stakeholders, and risks that exclude certain individuals. Using policy papers, interviews, and summary data, this chapter gives a full picture of where Bangladesh is on its digital social safety path.

### 6.4 Chapter Four: Measuring Success: Evaluating the Effectiveness of Digital Cash Transfers in Bangladesh's Social Safety Net Programs

In Chapter four, it is important to look at how well digital cash transfers work on two levels: the effects for the recipients and the success of the administration. From the user's point of view, it looks into how people feel about getting payments, taking into account things like ease of use, speed, dependability, ways to file complaints, and how fair they think things are. From a management point of view, it looks at things like streamlining processes, lowering scams, making better use of staff time, and lowering transaction costs. Survey results, administrative records, and discussions with key stakeholders, including UP representatives and NGO partners, are utilised in this chapter to provide a detailed assessment of success. We can tell how well Bangladesh is doing by examining how well it works in other nations, such as India, Kenya, and Brazil. This chapter creates a comprehensive framework for figuring out how effectively digital payments perform in SSN systems by integrating personal experience with statistical data.

### 6.5 Chapter Five: Enablers and Challenges: Key Determinants Shaping Digital Cash Transfers in Bangladesh's Social Safety Net Programs

This chapter examines the structural and environmental determinants that influence the success or failure of digital cash transfer initiatives within SSN programs. This chapter examines how these enablers and limitations impact the application of digital cash transfers. It achieves this by focusing on four key factors: technological infrastructure, digital literacy, governance methods, and the socio-economic context. The first section examines platform interoperability, internet connection, and the number of people with cell phones as requirements for digital entry. Then it examines at how digital skills, user interfaces, and efforts to raise knowledge can help or hurt user participation. The next group of problems is those that have to do with governance. These include institutional cooperation, accounting systems, reducing corruption, and regulatory help. Ultimately, it examines how differences in income, gender, and between rural and urban areas influence the transparency of digital payment systems. A database with poll responses from beneficiaries, administrative data at the UP level, and conversations with key informants gives real-world information. This section presents everything about the environment that works with digital cash transfers.

### 6.6 Chapter Six: Discussion: Integrating Findings with Theoretical Perspectives

Chapter Six goes over the results again through a theoretically-based view. It brings together the real-world lessons from Chapters Three to Five using the mental tools explained in Chapter Two. Digital cash transfers are evaluated using the Capability Approach to see whether they increase recipients' financial autonomy and agency. Digitalisation influences transparency, accountability, and efficiency in several ways, as the Good Governance Framework shows. On the other hand, technology adoption theories clarify user acceptance, resistance, and adaptation trends. This chapter investigates the synergies and tensions between theoretical viewpoints and normative objectives—e.g., inclusion empowerment—and practical limitations—e.g., digital divides and institutional inertia. It also makes people worry about unintended outcomes, like technology making exclusions worse or people relying too much on technocratic solutions. The chapter bridges the gap between the real world and the world of ideas, providing a comprehensive view of the book's strengths and weaknesses.

### 6.7 *Chapter Seven: Bridging the Gap: Key Findings, Challenges, Recommendations, and Conclusion*

The concluding chapter lays forth a plan for the future by putting together the key results of the investigation. It gives a brief overview of the major findings of how well digital currency transfer systems work, what causes problems, and where they happen. The chapter then gives policy suggestions based on evidence for a number of groups, such as government agencies, development partners, civil society groups, and local governments. Recommendations stress the need to improve digital infrastructure, encourage inclusive design, improve coordination across agencies, and pay for the growth of digital skills. The chapter also discusses areas that require further research, including evaluating long-term effects, comparing regions, and examining the impact of new technologies such as blockchain and artificial intelligence. It finishes by talking about how changes to digital wellbeing will affect long-term development, democratic governance, and social fairness. This chapter provides legislators with a practical yet crucial guide for building robust and inclusive digital safety nets in Bangladesh and other regions.

## 7 Conclusion

This chapter discusses how digital currency transfers operate within Bangladesh's Social Safety Net (SSN) initiatives, as well as their overall purpose, objectives, and design methodology. In doing so, it has highlighted the shortcomings of traditional cash-based delivery systems—especially their vulnerability to delays, lack of transparency, and inefficiencies—and positioned digital financial mechanisms as a possibly revolutionary substitute. The chapter has placed this investigation within the larger worldwide conversation on digital social protection, utilising a review of pertinent literature, stressing the contextual limitations and possibilities particular to Bangladesh. The chapter also outlined the qualitative research method used in the book, which comprised documentary analysis, key informant interviews (KIIs), and in-depth interviews. Emphasising its representativeness and relevance for understanding the grassroots-level implementation of digital payment systems, it justified choosing Gaibandha District as a case study site. This chapter lays the basis for critically exploring how digital cash transfers can improve SSN programs' inclusiveness, efficiency, and accountability in Bangladesh by including empirical, theoretical, and methodological issues. Building on this basis, the next chapter presents the theoretical framework to direct the research analysis.

## References


Aker, J. C., Boumnijel, R., McClelland, A., and Tierney, N. (2016). Payment mechanisms and anti-poverty programs: Evidence from a mobile money cash transfer experiment in Niger. *Economic Development and Cultural Change, 65*(1), 1–37.

Alam, M. A., and Hossain, S. A. (2016). Effectiveness of social safety net programs for poor people in the government level of Bangladesh. *International Journal of Social Sciences and Management, 3*(3), 153–158.

Ali, A. M., and Savoia, A. (2023). Decentralisation or patronage: What determines the government's allocation of development spending in a unitary country? Evidence from Bangladesh. *GDI Working Paper 2023-063*. Manchester: The University of Manchester.

Aziz, A. (2020). Digital inclusion challenges in Bangladesh: The case of the National ICT Policy. *Contemporary South Asia, 28*(3), 304–319. https://doi.org/10.1080/09584935.2020.1793912

Aziz, A., and Naima, U. (2021a). Rethinking digital financial inclusion: Evidence from Bangladesh. *Technology in Society, 64*, 23–31.

Aziz, A., and Naima, U. (2021b). Rethinking digital financial inclusion: Evidence from Bangladesh. *Technology in Society, 64*, 23–31.

Banerji, A., and Gentilini, U. (2013). Social safety nets: Lessons from global evidence and practice. *World Bank Symposium on Social Safety Nets in Namibia: Assessing Current Programs and Future Options*, 26 September 2013, Windhoek.

Bangladesh Bank. (2022). Annual report (2021–2022). Bangladesh Bank.

Bangladesh Telecommunication Regulatory Commission (BTRC). (2023). Internet subscriber report: 2023. Bangladesh Telecommunication Regulatory Commission.

Bold, C. E., Porteous, D., and Rotman, S. C. (2012). Social cash transfers and financial inclusion: Evidence from four countries. *CGAP Focus Note, No. 77*. Washington, DC: World Bank Group.

Chowdhury, A., Lawson, C., Kellison, E., Chia, H. S., Kharas, H., Fuller, J., Faye, M., Rutokowski, M., Salvado, R., and Dercon, S. (2022a). Accelerating digital cash transfers to the world's poorest. *Brookings*. Retrieved from https://www.brookings.edu/articles/accelerating-digital-cash-transfers-to-the-worlds-poorest/ (Accessed on November 23, 2024).

Chowdhury, A., Lawson, C., Kellison, E., Chia, H. S., Kharas, H., Fuller, M. F., Rutkowski, M., Salvado, R., and Dercon, S. (2022b). Accelerating digital cash transfers to the world's poorest. Brookings Institution. https://www.brookings.edu/articles/accelerating-digital-cash-transfers-to-the-worlds-poorest/

Gentilini, U. (2022). *Cash transfers in pandemic times: Evidence, practices, and implications from the largest scale-up in history*. Washington, DC: World Bank Group.

Global System for Mobile Communications (GSMA). (2022). State of the industry report on mobile money. GSMA.

Government of Bangladesh (GoB). (2015). National Social Security Strategy (NSSS) of Bangladesh: Mid-term Progress Report. General Economics Division (GED), Bangladesh Planning Commission.

Government of Bangladesh. (2021). National social security strategy. Ministry of Finance.

Haider, M. Z., and Mahamud, A. (2017). Beneficiary selection and allowance utilisation of social safety net programme in Bangladesh. *Journal of Human Rights and Social Work, 2*(1–2), 45–51.

Hossain, M. (2022). *Digital transformation and economic development in Bangladesh: Rethinking digitalisation strategies for leapfrogging*. Springer Nature.

Jack, W., and Suri, T. (2014). Risk Sharing and Transactions Costs: Evidence from Kenya's Mobile Money Revolution. *American Economic Review, 104*(1), 183–223.

Khera, R. (2017). Impact of Aadhaar on welfare programmes. *Economic and Political Weekly, 52*(50), 61–70.

Rahman, H. Z., Choudhury, L. A., and Ali, K. S. (2011). *Social safety nets in Bangladesh: Review of issues and analytical inventory (Vol. 1)*. Dhaka: A PPRC-UNDP Research Initiative.

Siddiquee, M. S., Faruk, A., and Matin, I. (2022). *COVID-19 Learning, Evidence and Research (CLEAR) for Bangladesh: Social Protection During Covid Times Research For Building Forward Better*. Scoping paper. Centre for Learning on

Evaluation and Results (CLEAR)/ BRAC Institute of Governance and Development (BIGD).
World Bank. (2020a). *The global Findex database 2017: Measuring financial inclusion and the fintech revolution*. Washington, DC: World Bank Publications.
World Bank. (2020b). *The global Findex database 2017: Measuring financial inclusion and the fintech revolution*. Washington, DC: World Bank Publications.
World Bank. (2022). The global Findex database 2021. World Bank.
Yin, R. K. (1994). *Case Study Research: Design and Methods* (2nd ed.). Thousand Oaks, CA: Sage Publications.

# Framing the Digital Shift: Theoretical Lenses and Conceptual Foundations

**Abstract** This chapter describes the concepts and methods that will be used to see how well Bangladesh's social safety net (SSN) programs work with digital cash transfers. The first step is to put into action three basic ideas: digital cash transfers, social safety nets, and financial inclusion. Then it places these concepts within the broader discussion about digitising welfare. The chapter then goes into greater depth regarding the main things that led to the empirical study. The dependent variables indicate how digital transfers impact how programs run and how people who receive them feel. Factors such as the level of satisfaction among program participants, the program's efficiency, and the cost of running a business are used to measure them. The independent variables are the structural and environmental elements that affect the outcomes of these activities. These include things like the technology infrastructure, digital skills, government processes, and socioeconomic situations. This chapter makes it clear that digital cash transfers will not work until there is more than simply new technology. It also relies on how strong the institutions are, how much people participate in society, and how good the government is. This framework provides a foundation for the subsequent research chapters. It lets the readers look at how digitisation is changing how help is given and how money is given to disadvantaged populations in Bangladesh.



P. K. Panday, A. H. M. K. Ahsan, *Digital Revolution for the Vulnerable*, https://doi.org/10.1007/978-981-95-7980-8_2

**Keywords** Digital cash transfers • Social safety nets • Financial inclusion • Digital literacy • Institutional capacity • Governance

## 1 Introduction

Digital technologies have grown so quickly that they have revolutionised how people, groups, and governments operate together. It has also transformed the way banks and other public agencies operate. This development, also known as a "digital shift," has made social safety and assistance more efficient, transparent, and accessible in new ways. It has raised several challenges, though, such as access, fairness, and control. To properly understand these developments, it is vital to put the discussion in solid theoretical and conceptual contexts. This chapter presents the study's theoretical framework. The first section examines the foundational notions of the discipline. These ideas originate from three interrelated domains: theories of financial inclusion, theories of governance, and theories of digital adoption. These models elucidate the reasons for the popularity of digital modifications to social safety and demonstrate the measurement of their impacts across various socioeconomic contexts.

The following section of the chapter presents three main themes from the study as real-world examples: digital cash transfers, social safety nets, and financial inclusion. The chapter makes sure that the concepts are obvious by defining these words. It also gives readers a common vocabulary to use in future studies. The chapter then summarises the study's dependent and independent variables, as well as the indicators that illustrate their nature. The dependent variable is how well digital cash transfers work, which may be quantified by things like how satisfied the receiver is, how well the system works, and how much it costs to send and receive money. The independent variables—technological infrastructure, digital literacy, governance procedures, and socioeconomic factors—subsequently delineate the conditions that enable or hinder digital acts. Finally, the chapter brings all these pieces together into a broader theoretical framework that underlies the observational research. This links academic ideas to real-world issues of delivering digital services, making sure that the study is both complete in its ideas and based on facts.

## 2 Theoretical Underpinnings

To put this study in its proper place, it is important to look at the ideas that explain the importance of digital cash transfers in the bigger picture of government reforms, financial inclusion, and social safety. Digitalisation is not just a new tool; it is also a significant shift in how governments interact with people and deliver services. When different but related ideas about financial inclusion, government, and digital use are put together, a full picture of this shift can be found. Some ideas about financial inclusion state that people are better off and can fully join the economy when they have access to reliable and affordable financial services. Governance theories describe the institutions, accounting systems, and policy frameworks that make digital changes possible. They also explain how these changes are planned and carried out. Lastly, theories of digital adoption look at how people and groups accept new technologies, what stops them, and how social or cultural factors affect this process. All of these theoretical lenses work together to support this study. They not only help make key ideas more concrete, but they also make sure that the analysis goes beyond simple descriptions of digitalisation and looks more closely at how it affects people, institutions, and the way things are distributed. In what comes next, we will first talk about financial inclusion, then move on to government and digital usage.

### 2.1 *Theories of Financial Inclusion*

Most people are aware that financial inclusion involves ensuring that individuals and groups who are less fortunate have access to and can utilise safe, affordable, and suitable financial products and services. Most importantly, it is about removing barriers that prevent people from using the official banking system. Financial inclusion is not a goal in itself for both researchers and people who work with it. It is a way to improve people's economic prospects, resilience, and sense of self-worth. Amartya Sen's Capability Approach (1999) is a powerful theory that helps us understand financial equality. Viewed this way, poverty is defined not merely by a lack of financial resources but by a lack of basic skills and the freedom to live a fulfilling life. Having money is important for helping people improve in various areas because it enables them to afford essential services such as education, healthcare, and better opportunities for earning a living. Digital cash transfers aim to eliminate the social and physical barriers that prevent low-income and rural populations from accessing traditional banking services.

Beck et al. (2007) demonstrated the importance of financial institutions in reducing inequality and promoting overall economic growth. Some people say that transparent financial institutions protect groups that are already at risk by making it easier for everyone to get access to economic possibilities. New research indicates that financial inclusion facilitates achieving broader development objectives, such as empowering women and enhancing community resilience (Demirgüç-Kunt et al. 2018; Gabor and Brooks 2020). There are problems that people, especially those with low incomes, face that are discussed in theories of financial inclusion. These problems include not having enough financial infrastructure, not knowing how to use technology well enough, high trade costs, and not trusting government institutions (Allen et al. 2016). Some people believe that digital innovations, such as fingerprint tracking systems, banks without physical branches, and mobile money, could help address these issues. Digital cash transfers may help social safety net programs reach more people by making them cheaper, easier to use, and able to get around problems that have always been there.

On the other hand, the research also warns against being too hopeful. Some researchers say that digital solutions can make people feel even more left out if problems with access, gender inequality, and regional differences are not fixed (Bateman 2012; Suri and Jack 2016). For example, women living in rural areas may not have easy access to cell phones or may be limited in their use of technology due to cultural norms. These ideas are especially useful for Bangladesh because social safety net programs are using digital cash transfer more and more. So, this study puts digital cash transfers in the bigger picture of the theory of financial inclusion. It examines whether and how digital tools improve economic independence, lower risk, and help close the gap between the rich and the poor. By using theories of financial inclusion to guide the study, it shows that digital solutions can have two effects: they can help impoverished groups, but they can also make things worse if structural and contextual barriers are not fixed.

### 2.2 *Theories of Governance*

There are different ideas about how institutions, rules, and practices affect how well public services are delivered. Governance theories help us understand these ideas. They help explain not only the systems of power but also how citizens can hold the government accountable, make the government more transparent, and get involved in politics. Governance theories are vital for making social safety nets (SSNs) better because they illustrate how new technology, like digital cash transfers, may change the way things are done and aid vulnerable individuals. The World Bank introduced the concept of "Good Governance" in 1992 (Crawford 2006). It is built on the concepts of being transparent, accountable, fast, fair, and quick to respond. This notion has been at the centre of discussions about expansion ever since, especially when it comes to making sure people are secure. These principles demonstrate the importance of SSN programs having strong organisations that can assist people in a fair, effective, and non-exploitative manner. These views are in line with what most people think about digitalisation: a way to fix long-standing problems with how help is given. If people pay for things online, it is less likely that their money will be lost or stolen. This makes things clearer and makes sure that resources get to the right people (Hanna et al., 2017a, 2017b).

Governance theories suggest that public participation is a crucial component of effective administration, complemented by executive efficiency. As Pierre and Peters (2020) state, governance is a change from bureaucratic, top-down control to more networked, bottom-up types of government. In this way, digital technologies like real-time monitoring, beneficiary feedback systems, and venues for resolving complaints can make it easier for people to hold institutions accountable. These kinds of systems give people who receive services the power to report problems, demand that they are fixed, and have more control over how those services are delivered (Fox 2015).

Different people have varying ideas about what "good governance" entails and how power operates, as well as the limitations of institutions. Hydén and Mease (2004) suggest that we should examine government from the perspective of social problems and power dynamics. From this point of view, technology is not fair; politics and institutions must work. Digital technologies may impede minor corruption; yet, they can exacerbate issues if access is inequitable for individuals of varying genders, classes, or regions (Scholl 2008). So, looking at things from the point of view of governance makes us think more deeply about whether digital cash transfers in Bangladesh promote fairness and accountability or accidentally keep some people from benefiting.

In conclusion, governance theories demonstrate how digitising SSN programs can transform institutions by integrating new technologies with changes in their operational processes. However, they also warn that for technology to make a real difference, it needs to be integrated into systems of government that support it, such as laws, mechanisms for holding people accountable, and public participation. These findings are very important for this study because they help us figure out how digitalised cash transfers in Bangladesh can meet world standards of good governance while also dealing with problems that are unique to the country's institutions.

## 2.3 *Theories of Digital Adoption*

Political, cultural, and physical factors also have a role in how digital platforms are employed in SSN initiatives, not only technology. Theories of digital acceptance elucidate the reasons behind individuals and organisations' acceptance or rejection of new technologies, as well as the circumstances in which these technologies effectively enhance conditions. The Technology Acceptance Model (TAM) by Davis (1989) and the Diffusion of Innovations Theory (DIT) by Rogers (2003) are two of the most influential ideas in this area. They are both still quite helpful for figuring out how digital cash transfers work.

From a user's point of view, the TAM stresses that how useful and easy something is to use is a significant factor in its acceptance. People who receive the money are more likely to use fingerprint or mobile money payment systems if they believe they are easy to use, safe, and enhance their ability to access resources. Adoption is also boosted by trust in digital platforms and the idea that deals are safe (Venkatesh and Davis 2000). People who live in rural areas of Bangladesh do not always have access to official financial institutions. To build user trust in digital systems, they need to be able to show real changes in ease and speed.

Rogers's (2003) DIT examines acceptance within a broader context, illustrating how social processes influence it. In order to explain how advances spread, it lists five main factors: relative benefit, compatibility, complexity, trialability, and observability. These factors show that acceptance of digital cash transfers relies on more than how well they work. They also depend on how well they fit in with current cultural practices, how easy they are to try out, and how clearly they help. People who benefit may be more likely to use mobile banking if their friends in the community do it successfully. This is called "social proof," and it boosts trust.

New versions of these ideas add to the study even more. Venkatesh et al. (2003) came up with the Unified Theory of Acceptance and Use of Technology (UTAUT). It combines parts of TAM and diffusion theory to show how social impact and enabling factors play a part. This shows how important digital knowledge, gender roles, and the readiness of infrastructure are in determining adoption trends. In rural Bangladesh, issues such as limited mobile service, power outages, and unequal access to mobile devices between men and women hinder beneficiaries, particularly women, from fully utilising digital systems (Donner and Tellez 2008; Grohmann et al. 2018).

Sociocultural issues are still very important to think about. People do not just accept new technology; social norms, trust in organisations, and shared digital experiences all play a role in how people adopt new technology. Studies show that building local networks of trust and running training and teaching programs at the same time can make something more acceptable (Chib et al. 2015). Without this kind of help, even well-designed digital solutions might not work as well as they should, making marginalisation worse instead of better. Theories of digital use explain the psychological, social, and structural factors that affect how well digital SSN changes work. Some people argue that adoption is not always a guaranteed outcome. People will use the tools if they are useful, simple, in line with local norms, and backed by institutions. By applying these academic ideas to Bangladesh, we can see both the pros and cons of using computers to send money to poor people.

It is not enough for people to accept new technology. Several factors come into play, including social norms, trust in the government, and shared internet experiences. Chib et al. (2015) say that building local trust networks and running training and education programs at the same time might make things more acceptable. Without this kind of help, even well-thought-out digital solutions might not work as well as they could, which would make things worse instead of better. Theories of digital use explain the social, psychological, and structural factors that influence the effectiveness of digital SSN changes. They might not always be able to adopt. People will use the tools if they are useful, easy to use, in line with local customs, and backed by institutions that make them possible. Using these academic ideas to look at Bangladesh helps us understand the pros and cons of digitising cash exchanges for poor people. This helps figure out how to put essential concepts into action, choose study parameters, and select what sort of analysis will be utilised to make sense of the research data.

## 3 Operationalisation of Key Concepts

Operationalisation is an essential process for transforming abstract theoretical concepts into tangible variables that can be examined, quantified, and analysed. This study does not see the key concepts of digital cash transfers, social safety nets, and financial inclusion as ambiguous notions. People regard them as quantifiable ideas with distinct dimensions and signals instead. By making these ideas clear, the study enables the assessment of the usefulness and importance of digital cash transfers in Bangladesh's SSN programs. It is also possible to look more closely at the program's effects on people from different social and economic backgrounds, especially on the weakest people in society. The study focuses on certain Social Security programs, such as the Old Age Allowance and the Allowances for Widows, the Deserted, and Destitute Women, which support those who are particularly vulnerable to economic and social instability. These initiatives can help us learn more about how digital solutions can simplify access, reduce unnecessary government work, and make it easier for individuals who are not already part of the economy to join it.

### *3.1 Digital Cash Transfers*

Digital cash transfers provide money electronically to individuals who need it, instead of using traditional methods that can be hacked, take too long, or result in a loss of money. Technologies like mobile money platforms, e-wallets, and direct bank transfers are used in these payments to make sure that funds get to their recipients quickly, safely, and clearly. To use digital cash transfers for a real-world study, there is a need to consider different factors that show both how well the system works and how the users feel about it. The first factor, **accessibility**, checks whether the people who will benefit from the payments, especially those living in rural or underdeveloped areas, have the necessary skills and tools to use the digital platforms set up for them. Access is affected by the number of available devices, how well they work with mobile or payment technologies, and how well people know how to use them (Rahman et al. 2011). The second factor, **timing**, refers to the frequency and punctuality of payments. Delays in payments can make social safety programs less effective, especially for people who rely on allowances to meet their daily needs. The third factor is **reliability**, which is how well and regularly the system can send payments. It includes the ability to prevent technology problems, mistakes, and incorrect distributions, ensuring that the right people receive the right amounts without any additional issues. Lastly, ease of use measures how simple the digital method is for people to use. Some of the factors that enable receivers to accomplish this independently include literacy, digital skills, and the ease of use of the platform (Alam and Hossain 2016). All of these useful details make it possible to assess how effectively Bangladesh's SSN systems handle transactions involving digital currencies. They help us figure out how well management is doing its job and give us details about the issues and experiences of people who use the services. The discussion offers a comprehensive understanding of how digital tools can help individuals access financial resources and social security.

### 3.2 Social Safety Nets

SSNs are programs run by the government that help people and families who are having trouble with money by giving them money and other social services. Some of these include food stamps, cash transfers, loans, and other forms of assistance. In Bangladesh, social safety nets are especially important for reducing poverty, promoting fairness, and helping people who cannot work in the formal sector (Alam and Hossain 2016). Allowances for Widows, the Deserted, and Destitute Women, as well as the Old Age Allowance, are what this study is mostly about. These services are meant to help people who really need them. The goal of the Old Age Allowance program is to assist older people who are having a hard time meeting their basic needs and do not have enough money or family support to do so. The goal of the program is to improve people's health, reduce their reliance on local support networks, and protect their finances by providing them with a monthly stipend (Choudhary 2013). Widows, deserted women, and poor women can get money from the government to aid them with their financial troubles. The purpose of these prizes is to aid women who do not have steady jobs or family support by meeting their basic requirements and getting them more involved in social and economic activities (Pradhan and Afrin 2015).

To use these SSNs for actual research, it is important to look at many factors that show how the program is used and how well it works. Program coverage measures how many qualified people are a part of these programs, especially those who live in rural or impoverished areas. Targeting correctly is also crucial because it ensures that resources are allocated to individuals who meet the specified requirements, thereby preventing people from being left out and ensuring that resources are not wasted (Salam 2022). Another crucial clue is that management expenses are going down. Digital cash transfers can help programs function more smoothly, cut down on the need for physical equipment, and cut down on the amount of labour that needs to be done by hand. These kinds of efficiencies not only save operational expenses but also optimise the use of resources that may be directly employed by beneficiaries (Banerjee et al. 2024). In order to show the link between digital technology and social safety, this study looks at specific issues. It highlights how digitalisation can make it easier for populations that have been hindered in the past by institutional hurdles to access services. The operationalisation framework gives us a structured means to find out if digital cash transfers improve coverage, target better, and lower administrative costs. This would make Bangladesh's social safety net system more effective and available to everyone.

### *3.3 Financial Inclusion*

People with low incomes can access quick and affordable banking, loan, and insurance services when they are part of the formal financial system. This word means "financial inclusion." The main focus of this study is on how digital cash transfers affect Bangladesh's SSN programs for financial inclusion. To make financial inclusion a reality, we need to look at a lot of different factors that show both how easy it is for people to get financial services and how involved they are with the official financial system. The most important thing is to use banking services. People who receive digital payments must have bank accounts. For this to work, banks must be able to access computer SSN systems. Not having an account could make it harder for digital solutions to spread and for people to use banking services (Demirgüç-Kunt et al. 2018). Another important factor is the increasing ease of access to mobile wallets, which are being used more frequently as a valuable tool for sending money to people in remote or underserved areas. Mobile financial services not only make payments easier, but they also help people get started with digital financial tools, which leads to more widespread financial inclusion.

Another important sign is how often digital transfers happen, which shows how much recipients use digital platforms for things other than getting allowances. People who use digital financial services regularly are more likely to be financially literate, have more power, and be involved in the economy (Beck et al. 2007). By looking at these measures, we can see if digital cash transfers help users become more financially independent, especially those from groups that have not had access to official financial services in the past. The gender aspects of this study are given extra attention because women make up a big part of SSN recipients and often face extra problems when they try to get financial help. Looking into how women use and access digital financial services can help show where structural inequality exists and how digital solutions can help close the gaps between men and women when it comes to financial access and independence (Suri and Jack 2016). This study fills in the blanks between theory and measurable results by looking at things like ease, program coverage, banking usage, and transaction frequency as ways to measure digital cash transfers, social safety nets, and financial inclusion. It looks at programs like the Old Age Allowance and the Allowances for Widows, Deserted, and Destitute Women to make sure that the views of the poorest and most vulnerable people are heard. We can use this method to clearly see how digital financial systems can make Bangladesh's social safety net better by making it more effective, transparent to everyone, and powerful. It demonstrates how ideas from the theory can have real-world effects.

In this study, the connection between theory and real-world research is the operationalisation of important concepts such as digital cash transfers, social safety nets, and financial inclusion. The study makes it easy to see how well digital changes to Bangladesh's SSNs are working by listing things like how easy they are to use, how often they happen, how reliable they are, how many people they cover, how well they target people, how much money they save on administration, how easy it is to get to a bank, how often people use their mobile wallets, and how often they make transactions. For example, focusing on programs like the Old Age Allowance and Allowances for Widows, Deserted, and Destitute Women keeps the research on the most vulnerable groups. It includes both the pros and cons of digitisation. This framework not only makes it possible to evaluate program success in an organised way, but it also gives us a better understanding of the study's larger goals of financial freedom, transparent access, and institutional efficiency. It sets the stage for the study's later analysis parts.

## 4 Variables of the Study

To fully understand how digital cash transfer systems work in Bangladesh's SSN programs, we first need to define and describe the key factors used in this study. Any study is predicated on aspects that establish the framework for data collection and analysis. In this study, we analyse both dependent and independent variables to explore the relationships between digital cash transfer systems and their effects on the social safety net. The dependent variables are what we want to look at and assess in this study. These are ways to send money digitally. These numbers suggest that the initiatives helped people acquire financial services, keep their money safe, and grow healthier overall. The independent factors, on the other hand, are the aspects that determine how effectively the digital cash flow systems perform and what they do. Some of these things include how well the administration works, how much the users know, the technological foundation, and how easy it is to get in. This section will go into more depth about these variables so people can understand how digital cash transfers fit into the bigger picture of social safety nets and how they influence the social and economic conditions of disadvantaged populations in Bangladesh.

### *4.1 Dependent Variable: Effectiveness of Digital Cash Transfers*

The dependent variable in this study is the effectiveness of digital cash transfers, which assesses the extent to which these instruments achieve their intended objectives within social safety net programs. This idea is crucial when utilising digital financial tools to enhance transparency, reduce waste, and empower those who lack access to power. The section examines how digital technologies can impact the delivery of welfare benefits, focusing on recipient satisfaction, computer compatibility, and the associated costs of business operations. We can use these measures to figure out how digital payments might change SSNs. There are many ways that digital cash exchanges are useful. Looking at how these systems work in terms of how users feel, how well they work, and how much money they make helps understand each other. The switch to digital distribution systems aims to address the issues with traditional cash transfer systems, such as fraud, delays, and poor logistics, thereby making the process easier (Rahman et al. 2011). Digital cash transfers have shown much promise for making help programs easier to run by reducing the human and administrative problems that have traditionally come with them. These systems use technology to try to improve service delivery, especially for the poorest and most vulnerable people (Gentilini 2022).

#### *4.1.1 Indicators to Measure the Effectiveness of Digital Cash Transfer*

For digital cash transfers to be successful, there is a need to look at more than just the technical aspects of how they are delivered. It is important to consider how the recipients of the SSNs feel and how effectively the system operates. In this case, "effectiveness" refers to how well digital platforms fulfil their intended purpose, which is to help vulnerable groups access money in a fast, reliable, and transparent manner. Digital payments are supposed to make things easier, cheaper, and clearer than standard cash-based systems, while also making users happier and more trusting. To put this idea into practice, the study proposes a set of measures that examine the success of Digital cash transfers from various angles. These include ensuring **beneficiaries are satisfied**, **ensuring efficient administration**, and **reducing transaction costs**. Each of these sheds light on a different but related part of system performance. These factors can be used together to get a full picture of how well digital actions in Bangladesh's social safety nets are meeting their goals of being accessible, fair, and long-lasting. Beneficiary Happiness

**Beneficiary Satisfaction**

**Beneficiary satisfaction is** a key indicator of how well digital cash transfer programs work, as it reveals how recipients truly feel, rather than just how well the programs were administered. Not only is the amount of money sent or the speed of delivery often used to judge the success of a digital solution, but also how well the system fits the users' wants, needs, and abilities (Kaiser et al. 2023) in many situations. A user-centred method puts program users at the centre of review, because how they feel about the program's accessibility, trustworthiness, and ease of use are crucial for both short-term results and long-term sustainability.

**Ease of use**, which measures how well beneficiaries can use digital tools to get to their benefits, is a key sign of satisfaction. For many rural and older users, digital literacy is still low, which makes it hard for them to use complicated interfaces or words they do not know. Yoshino and Morgan (2017) state that user-friendly design, local language choices, and simpler displays all contribute to people accepting and trusting digital systems. When systems are made with the end user in mind, the people who will use them are more likely to see them as trustworthy and helpful, rather than scary.

**Timeliness and dependability** are also very important. Beneficiaries can plan their spending, meet their basic needs, and avoid going back into cycles of fear if they get their money on time and regularly. However, delays, uneven payments, or technology problems can not only make it harder to survive each day but can also make people lose faith in the system (Nikey 2024). A steady flow of resources makes things more predictable, which is crucial for groups that lack other safety nets.

**Reduction in access challenges** is another way to measure how well something works. A long time ago, people who got government benefits often had to drive far, wait in lines, or pay for transportation to get their benefits. Digital systems make this easier by letting people send money directly to bank accounts or mobile wallets. This saves time and money. This ease of use makes things a lot better for the receiver because it gets rid of many of the hidden costs that come with traditional cash transfer methods. By making digital cash transfer programs easier to use, more reliable, more accessible, and more on time, program managers can not only make users happier right away, but they can also boost the programs' trustworthiness and long-term value. To make these systems effective, we need to make sure they are not only technologically advanced but also quick, transparent to everyone, and trusted by the people they want to help.

### Administrative Efficiency

Another important factor in judging how useful digital cash transfers are is their **administration efficiency**, which shows how well a program can use its resources, simplify processes, and get rid of extraneous complexity. Administrative efficiency is important for both people who run programs and the people who receive services. It affects the experiences of both groups by making sure that services are provided easily, clearly, and without too much unnecessary red tape. Digitisation has become an important part of governance changes in social safety nets because it can make them more efficient, hold governments more accountable, and help more people (Sarwar et al. 2023).

One clear result of better management is **a reduction in time**. Automation cuts down on the work that needs to be done by hand, gets rid of long lines of middlemen, and speeds up the payment process. Studies (Sarwar et al. 2023) show that digital payment systems can cut the time it takes to send money from weeks to days or even hours. This means that vulnerable families can get help when they need it most. This efficiency not only helps managers by making their jobs easier, but it also makes the system more stable and predictable for users.

**Simplifying the procedures** is a second important factor. Traditional section-based systems often have long lines, multiple levels of proof, and the chance for people to be harmed by decisions that are made without their input. Paperwork, recipient identification, and verification processes can be digitised to make payments faster and clearer. This also reduces the likelihood of cheating and rent-seeking (Demirgüç-Kunt et al. 2018). For receivers, streamlined processes mean less time spent navigating red tape, and for managers, they mean fewer mistakes and disagreements.

**Cost-effectiveness** is also very important. Digital cash transfers can cut costs by a large amount because they do not need as much real equipment or human intermediaries. When governments and executing agencies have lower administrative costs, they can allocate funds to support more services, larger programs, or enhanced tracking. Over time, this makes the safety net system more financially stable, allowing it to help more people with the same amount of money or less. Digital currency transactions are faster and more transparent. They also enhance financial management by saving time, simplifying processes, and promoting prudent spending. Increasing administrative efficiency is not just a technical goal; it is also a key part of changing how the government works, making sure that social safety nets work, cutting down on waste, and giving people and governments more value.

### Reduction in Transaction Costs

A big sign of how well digital cash transfers work is a **reduction in transaction costs**. These costs include both the money and time that managers and recipients have to spend on getting and using benefits. In the past, giving out cash transfers came with a lot of hidden costs, like fees for middlemen, transportation, and paperwork, that made the benefits less valuable for the people who got them. Digital payments try to make the system fairer and more cost-effective by lowering these costs as much as possible. This way, more of the money that is given gets to the right people. Indeed, research on digital inclusion reveals that lowering transaction costs is one of the most obvious and tangible benefits of digitalised welfare measures (Sarwar et al. 2023).

The **elimination of intermediary fees** is a significant reason for these savings. In the old way of doing things, payments were usually made through local agents or brokers who charged fees or, in some cases, stole some of the allowance by renting out their services. By sending money directly to recipients' bank accounts or mobile wallets, these middlemen are cut out. This makes things clearer and less likely for fraud and abuse (Haider and Mahamud 2017). This not only gives the people who benefit the most money, but it also builds trust in the system.

**Lower travel and documentation costs** of paperwork are two additional ways to save money. In the past, people who were supposed to get benefits often had to drive long distances to specific collection points, which cost them money and time. Many people also had to fill out and resubmit section documents, which added to the costs. By letting users access funds online, through mobile banking agents or nearby ATMs, the method greatly reduces these costs. This drop in out-of-pocket costs can make a big difference in the general health and happiness of low-income families, especially those that live in rural areas.

Digital methods also save a significant amount of money because they reduce management costs. In the past, keeping records, verifying payments, and monitoring for fraud required a significant amount of manual work, diverting resources that could have been used to assist recipients. A lot of this work is done automatically by digital tools, which makes tracking more effective and less resource-intensive (Chowdhury et al. 2022). The result is a leaner system that gets more money straight to the people who need it while also making everyone more accountable.

Digital cash transfer makes the system more efficient, fair, and financially stable by cutting down on fees for middlemen, travel and paperwork costs, and management overhead. These savings not only keep the value of benefits for people who get them, but they also let program managers increase access or service quality without having to raise budgets by the same amount. Taking the measures of recipient satisfaction, administrative efficiency, and lower transaction costs together, it provides a good picture of how well digital cash transfers work. They demonstrate both how users perceive things and how systems operate, illustrating how technology can enhance social safety nets and improve outcomes. Bangladesh must comprehend and tackle these challenges to enhance digital initiatives in a sustainable, inclusive, and enduring manner.

To sum up, we can tell how effective digital cash transfers are by how happy the people who get them are, how smoothly the system works, and how much it costs to send and get money. User-centred design and trust in digital platforms are important because beneficiary satisfaction shows how important they are. Administrative efficiency shows how important clear, streamlined processes are for making sure services are delivered on time and at a low cost. Reducing transaction costs shows how digitisation makes the system fairer, which increases the value of benefits for both recipients and administrators. By putting these factors together, this study not only shows how digitalised welfare programs work, but it also shows how they have the power to change the way social safety is provided. Recognising and improving these aspects will be important for Bangladesh to increase digital cash transfers in a way that benefits everyone and lasts. This will make sure that the most vulnerable people continue to benefit from social safety nets even as the country's government changes.

## *4.2 Independent Variables*

To fully understand how well digital currency transfer systems work, we need to examine the various factors that either facilitate or hinder their use. These situations are mirrored in the independent factors, which affect how well these kinds of systems help people. Digitisation makes things more transparent, faster, and easier to get involved in, but how well it works relies a lot on the quality of the technological infrastructure, the digital skills of the users, the strength of the systems that manage things, and the social and economic positions of the people who benefit. By turning these factors into measured signs, this study provides a structured way to look at how external and systemic factors affect how well digital cash transfer works. This strategy enables us to examine the strengths and weaknesses of Bangladesh's social safety net initiatives more closely. It also makes sure that the study goes beyond the technology itself and looks at how it works in the actual world.

### *4.2.1 Technological Infrastructure*

The infrastructure for technology is a significant outside aspect that has a direct effect on how successfully digital cash transfers operate. It includes both the digital and physical technologies that make financial transactions go smoothly. The technological infrastructure decides how easy it is for individuals to use, depend on, and access technology in the context of social safety nets. This is particularly applicable in rural and underdeveloped regions. The research investigates the impact of this variable on the efficacy of digitalised social initiatives through the use of certain metrics. Digital cash transfers rely significantly on the quality and accessibility of the technological infrastructure. Good execution depends on robust systems that make it easy for users to become engaged, work around connection issues, and make sure that transactions are safe. Hasan et al. (2017) found that digital social solutions are harder to use and less successful when the infrastructure is not good enough, especially in countries that are not very well developed. Strong technology infrastructure makes it simpler for people to access what they need, especially those who reside in distant places. One strategy for program administrators to ensure that cash transfer systems are utilised effectively is to invest in stronger connections, reasonably priced mobile devices, and always-on digital platforms. This variable is the foundation of all digital aid programs since it makes sure that everyone has equal access to services and that operations function more smoothly. The foundation of technology is what enables digital cash transfers to work. It is possible to tell how well a program works by looking at factors like how many people have internet access, how many people possess cell phones, and how safe the platform is. Connecting the goals of digital inclusion and financial freedom hinges on addressing infrastructure issues, particularly in rural or underdeveloped areas. By focusing on this variable, the study shows how important it is for Bangladesh's social safety nets to keep getting better through technological progress.

**Indicators of Technological Infrastructure**

**Internet Connectivity:** Access to the internet is needed for digital cash transfer methods to work properly. The success and transparency of the program are shown by the number of people who can consistently connect to the internet. Connectivity problems often keep people from getting to their rights on time, especially in remote areas. As Sarwar et al. (2023) demonstrate, significant disparities persist in internet access among rural Bangladeshis. These differences affect poor groups more than others. Broadband needs to be widely available in order to reduce digital inequality and improve program reach.

**Mobile Phone Ownership:** Having a cell phone, especially a feature phone or a smartphone, is one of the main things that makes digital interactions possible. For cash transfers, the recipients must have devices that can run mobile banking apps, SMS-based systems, or USSD codes. A study by Chowdhury et al. (2022) found that over 75% of Bangladeshi users have at least one main cell phone. However, smartphone use is still low in rural areas. As a top concern, programs should make sure that their technology is easy to use on a variety of platforms.

**Platform Stability:** Platform security in digital systems refers to the technology's ability to handle transactions without errors or issues. According to a study by Chowdhury et al. (2022), frequent problems or downtime can make users less likely to trust the system, which in turn may deter people from using it. Technical problems during times of high demand could cause funds to be late, making customers unhappy. To keep things stable, rules must be made to protect private user data and stop scams.

### *4.2.2 Digital Literacy*

How well digital money transfer methods work depends a lot on how well people know how to use technology. The test assesses how effectively people can utilise digital tools to locate and comprehend banking services. People who use social safety net programs are judged on how well they can use technology to buy things, fix problems, and do other things. This is called digital literacy. The study uses certain measurements to find out how much this factor makes digital currency deals more useful and popular. For digital money movement to work effectively, there is a need to have a good understanding of technology. People might make mistakes when they buy things, need help from other people, or have trouble using digital tools well if people are not good with technology. Studies show that digital expertise is the most significant factor affecting customer satisfaction and the effectiveness of digital assistance services (Aziz 2020).

Higher levels of digital knowledge are linked to higher rates of acceptance and happiness with technology. People who know how to use technology well are more likely to be able to use platforms successfully, which means they will depend less on middlemen and have more financial freedom. Literacy programs also equip people with the necessary tools to become more engaged in the digital economy, laying the groundwork for sustained digital inclusion. Digital knowledge is what makes it possible for digital currency transfer systems to operate. Basic digital skills, efforts to improve understanding, and feedback on usability all help people determine how it will affect them. Social safety net initiatives may make the system more accessible, happier for users, and more efficient by filling up gaps in computer literacy, especially in rural and poor areas. Because of this, this part is very important for closing the digital gap and making sure that everyone gets the same level of care.

**Indicators of Digital Literacy**

**Basic Digital Skills**: Basic digital skills mean that the recipients can use their phones or tablets to do cash activities. Some of these skills are using user interfaces, giving and getting money, and fixing small problems. Ahmed (2023) showed that many rural recipients in Bangladesh did not have the basic digital skills they needed to do their jobs. This shows the importance of focused skill-building programs. According to Babar et al. (2023), programs that teach people how to use technology properly have higher usage rates and fewer transaction mistakes.

**Awareness Campaigns:** Much of what happens on digital sites depends on how much people know about their features and benefits. Usually, these initiatives employ local languages and hands-on demonstrations to build confidence, dispel myths, and provide people with meaningful training (Aziz and Naima 2021). The most effective awareness initiatives are customised to the social and cultural contexts of the target audience. Aziz (2020) discovered that individuals engaged in organised information initiatives experienced increased comfort with digital platforms, resulting in elevated satisfaction levels.

**Usability Feedback:** Usability input refers to the difficulty people encounter when using digital products and how effectively they can communicate these issues to program managers. Commonly used feedback tools help improve the user experience and identify areas where work needs to be done. Leporini et al. (2012) conducted a study that indicated that benefit remarks in platform design make it much simpler for individuals to use and access, especially for groups who are not as well-off. Feedback can also help find problems, like problems with technology, bad user interfaces, and language barriers.

### *4.2.3 Governance Mechanisms*

Some rules must be followed for digital cash transfers to operate. These systems work well due to several factors, including rules, legislation, and management procedures. Good governance ensures that digital cash transfers are made in a fair, transparent, and efficient way. This builds confidence among beneficiaries and makes the system work better. This chapter talks about the most important factors that affect how governments work and how those factors affect and what happens with digital money exchanges. For digital cash transfer systems to work, the systems that control them need to be secure. Systems need to be transparent and accountable if people are to believe them, for scams to decrease, and for the government to work better. If there are no tight rules in place, trades in digital money could be held up, stolen, or treated wrongly. According to Chowdhury et al. (2022), effective management ensures that resources are allocated to the neediest groups and enhances the functionality of digital systems.

To work well, digital methods for sending money need strong ways to keep track of things. There should be clear rules about who is accountable for what, how to do things, and rules that encourage everyone to work together to keep the system running smoothly. Strong governments are less likely to be crooked, run badly, or cause delays. This makes the service work better, gives people more trust, and spreads the word about the app. How well digital currency transfer systems work rests on things like how transparent the government is, how jobs are distributed, and how much help they get from the government. A program is doing its job if it shares money freely, protects against fraud, and has clear rules for how it should work. Digital money transfer systems can help poor people and make sure that everyone can use financial services by making sure that government tools are strong and work properly.

### Indicators of Governance Mechanisms

**Transparency:** Many parts of digital cash transfer methods are easy for anyone to learn about if the government is transparent and honest. There are due dates for payments, requirements to meet, and ways to file concerns. Researchers have found that the public's trust in these programs is greatly affected by how clear the payment directions and program limits are (Khan et al. 2022). Digital options that make it simple to understand payment plans, who can use them, and the current payment state are better. According to Chowdhury et al. (2023), making it simple for customers to report problems or delays builds trust in the system.

**Accountability Structures:** There are no effective ways to hold individuals accountable for digital currency, identify flaws, and address fraud or misuse. To make sure that the money goes to the proper persons, the following measures must be taken. Regular inspections or support from outside watchdogs can help reduce fraud, cheating, and the waste of valuable resources. According to Chowdhury et al. (2022), user feedback loops and data-driven tracking systems help identify bugs early on, making the system more reliable. It is essential to establish clear guidelines for addressing mistakes, scams, and complaints. Systems that enable receivers to identify issues with payments or incorrect transfers quickly significantly reduce the likelihood of people being taken advantage of or making mistakes (Haider and Mahamud 2017).

**Policy Support:** Policy support refers to national or local rules that facilitate access to the internet and enable individuals to modify social safety net programs. Digital cash transfer systems that are transparent to everyone, long-lasting, and in line with larger development goals are guaranteed by well-thought-out policy designs. Haider and Mahamud (2017) say that strong policy support can be seen in the fact that national programs that encourage digital financial inclusion are accepted. These include internet payment methods and mobile banking, which the government requires. Plans like the Digital Bangladesh Vision 2021 have made it possible for a lot of digital banking services to launch in Bangladesh. These measures have also made it easier for social safety nets to use digital money as a form of payment (GoB 2019).

#### *4.2.4 Socioeconomic Factors*

How people use and make money from digital currency trade methods depends on how much money they have. Because of these things, these strategies might be harder to use, less accepted, and less successful, especially with sensitive groups of people. This part looks at some important social factors, like income levels, differences between men and women, and differences between regions, to see how they affect the use and success of digital currency transfer programs. By examining these factors, we may be able to determine what makes digital financial inclusion beneficial or detrimental to different individuals. What kind of money people have a lot to do with how easy it is for them to get and use good digital currency transfer technology. It depends on their income, gender, and where people live, as well as how big the tech gap is. Some people will find it harder to use banking services and tools because of this. Several studies show that digital currency markets must deal with these societal and economic problems if they are to achieve their goals of supporting social justice and financial inclusion (Chowdhury et al. 2022).

The ease of accessing and using digital currency trading sites depends significantly on socioeconomic factors. Some people, especially those with lower incomes, may find it hard to be physically active because of worries about money, social values, or unfair access to resources. To maximise the benefits of digital cash transfers in helping more people access money, it is essential to address certain challenges. What can be done is to make technology easier for low-income families to access, fight for policies that include both men and women, and improve facilities in rural areas. Wealth, gender roles, and location may all affect efforts to send money digitally. Some people who could benefit from these services might not be able to use them because of where they live, their gender, or their lack of money. If these problems were addressed, digital money transfer methods would be fairer and more accessible to a wider range of people. Digital banking will be able to be used by people.

**Indicators of Socioeconomic Factors**

**Income Levels:** If someone wants to use a digital currency exchange, they need to have enough cash to pay for the services, tools, and internet plans they need. People who do not have much money might not be able to obtain the cell phones, mobile internet, and other equipment they need to utilise digital currency. People need to be able to utilise current instruments that are not too pricey so that most people can afford them. Not having much money can make it hard to get the most out of digital currency purchases, according to the World Bank (2020). This is because they do not have the right tools. People with restricted funds may have trouble getting to digital platforms, especially if they are not familiar with the technology (Haider and Mahamud 2017).

**Gender Dynamics:** The disparity between men and women is a key social aspect that impacts how successfully digital money transfer systems perform. Women, especially those who live in rural regions, may have trouble using digital banking services because of cultural, economic, and educational limitations. Gender not only affects digital understanding, but it also affects who can use technology well. Studies indicate that women are less inclined to utilise digital payments due to a lower likelihood of possessing mobile phones or internet access (Aziz 2020). Women can trade digital currency, but societal gender conventions may make it difficult for them to manage their money (Aziz and Naima 2021). Giving women mobile phones or putting greater emphasis on teaching them about money might help digital initiatives move forward by making them more successful and erasing gender inequalities.

**Regional Disparities:** The gap between locales, especially between urban and rural regions, is another big social and economic challenge. People who live in remote locations may have a tougher time accessing digital infrastructure that benefits them, such as safe mobile phone and internet networks. People can only transmit digital money if they have a cell phone network and an internet connection. They do not operate as well outside of cities (Haider and Mahamud 2017). People who reside in remote regions may also have trouble using digital currency transfer systems because they typically have limited access to banks and programs that educate them on how to use technology. Khan et al. (2022) discovered that inadequate infrastructure in rural regions hinders timely access to digital monies. This makes it harder for them to make money from these ventures.

There is a need to look at four separate things to figure out why digital cash transfers succeed or do not work: the technology behind them, how well people know how to use computers, how the government works, and socioeconomic considerations. These four things all function together. Each variable represents a distinct aspect of the environment in which these programs operate. For example, infrastructure makes it easier for people to get involved, literacy encourages meaningful participation, good governance builds trust and responsibility, and socioeconomic conditions affect how fair and inclusive the results are. The study demonstrates that digitalisation alone cannot rectify the issue of inequality; it needs continuous investments in infrastructure, targeted skill development, robust institutional frameworks, and context-specific remedies. This multimodal method not only makes it easier to analyse the study better, but it also makes it easier to give good ideas on how to make Bangladesh's digital safety net services better in a way that benefits everyone.

In short, both dependent and independent factors have been analysed in this chapter. This tells us everything that is needed to know about how Bangladesh's digital cash transfer methods help its SSNs. Beneficiary satisfaction, administrative efficiency, and lower transaction costs are some of the indicators of the dependent variable that demonstrate how digital activities directly impact program beneficiaries and managers, as well as their effectiveness. However, the independent variables—which include technology infrastructure, digital skills, government processes, and socio-economic factors—show the structural and contextual factors that affect how well these systems work in real-life situations. The study develops a comprehensive analytical framework by examining the relationship between these two groups of characteristics. It aims to determine both the effectiveness of digital cash transfers and what factors make them more or less useful in various situations and among different groups of people. This two-sided method shows how digitisation affects social safety, relying on how outcomes are measured as well as the structural factors that those outcomes are based on. Together, these things give us an organised way to think about the pros, cons, and long-term viability of sending money using digital currency. This is especially helpful for improving social safety net services in Bangladesh and other areas.

## 5 Analytical Framework

This study's analytical framework focuses on how the dependent and independent variables that affect how well digital cash transfers work with each other. How well digital cash transfers work is the dependent variable. The framework is meant to show how different factors, like technology infrastructure, digital literacy, governance systems, and socioeconomic factors, affect the dependent variable. This system is based on how well digital cash transfers function, which is influenced by several key external factors. Technological infrastructure is a crucial, separate factor because it determines the reliability and ease of access to digital platforms required for smooth cash flow performance. Digital money transfers cannot function effectively without stable mobile apps, a reliable internet connection, and systems that people can rely on. Digital knowledge is very important for these trades to go well. How happy receivers are and how ready they are to utilise digital currency transfer schemes depends a lot on how well they can connect to digital platforms. This is true whether they have extensive knowledge of digital systems or are only familiar with operating a phone. Governance strategies assist in making these systems even more valuable by giving them the rules, accountability frameworks, and transparency they need. Strong governance systems make sure that the right people get help quickly and properly. This builds trust while reducing mistakes, scams, and delays.

Finally, the person who receives the money may not be able to receive digital cash transfers depending on their gender, income, or where they live. These things decide if someone can do business online and what can go wrong with their transactions, including not having enough infrastructure in their location or being worried about the cost. The way that digital cash transfers function in real life is controlled by a sophisticated network of connections between these different aspects. This graph illustrates the connection between these factors, showing how each one contributes to the overall performance of digital currency exchange systems (Fig. 1).

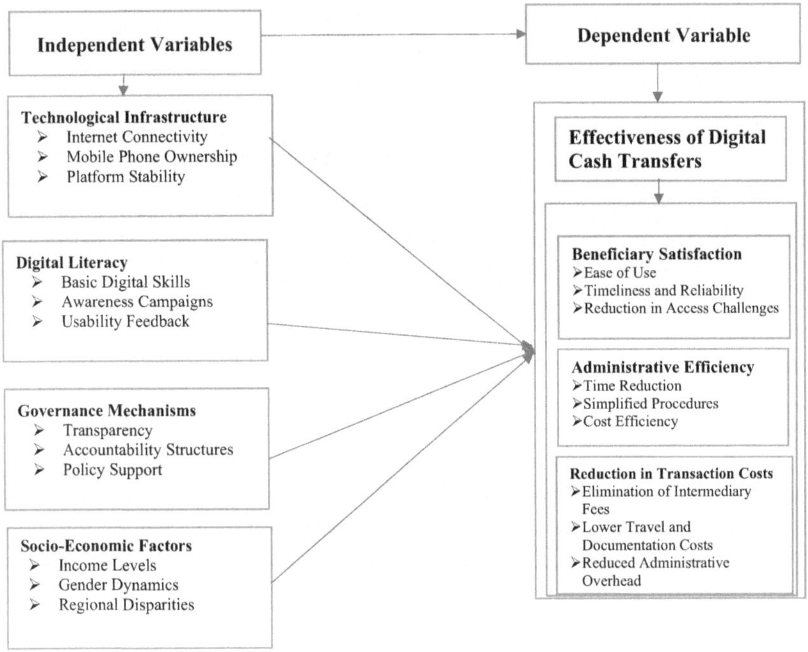


**Fig. 1** An analytical framework of the study. Source: The figure was drawn by the authors

## 6 Conclusion

This chapter explains the basic ideas and steps required to assess the effectiveness of digital cash transfers in Bangladesh's social safety net programs. The study developed a clear framework for further research by breaking down the main ideas—including digital cash transfers, social safety nets, and financial inclusion—into measurable measures. The dependent variable has been discussed, and it became clear that results like satisfied beneficiaries, streamlined administration, and lower transaction costs show how technology has changed service delivery and the experience of recipients. Additionally, identifying independent variables such as technical infrastructure, digital skills, governance mechanisms, and socioeconomic factors revealed the structural barriers and enabling conditions that influence the effectiveness of these programs and the number of people who can participate in them. When viewed as a whole, this approach suggests that output indicators alone are insufficient to determine the effectiveness of digital social safety. Instead, we need to look at how results interact with the factors that cause them. Digital cash transfers are not just fixes for technical problems; how well they work depends on the community they are part of. This chapter provides the analytical tools necessary to examine both the benefits and drawbacks of technology in Bangladesh's social safety nets, situating the research within a multidimensional framework. This then sets the stage for the next empirical study, which will use the operationalised variables to look at how digital measures are changing the way aid is given to some of the most vulnerable groups in the country.

## References

Ahmed, W. (2023). Understanding self-directed learning behavior towards digital competence among business research students: SEM-neural analysis. *Education and Information Technologies, 28*(4), 4173–4202.

Alam, M. A., and Hossain, S. A. (2016). Effectiveness of social safety net programs for poor people in the government level of Bangladesh. *International Journal of Social Sciences and Management, 3*(3), 153–158.

Allen, F., Demirgüç-Kunt, A., Klapper, L., and Martinez Peria, M. S. (2016). The foundations of financial inclusion: Understanding ownership and use of formal accounts. *Journal of Financial Intermediation, 27*, 1–30. https://doi.org/10.1016/j.jfi.2015.12.003

Aziz, A. (2020). Digital inclusion challenges in Bangladesh: The case of the National ICT Policy. *Contemporary South Asia, 28*(3), 304–319. https://doi.org/10.1080/09584935.2020.1793912

Aziz, A., and Naima, U. (2021). Rethinking digital financial inclusion: Evidence from Bangladesh. *Technology in Society, 64*, 23–31.

Babar, Z. N., Al-Sulaiti, K., Aldereai, O., Abbas, J. and Al-Sulaiti, I. (2023). Financial Inclusion, Leadership Abilities, Family Support, and Country of Origin Effects Empower Female Entrepreneurs. *Journal of Excellence in Business Administration*, 1(2):39–63

Banerjee, A., Hanna, R., Olken, B. A., and Lisker, D. S. (2024). Social protection in the developing world. *Journal of Economic Literature, 62*(4), 1349–1421.

Bateman, M. (2012). The role of microfinance in contemporary rural development finance policy and practice: imposing neoliberalism as 'best practice'. *Journal of Agrarian Change, 12*(4), 587–600.

Beck, T., Demirgüç-Kunt, A., and Levine, R. (2007). Finance, inequality, and the poor. *Journal of Economic Growth, 12*(1), 27–49.

Chib, A., van Velthoven, M. H., and Car, J. (2015). mHealth adoption in low-resource environments: A review of the use of mobile healthcare in developing countries. *Journal of Health Communication, 20*(1), 4–34. https://doi.org/10.1080/10810730.2013.864735

Choudhary, M. S. R. (2013). Impact of old age allowance among rural aged: An empirical investigation. *International Journal of Sociology and Anthropology, 5*(7), 262.

Chowdhury, A., Lawson, C., Kellison, E., Chia, H. S., Kharas, H., Fuller, J., Faye, M., Rutokowski, M., Salvado, R., and Dercon, S. (2022). Accelerating digital cash transfers to the world's poorest. *Brookings*. Retrieved from https://www.brookings.edu/articles/accelerating-digital-cash-transfers-to-the-worlds-poorest/ (Accessed on November 23, 2024).

Chowdhury, S., Joel-Edgar, S., Dey, P. K., Bhattacharya, S., and Kharlamov, A. (2023). Embedding transparency in artificial intelligence machine learning models: managerial implications on predicting and explaining employee turnover. *The International Journal of Human Resource Management, 34*(14), 2732–2764.

Crawford, G. (2006). The World Bank and good governance. *The IMF, World Bank and policy reform, 48*, 115.

Davis, F. D. (1989). Perceived usefulness, perceived ease of use, and user acceptance of information technology. *MIS Quarterly, 13*(3), 319–340.

Demirgüç-Kunt, A., Klapper, L., Singer, D., Ansar, S., and Hess, J. (2018). *The Global Findex Database 2017: Measuring financial inclusion and the fintech revolution*. World Bank Publications.

Donner, J., and Tellez, C. A. (2008). Mobile banking and economic development: Linking adoption, impact, and use. *Asian Journal of Communication, 18*(4), 318–332. https://doi.org/10.1080/01292980802344190

Fox, J. (2015). Social accountability: What does the evidence really say? *World Development, 72*, 346–361. https://doi.org/10.1016/j.worlddev.2015.03.011

Gabor, D., and Brooks, S. (2020). The digital revolution in financial inclusion: international development in the fintech era. In *Material cultures of financialisation* (pp. 69–82). Routledge.

Gentilini, U. (2022). *Cash transfers in pandemic times: Evidence, practices, and implications from the largest scale-up in history.* Washington, DC: World Bank Group.

Government of Bangladesh (2019). *Digital Bangladesh Vision 2021: National ICT Policy.*

Grohmann, A., Klühs, T., and Menkhoff, L. (2018). Does financial literacy improve financial inclusion? Cross country evidence. *World Development, 111*, 84–96. https://doi.org/10.1016/j.worlddev.2018.06.020

Haider, M. Z., and Mahamud, A. (2017). Beneficiary selection and allowance utilisation of social safety net programme in Bangladesh. *Journal of Human Rights and Social Work, 2*(1–2), 45–51.

Hanna, E., Ward, L. M., Seabrook, R. C., Jerald, M., Reed, L., Giaccardi, S., and Lippman, J. R. (2017b). Contributions of social comparison and self-objectification in mediating associations between Facebook use and emergent adults' psychological well-being. *Cyberpsychology, Behavior, and Social Networking, 20*(3), 172–179.

Hanna, R., Kreindler, G., and Olken, B. A. (2017a). Citywide effects of high-occupancy vehicle restrictions: Evidence from "three-in-one" in Jakarta. *Science, 357*(6346), 89–93.

Hasan, N., Ashraf, M., Ahmed, E., Hasan, M. R., and Bhattacharjee, V. (2017). The impact of information and communication technology (ICT) on the lives of disabilities: a case in Bangladesh. *International Journal on Disability and Human Development, 16*(3), 301–310.

Hydén, G., and Mease, K. (2004). *Making sense of governance: empirical evidence from sixteen developing countries.* Lynne Rienner Publishers.

Kaiser, Z. R. M. A., Uddin, N., and Yaquib, M. (2023). Governance of social safety net in Bangladesh: A study on the employment generation programme for the poorest. *Indian Journal of Public Administration, 69*(2), 1–15.

Khan, M., Parvaiz, G. S., Dedahanov, A. T., Abdurazzakov, O. S., and Rakhmonov, D. A. (2022). The impact of technologies of traceability and transparency in supply chains. *Sustainability, 14*(24), 16336.

Leporini, B., Buzzi, M. C., and Buzzi, M. (2012). Interacting with mobile devices via VoiceOver: usability and accessibility issues. In *Proceedings of the 24th Australian computer-human interaction conference* (pp. 339–348).

Nikey, R. (2024). Digital Landscape and Women Entrepreneurship Development in Bangladesh. An Unpublished Bachelors in Business Administration Dissertation. Dhaka: BRAC University.

Pierre, J., and Peters, B. G. (2020). *Governance, politics and the state.* Bloomsbury Publishing.

Pradhan, M. A. H., and Afrin, S. (2015). A review of social safety nets programs for women in Bangladesh: Issue and challenges. *Advances in Economics and Business, 3*(4), 149–156.

Rahman, H. Z., Choudhury, L. A., and Ali, K. S. (2011). *Social safety nets in Bangladesh: Review of issues and analytical inventory (Vol. 1).* Dhaka: A PPRC-UNDP Research Initiative.

Rogers, E. M. (2003). *Diffusion of innovations* (5th ed.). Free Press.

Salam, M. A. (2022). *Social Protection for Well-Being. The effectiveness of social protection programmes in Bangladesh* (Doctoral dissertation).

Sarwar, M. B.; Diepeveen, S.; Moreno, D. B. (2023): Cash transfers and digital financial inclusion: Regional evidence from Asia Pacific with a focus on Bangladesh, Cambodia, and Nepal, ODI Report, Overseas Development Institute (ODI), London.

Scholl, H. J. (2008). Discipline or interdisciplinary study domain? Challenges and promises in electronic government research. In *Digital government: E-government research, case studies, and implementation* (pp. 21–41). Boston, MA: Springer US.

Sen, A. (1999). *Development as freedom*. Oxford University Press.

Suri, T., and Jack, W. (2016). The long-run poverty and gender impacts of mobile money. *Science, 354*(6317), 1288–1292. https://doi.org/10.1126/science.aah5309

Venkatesh, V., and Davis, F. D. (2000). A theoretical extension of the technology acceptance model: Four longitudinal field studies. *Management Science, 46*(2), 186–204. https://doi.org/10.1287/mnsc.46.2.186.11926

Venkatesh, V., Morris, M. G., Davis, G. B., and Davis, F. D. (2003). User acceptance of information technology: Toward a unified view. *MIS Quarterly, 27*(3), 425–478. https://doi.org/10.2307/30036540

World Bank. (2020). *The global Findex database 2017: Measuring financial inclusion and the fintech revolution*. Washington, DC: World Bank Publications.

Yoshino, N. and Morgan, P.T. (2017). Financial Inclusion, Regulation, and Education. Japan: Asian Development Bank Institute.

# Digital Cash Transfer Systems in Social Safety Net Programs in Bangladesh: An Overview

**Abstract** This chapter examines the effectiveness of digital cash transfer methods employed by Social Safety Net (SSN) programs in Bangladesh in facilitating access to money for low-income people. This chapter examines the advantages and disadvantages of digital cash transfers, as well as their effects on user convenience, speed, and security. It addresses issues like unequal distribution throughout the country, limited access to technology, and low levels of digital literacy. This chapter explores how digital technology can enhance government operations, reduce costs, and foster accountability and transparency. With a particular focus on programs such as the Old Age Allowance and the Allowance for Widows, this chapter illustrates how digital technologies can be effectively integrated into a country's social welfare system. Ultimately, it offers recommendations that would strengthen the safety net, expand access to financial services for a broader population, and remove barriers to digital money transfers.

**Keywords** Digital cash transfers • Social Safety Net programs • Bangladesh • Financial access • Digital literacy • Governance



P. K. Panday, A. H. M. K. Ahsan, *Digital Revolution for the Vulnerable*, https://doi.org/10.1007/978-981-95-7980-8_3

## 1 Introduction

For a long time, Bangladesh's Social Safety Net (SSN) programs have played a crucial role in reducing poverty and improving living standards. They assist those in need, including older adults and children. These programs are crucial because they prevent people from falling into extreme poverty in a society where many people remain concerned about their financial security. The government has updated and expanded these programs to meet new policy goals and evolving social and economic demands. The way things work has changed recently with the addition of digital cash transfer options to SSN systems. Now that they are more widely available, anyone can take part. These strategies utilise technology to minimise leakage, lower transaction costs, and ensure that beneficiaries receive their payments on time. The SSN programs in Bangladesh are described in this chapter. Their history, existing service practices, and the consequences of digital transformations have been the main topics of discussion. This chapter discusses the two primary SSNs in Bangladesh: the Old Age Allowance (OAA) and the Allowance for Widowed, Deserted, and Destitute Women. These initiatives demonstrate the government's commitment to supporting the most vulnerable. They also demonstrate how to evaluate the usefulness and effectiveness of using digital transfers versus cash. The history of SSN programs in Bangladesh is covered first, followed by an analysis of digital system integration. Ultimately, it discusses the advantages and disadvantages of the current system. We will learn a great deal about how to help Bangladesh's poor people by combining social assistance with contemporary technology.

## 2 History and Evolution of Social Safety Net Programs in Bangladesh

Bangladesh primarily relies on SSN programs to fight poverty, guarantee that everyone has access to money, and promote social justice. These programs have evolved in response to new legislation, demographic shifts, and budgetary constraints. To completely understand their current shape and relevance, it is essential to have a solid understanding of their history and evolution.

### 2.1 *The Post-Independence Era: Foundations of Social Protection*

As soon as Bangladesh gained its independence in 1971, SSN programs were started. Access to food was hindered by the country's highly unstable economy and its large population of impoverished people. The government responded by launching initiatives to provide minor aid to needy populations. One of the first notable initiatives launched in 1974 was the Food for Work (FFW) program. In return for their labour on public works projects, including irrigation and road building, they received food goods (Khuda 2011). Even though it was small and had limited resources, this marked the beginning of safety nets as an integral part of Bangladesh's social policy. Because the government prioritises reducing poverty in the short term over long-term growth, these projects were primarily aimed at addressing major disasters.

### 2.2 *Expansion During the 1980s and 1990s: Institutionalisation of SSN Programs*

In the 1980s and 1990s, SSN programs became more formalised and grew significantly. By that time, the country's economy had begun to recover, enabling the government to expand and refine its social security programs. During this time, cash-based solutions were used in conjunction with food-based ones. When it began in the fiscal year 1997–1998, the traditional Old Age Allowance was intended to assist low-income older adults with their financial needs. With its small weekly payments, the program recognised the growing problems that come with an older population, especially in rural areas. At the same time, the Widow pension was created in the fiscal year 1998–1999 to help women who were struggling financially after the death of their husbands (Khuda 2011). The goal of these payments was to help widows deal with social shame and being left out, as well as to meet their immediate cash needs.

### 2.3 *The Role of International Donors and Development Partners*

Donors from outside of Bangladesh have had a significant impact on SSN programs in the country. There was assistance with funding and professional expertise from the World Bank, the Asian Development Bank

(ADB), and the United Nations Development Program (UNDP). For instance, the World Bank's assistance for poverty alleviation systems has led to program design changes that better align with poverty reduction objectives (Anwar and Cho 2019). These connections also provided people with access to international best practices, including methods for tracking and evaluating the effectiveness of programs and initiatives. Changes were implemented during this period to prevent leaks, clarify procedures, and ensure that the appropriate people were provided with the necessary resources and support.

### 2.4 *Integration with National Development Strategies*

As the twenty-first century began, SSN projects have evolved, as they are now incorporated into larger national development goals. According to the government, improving social protection through its Five-Year Plans is the best approach to boost the economy. In the 2000s, the Poverty Reduction Strategy Papers (PRSPs) formalised this approach by linking SSN initiatives to broader objectives, such as eradicating poverty, promoting gender equality, and enhancing women's economic empowerment (Government of Bangladesh 2005). The National Social Security Strategy (NSSS), released in 2015, altered the process. The primary objective of this comprehensive policy framework was to consolidate and streamline the various SSN systems across the nation. This would make things run more smoothly and less divided. It also stated that transitioning to digital platforms could help the government become more transparent and save money (Government of Bangladesh 2015).

### 2.5 *Recent Developments: Digitalisation of SSN Programs*

Technology has improved Bangladesh's SSN services over the last few years. People are increasingly using digital cash because governments are supporting it. It is now possible to pay for the Old Age Allowance and the Allowance for Widowed, Deserted, and Destitute Women digitally (Choudhury et al. 2019). Mobile banking and fingerprint recognition are utilised in these systems to ensure that transfers are quick and accurate. These new ideas address long-standing problems, such as the misblending of people, lengthy money transfer processes, and cheating. Digitisation has reduced transaction costs and improved aiming accuracy by eliminating the need for middlemen and routine tasks.

Bangladesh's SSN systems continue to experience problems, despite significant progress. They are still not working because they do not cover enough people, do not provide sufficient rewards, and operate in different areas at varying levels. Due to inadequate management or a lack of expertise, many legitimate users are rejected (Ahmed et al. 2014). This is particularly true in rural areas. These efforts will not be successful until these issues are fixed and more people have access to the newest digital technologies. To ensure that SSN activities are successful and long-lasting, it is crucial to enhance governance, train personnel on how to utilise technology efficiently, and foster partnerships with businesses. Lastly, the numerous SSN programs in Bangladesh underscore their importance in combating poverty and promoting equity. These programs have changed over time to meet the needs of the country's society and economy. They began in the 1970s with limited resources and have since evolved into digital money transfer specialists. The relevance and utility of these tools as catalysts for advancement, benefiting all stakeholders and making loans more accessible, are underscored by their connection to the global development goals.

## 3 Overview of Current SSN Programs in Bangladesh

SSN programs are crucial to Bangladesh's efforts to combat inequality, alleviate poverty, and support those who are marginalised or excluded from the system. These programs help achieve the Sustainable Development Goals (SDGs), which align with the government's primary objective of promoting individual growth and development. The Government of Bangladesh's Finance Division (2023) states that 23 different ministries and departments are implementing 113 social safety net programs. By addressing problems and chances for growth in both business and society, these programs benefit a wide range of people.

### *3.1 Categories of SSN Programs in Bangladesh*

Bangladesh has numerous programs that aim to protect people from unfair treatment, enhance public safety, and assist those in need. People and families with low wages can get help from these services. These groups can ultimately benefit people by providing them with financial assistance, social support, and opportunities for personal growth. The country's SSN programs, which take a different method, are meant to help more people who are having trouble with money. These groups include activities that aim to have a greater impact on society, such as food security programs and job growth initiatives. All of them are different and are designed to meet specific needs while also working towards the primary goals of eradicating poverty and empowering people in communities. This section lists the most significant projects from each group, along with their primary objectives, outcomes, challenges, and proposed solutions. This is a comprehensive list of all the ways the SSN system assists people in need and how it operates nationwide.

### *3.1.1 Cash Transfer Programs*

Bangladesh's SSN utilises money transfer methods to assist some of the nation's poorest citizens directly. These services are crucial to assisting them in a society where economic inequality and poverty remain major problems. The goal of these programs is to help low-income people escape poverty, become less vulnerable, and lead more fulfilling lives. These services are crucial for maintaining security and empowering staff to perform their jobs efficiently. Many of these people, such as the elderly, women who have been separated or abandoned, and people with disabilities, are prohibited from receiving assistance in order to work lawfully. In order to alleviate poverty and assist those who are most in need, SSN programs are crucial. The two most significant programs are Old Age Security (OAS) and the Allowance for Widowed, Deserted, and Destitute Women (Widows' Allowance), which assist older adults and women. This section provides comprehensive information about these programs, including their objectives, target audience, operational methods, and impact on poverty. This group is engaged in several significant projects:

**Old Age Allowance (OAA)**

Bangladesh has developed a plan to address its social and economic challenges by implementing specific policies. The OAA and the Widows' Allowance are two crucial components of this plan. These programs provide financial assistance to help elders and children, two of society's most vulnerable groups. Their life will be safer, more pleasant, and filled with social activities if they have them. A significant portion of the SSN system is comprised of these efforts. They demonstrate that the government is attempting to assist people who lack alternative means of support by providing them with additional resources and establishing a safety net in the event of unforeseen circumstances.

Bangladesh has developed a plan to address its economic and social challenges by implementing specific policies. The OAA and Widows' Allowance are two important elements of this plan. Older adults and children, two of society's most vulnerable groups, receive financial assistance from these programs. Furthermore, they enable people to live a safer, more polite, and socially active existence. The SSN system comprises numerous projects. They demonstrate how the government is attempting to assist people who lack alternative options by providing additional support and establishing a safety net in case unforeseen events occur in their lives. The program also directly helps older people who are impoverished, a significant issue in rural areas where the economy is not performing as well. There is a slightly lower age limit for women, at 62 years old, but the program is primarily intended for people 65 years or older. People who lack family or other means of support often seek help first. Approximately 5.8 million adults currently receive support from the program, with most residing in rural areas (GoB 2023a). This wide reach makes the program even more crucial for enhancing the financial well-being of seniors, particularly those who are most vulnerable to financial hardship

The OAA's operating methods make sure that the program helps the people who need it the most. Monthly payments are sent from bank accounts or mobile financial services (MFS) to ensure efficiency and prevent delays or leaks. Beneficiaries, mostly those from families living below the poverty line, are selected based on their income, age, and level of vulnerability. With this technology, the sharing process is now much faster and clearer, making it more efficient. As the program becomes increasingly important in the SSN system and more people realise that older people need this type of targeted financial assistance, the government allocated BDT 33 billion for it in the 2022–2023 budget (Bangladesh Bureau of Statistics 2023).

The OAA has made a significant difference in many areas. Eliminating poverty is one of the most significant effects. Studies show that the program has significantly reduced the number of impoverished people among its users, particularly in rural areas where the elderly are more likely to be impoverished (Uddin 2013). The program also helps people afford essential medical care by providing them with financial assistance. This improves their general quality of life. The scheme could provide people who receive help with a steady stream of financial support, thereby enhancing their freedom and dignity. They have more freedom and are better known within their groups as a result. The OAA is crucial for older citizens in Bangladesh, as it enables them to enhance their financial situation and become more actively engaged in their communities.

**Allowance for the Widowed, Deserted, and Destitute Women**

The Widows' Allowance program is a vital initiative that enhances the financial stability and independence of women who have lost their primary source of income. This is for women who have been abandoned, are in need, or have lost a loved one. These women are among the most vulnerable people in Bangladesh. The program's primary objectives are to enhance the financial security of these women, equip them with the ability to make informed decisions, and promote their development of independence and self-reliance. The initiative aims to empower these women by providing them with direct financial support, encouraging their participation in family and community activities, and removing barriers to their involvement. This service is available to women over the age of 18 who have lost a loved one and are below the poverty line. As of 2023, more than 24.75 lakh women (Bangladesh Bureau of Statistics 2023) are getting this income. Many of them live in rural or underdeveloped areas. Some of the significant socioeconomic challenges these women may face include being excluded from social groups and having limited opportunities for earning a living. They depend heavily on the Allowance they receive to cover the expenses necessary for their own care and that of their families.

The working methods of the Widows' Allowance program ensure that the right people who are supposed to receive help can access it quickly and easily. While interacting with neighbours, local government representatives select qualified women according to socioeconomic criteria. Because of this tactic, the weakest people are chosen first. Regular payees have the option to have their money transferred directly to their bank accounts or use mobile banking services. This digital strategy lowers the risk of fraud, expedites money transfers, and makes transactions more transparent. Frequent evaluations and input from the community support the program's goals, ensuring that everyone is held accountable for their efforts.

The Allowance for Widows program has a major impact on many factors. It provides them with a steady stream of income, enabling them to make timely bill payments and reduce their reliance on charity or illegal loans. People can afford the necessities, including food, medical care, and transportation, because they have enough money. The program has a significant impact on people's social lives, as it boosts their self-esteem and confidence. Giving these women money reduces the stigma associated with abandonment or losing a loved one, which aids in their reintegration into society. The Allowance is essential for mothers with dependent children because it enables them to ensure their children have better access to food, healthcare, and education. The following generation is therefore healthier and has a higher chance of success. The Allowance for Widows supports both immediate and long-term goals for social and economic advancement.

**Disability Allowance**

This benefit has been in place since the fiscal year 2005–2006. Providing financial assistance to people with physical or mental disabilities is one way it helps them. The monthly BDT 850 helps people cover their basic needs and reduces their dependence on family. According to the Government of Bangladesh (2023), 20.08 lakh people got help through the program in the fiscal year 2022–2023. This grant does more than provide financial assistance to people with disabilities; it demonstrates the government's commitment to meeting their rights and needs. Bangladesh's cash transfer programs have had a positive impact, particularly in reducing poverty, empowering individuals, and improving their health. Due to these programs, poverty has decreased, particularly in rural areas where many beneficiaries reside. Bangladesh is committed to addressing the social needs of all its citizens, as demonstrated by the OAA, Widows' Allowance, and Disability Allowance. These initiatives combat poverty, improve lives, and promote social justice by supporting women and older adults who are struggling. Those who received both projects are now in a better position.

Nevertheless, there are still areas for improvement, including poor management, insufficient coverage, and the need to adjust the regular payment level. Better financing, digital tools, and channels for community members to stay informed about these initiatives could help them. This will help ensure that Bangladesh's efforts to improve social justice do not overlook any groups that are already facing challenges.

Sarwar et al. (2023) suggest that providing people with money has significantly helped many of them escape extreme poverty. Financial assistance has improved the lives of the poorest people and helped maintain societal stability. Poor women and widows also benefited from entitlements that dramatically increased their financial independence. People who receive this support are better equipped to manage their finances and make informed decisions independently, which affords them greater influence in society and the economy. Additionally, people who have participated in programs like the OAA report having better access to food and medical care, which has improved their overall health and quality of life (Ahmed et al. 2014).

Although these are positive results, Bangladesh's cash transfer programs are limited in several ways that prevent them from reaching their full potential. One of the significant problems is the small amounts of money that are given. The regular funds these programs offer are very important, but they are often not enough to cover rising living costs. This makes it much harder for them to reduce poverty. It is also hard for these projects to succeed when people focus on mistakes. Due to errors in the beneficiary selection process, some eligible people were excluded, rendering the assistance less effective. Moreover, administrative problems significantly hinder the effectiveness of cash transfer programs. Delays and leaks can occur in cash transfer programs depending on human disbursement methods, which makes the program less efficient overall. Also, women still cannot get the benefits they deserve because of cultural and practical issues. This is especially true in rural regions, where women face greater challenges in accessing these programs due to cultural norms and inadequate infrastructure (Choudhury et al. 2019).

To address these issues, Bangladesh's government has initiated the digitisation of money transfer methods. One of the best aspects of going digital is that people can send money directly to anyone who needs it. Electronic payments make things run more smoothly by ensuring that the right people receive their money on time and in the correct amount. This cuts down on delays. Research indicates that online courses are also more affordable. Digitalisation makes it easier to run a program by eliminating the need for intermediaries. Asma et al. (2023) also note that linking funds to mobile banking accounts makes them more accessible, especially for people residing in rural areas who may not have easy access to traditional banking services. Cash transfer programs comprise a significant portion of Bangladesh's SSN system. Millions of people in need receive the money they require, thanks to them. Problems have included inadequate targeting, administrative slowdowns, and insufficient support. Still, the initiatives have brought people together, strengthened their ability, and reduced poverty. These programs aim to be more accessible, practical, and stable as they go to a digital platform. This will ensure that those who need help the most receive it, thereby improving the country's safety net.

### *3.1.2 Food Security Programs*

The food security efforts of Bangladesh's SSN program are also very important. They help poor people fight hunger and bad diets. The primary objectives of these programs are to provide food to as many people as possible, particularly low-income women and farmworkers, and to help people become stronger and more self-sufficient over time. People can earn money through these programs, which provide them with food and teach them new skills. This helps with the current food problems. These projects are the most important ones:

**Food for Work (FFW) Program**

The primary objectives of the Food For Work (FFW) program are to help people overcome food poverty and provide them with short-term employment opportunities. This initiative provides meals to workers who do not own property and are financially disadvantaged in exchange for their participation in community development projects, including road construction, irrigation system upgrades, and canal digging. The FFW program plays a significant role in promoting local development by enhancing infrastructure. This increases farming output, reduces the risk of flooding, and improves rural traffic efficiency. It not only helps alleviate hunger immediately, but it also strengthens rural economies (Ahmed et al. 2014). Although the program has benefits, it faces logistical challenges, including difficulties reaching remote areas, resulting in late food deliveries. Changes in the demand for workers during different times of the year also affect participation rates and program outcomes.

**Vulnerable Group Development (VGD) Program**

The Vulnerable Group Development (VGD) program, which began in 1975, is one of Bangladesh's largest food-based safety nets. Its main goal is to protect women from poverty. In addition to learning new skills that will help them earn a living in the long term, members receive monthly food rations, such as rice or wheat. The VGD program now assists approximately 750,000 women annually (GoB 2023a) and focuses on widows, divorcees, and low-income families. In addition to providing food, the program teaches people how to generate income through various means, including small-scale business ownership, sewing, and raising chickens.

Reading, writing, and health lessons help people get ready to be more involved in society and the economy. By combining food aid with programs that teach people new skills, the VGD program helps people become less reliant on outside assistance over time.

Due to programs like FFW and VGD, people in Bangladesh who are poor now have access to better food and are less likely to go hungry. The people who get food through these programs—mostly women and children—need it, and it meets their basic needs. Asma et al. (2023) state that the programs have improved the health of low-income people by providing them with access to basic food and essential minerals. This has helped them avoid hunger and the associated health problems. These programs enable individuals to meet their basic needs while also helping them achieve financial independence. One way the VGD program helps them is by giving them food and teaching them new skills. This helps them achieve long-term financial stability. This method makes it more possible for people to escape poverty and become less dependent on others. The FFW program has also helped the town grow by providing funding for building renovations. Ultimately, these programs have benefited entire communities by enhancing farm productivity, expanding market access, and improving the standard of living for rural residents. All of these things have made a significant difference in the success of the local business.

Food security programs yield numerous positive outcomes, but long-term issues frequently compromise their effectiveness. One of the main stops is the price of things. A lack of funding and resources could hinder the program's effectiveness, reducing the number of people who can receive help and ultimately making the program less effective overall. It is also unfair to continue with these projects after mistakes have been made. It remains challenging to ensure that food assistance reaches the poorest people, as mistakes in identifying recipients often result in benefits not being distributed equally. Food transportation delays, inefficient government, and greed can sometimes make programs less useful (Sarwar et al. 2023). More open and successful methods are needed in food security efforts because of these problems.

The government is developing new ideas to address these challenges and enhance the effectiveness of food security programs. One way to do this is to give people digital food coupons that they can easily access by linking them to their smartphones. This digital approach aims to simplify sharing, reduce waste, and ensure that the right people receive assistance when they need it. The use of significant data and geographic information systems (GIS) together to improve targeting is another interesting new trend. These tools can be used to identify who needs food aid, allowing resources to be directed to those who need them most. Companies are also being considered as potential partners to help food security programs reach more people and work more effectively. There are not as many people taking part in government projects as there should be. To address some of these issues, they can collaborate with private companies on initiatives such as sharing resources, transportation, and managing the supply chain. The FFW and VGD programs are essential parts of Bangladesh's food security and SSN systems. They support both current food needs and long-term economic growth. These programs help combat hunger by providing food and teaching people new skills simultaneously. They also strengthen neighbourhoods and combat poverty. There is a need to optimise the process, improve their aim, and make tool investments if people want to achieve the most. These initiatives tackle Bangladesh's ongoing hunger and malnutrition problems by utilising digital tools and cooperative approaches.

### *3.1.3 Employment Generation Schemes*

The foundation of Bangladesh's SSN structure is initiatives that provide short-term employment to help people escape poverty. These programs' main goals are to help rural poor people, lower seasonal unemployment, and preserve their financial security. SSNs based on employment also help build long-term infrastructure that helps communities' socioeconomic levels. Here are some key projects that fall within this category.

**Employment Generation Program for the Poorest (EGPP)**

The main project, named the Employment Generation Program for the Poorest (EGPP), commenced in 2008 to support people in rural areas in securing employment and overcoming poverty. During lean farming seasons, the EGPP assists low-income families who face limited job opportunities. The EGPP focuses on families that are below the ultra-poor level. It does this to help underprivileged groups, such as women-headed households and landless workers. The EGPP provides approximately 2 million people with casual jobs every year and offers important financial security during key off-seasons in agriculture (Anwar and Cho 2019). Maintenance work on roads, repairs to embankments, and building community centres are some of the hard infrastructure projects that recipients work on. These initiatives generate revenue and strengthen connections in isolated communities, ultimately making them more resilient and sustainable.

The primary objectives of the EGPP centre are to address pressing issues, including reducing poverty, building infrastructure, and empowering people. It also works on other projects that create jobs. These initiatives will provide both direct and indirect assistance to those who are struggling. This is particularly true for people living in rural areas, where unemployment and poverty are prevalent. There is a lot of seasonal poverty among farm workers during the off-season. These programs are meant to help reduce this. In these challenging economic times, the EGPP is a vital means for families to earn a living and avoid poverty. This income helps with financial matters and reduces the need for illegal loans, which many people resort to during times of seasonal unemployment. Additionally, the program mitigates the adverse effects of seasonal migration, such as increased city traffic and family separation, which can have lasting impacts on society (Ahmed et al. 2014). In this way, the EGPP is crucial for maintaining economic stability during periods of low demand.

Also, the most important benefits of policies that create jobs are linked to improving infrastructure. These projects enhance essential community resources while also providing direct funding to the initiatives. Repairing embankments is one example of a project that helps lessen the damage that natural disasters can do to rural areas. Similarly, projects to repair roads make it easier for people to access markets, which in turn help distribute farm goods to a wider audience and support local economic growth. While these infrastructure improvements were originally part of the program's short-term goals, they will have long-term economic benefits by supporting rural development and creating jobs in the community that will last (Raihan et al. 2021). Building facilities and helping people earn a living simultaneously is beneficial for rural communities in both the short and long term.

Programs like the EGPP, which are designed to create jobs, also focus on social security and empowering people. These projects help close gaps in entry to the job market by focusing on poor groups, especially women and landless workers. Since many of the people who will benefit from these programs are women, the fact that they emphasise the inclusion of both men and women is noteworthy. Women's place in society rests a lot on their ability to make their own money and be accepted by others, which participation in society gives them. Many people also acquire non-formal skills, such as project management or building, even though the primary focus is on physical work. These skills make them more marketable in several areas and give them useful tools for their next job search.

Nevertheless, programs that create jobs face several challenges that reduce their effectiveness, despite their successes. One significant problem is that there is insufficient coverage, which means that many suitable families do not receive the benefits due to limited funds, poor targeting, and inadequate program capabilities. Even when the program's recipients are identified, the pay they receive is often insufficient to cover their basic needs, which limits the program's ability to eradicate poverty (Rahman and Choudhury 2012). Additionally, delays in distributing funds and implementing projects hinder the program's objectives, particularly during challenging times when people require assistance the most. Corruption and leaks, poor management, favouritism in beneficiary selection, and misallocation of funds are also significant issues that compromise the programs' fairness and effectiveness, erode trust, and diminish their impact.

Several measures can be taken to enhance the effectiveness of programs that create jobs. Using digital methods alongside these efforts helps reduce leaks, enhances transparency, and shortens the time it takes to distribute wages. By utilising Geographic Information Systems (GIS) and current data analytics, the targeting process can be made more accurate, enabling the identification and assistance of the most vulnerable people. Additionally, ecology is of great importance. When long-term programs are combined with short-term job opportunities for skill development, they can help people secure higher-paying jobs and become less reliant on casual work.

Lastly, improving tracking systems and establishing robust mechanisms for people to file complaints will help reduce cheating and ensure that everyone who benefits from the program can use their benefits fairly. Bangladesh has two issues: poverty and unemployment. Programs like the EGPP help solve both of these problems. Poor people receive much-needed help from these programs, which combine quick cash aid with infrastructure improvements to boost long-term economic growth in rural areas. To have the most impact, they need to continue investing in technology, focus their efforts more effectively, and manage their programs more efficiently. By utilising digital technologies, implementing improved monitoring methods, and prioritising sustainability, these programs can become more transparent, effective, and capable of helping to reduce poverty and improve the lives of the most vulnerable people.

### *3.1.4 Social Empowerment Programs*

Bangladesh's SSN framework is based on programs that empower people. The goals of these projects are to promote social justice and address the root causes of social problems. The goal of these programs is to address structural issues that hinder disadvantaged groups from achieving long-term growth, thereby increasing their chances of success and overall well-being. Millions of people nationwide have benefited from two well-known programs: the Maternity Allowance Program (MAP) and the Primary Education Stipend Program (PESP). The most crucial actions to take in this area are as follows:

**Maternity Allowance Program (MAP)**

The MAP helps new parents and pregnant women who are struggling with financial difficulties by providing them with financial assistance. By allocating funds over a predetermined time frame, the program aims to reduce the costs of childcare, food, and medical care. Mothers and children must be healthy, particularly in regions experiencing economic hardship. MAP's main goal is to improve the health of mothers and babies by lowering the number of deaths of mothers and babies. The program tells women who are pregnant to get prenatal care and follow safe ways to give birth. For better births and fewer problems during birth, these are very important. Supporting these health efforts and improving the lives of mothers and children is part of the initiative's response to a major public health problem.

It is beneficial for women's and children's health because the MAP helps them eat healthier. People in many poor areas are not getting enough healthy food. The program helps to alleviate this problem by providing people with the necessary funds to purchase healthy food and maintain a healthy diet during pregnancy and after giving birth. This part of the program is necessary to achieve better health outcomes because good nutrition is crucial for both the mother's and child's recovery and growth (WHO 2020). During a particularly challenging time, the service helps families feel more secure about their finances. Many low-income families struggle to keep the costs of having a child under control because giving birth usually costs a lot of money. The MAP helps families with their financial problems by providing them with money. This allows women to focus on their health and care for their children without worrying about financial concerns. This helps ensure that people who are already struggling financially do not fall even further into poverty.

Statistics from the Ministry of Women and Children Affairs (2023) show that the program has a significant effect, helping nearly 1.1 million women each year. This large group of people demonstrates the program's importance in helping low-income families and addressing health issues that affect mothers. It has worked well so far, but it still has problems. There are still issues with the program, such as insufficient service and late payments, so it cannot help everyone who needs it as much as they should. These problems indicate that the program requires improved management to ensure that all qualified women receive the necessary assistance in a timely and straightforward manner. The MAP is very important for low-income families because it helps them access healthcare, eat healthier, and manage their finances. The program is a crucial component of Bangladesh's social safety net, as it enhances the health of women and children, thereby helping to close the health gap between mothers and their babies. Addressing current issues and expanding the program will benefit mothers and children across the nation.

**Primary Education Stipend Program (PESP)**

A very important and useful safety net program in Bangladesh is the Primary Education Stipend Program (PESP). It examines the relationship between poverty and schooling. To make it easier for children from low-income families, especially those facing financial difficulties, to participate, the program encourages them to do so. All children can gain from basic schooling this way. Bangladesh aims to enhance its educational system and alleviate poverty, particularly in underserved areas. PESP is in the middle of its plans to reach these goals. Approximately 14.3 million low-income children are supported by the PESP, which is well-known for its assistance to many. The quantity of money kids get from the program depends on their attendance and academic performance. This drives their interest in academics and motivates them to succeed. By lowering the cost of education and keeping children involved and active till they graduate from elementary school, this approach benefits families. The Bangladesh Bureau of Educational Information and Statistics (2023) reports that the widespread use of the project demonstrates the desperate need for education among millions of Bangladeshi youngsters.

By reducing the financial obstacles that prevent some families from sending their children to school, the PESP promotes education. For many low-income households, the cost of education—such as books, clothes, and transportation—is too high to be met. The payment lowers these costs, enabling families who usually prioritise near-term financial demands over long-term educational objectives to access education more readily and become more engaged. The program encourages families to enrol their children in school and keep them there by providing cash assistance, thereby improving reading and mathematics outcomes.

One of the main goals of the PESP is to promote gender equality in schools. The primary objectives of the program are to increase the number of female students and address past issues with gender inequality in school enrolment. The PESP aims to close the achievement gap between girls and boys by providing girls with extra support and ensuring they have the same opportunities as boys to attend school and excel academically. This part of the program is crucial for empowering women because education is one of the most effective ways to break the cycle of poverty and promote gender equality.

Lastly, PESP helps future generations secure better jobs by providing young people with more opportunities to attend school, thereby breaking the cycle of poverty. Education is the main reason for the rising movement. The program helps kids build a solid foundation for future success by enabling them to excel in basic education. In the long run, the PESP is beneficial to society because it creates more job opportunities and accelerates the country's economic growth. The PESP is crucial for enabling children in Bangladesh to access education and escape poverty. The primary objectives of the project are to break the cycle of poverty, promote gender equality, and provide children with incentives to excel academically. It is changing the lives of millions of kids. The PESP's success demonstrates the importance of investing in education for long-term growth and improved social mobility nationwide.

Two initiatives aimed at improving social justice are the MAP and the PESP. They have had a significant impact on Bangladesh's efforts to reduce socioeconomic disparities. These projects have made significant contributions to improving health, education, and reducing poverty. The MAP has made maternal health much better by lowering the number of deaths among mothers. The number of deaths per 100,000 live births in Bangladesh dropped from 240 in 2010 to 173 in 2020 (WHO 2020). Based on this new information, the program is helping to improve prenatal care, reduce the risk of complications during childbirth, and generally improve women's overall health. Importantly for the health of both mothers and babies, the program has improved the diet for mothers and babies, combating malnutrition in underdeveloped areas. The PESP has been especially helpful in education, as it has increased the number of kids who start and stay in basic school. In 2022, approximately 98% of children in low-income families were enrolled in school, indicating that the program was successful in encouraging families to send their children to school. Children who may not be able to attend school due to financial difficulties benefit from the stipends. While the number of women staying in school has increased, the number of children dropping out has decreased significantly. The PESP's focus on gender equality is especially beneficial for closing the educational gap between men and women, as it motivates female students to stay in school and complete their education, thereby reducing the gender gap.

By strengthening families, both the PESP and the Maternity Allowance help reduce poverty. These programs help families navigate challenging financial situations and provide support to groups that often lack sufficient resources. By lowering the cost of essential services such as childcare and maternal care, these programs have long-term positive effects on the economy and society. This provides many families with the peace of mind they need to escape poverty, enabling them to invest in their children's futures and enhance their overall standard of living. Although they have had some success, social development programs have several major issues that need to be addressed before they can be even more effective. Scope and targeting are two of the hardest problems to solve. Even though programs like the PESP help many people, there are still problems with finding the homes that need help the most. This leads to mistakes where qualified people do not get help. Additionally, distributing resources to the right places is challenging because these programs cannot grow as quickly as they would like due to a lack of funding, especially in areas that need it the most. Administrative delays continue to weaken the impact of these projects, as they affect the speed and effectiveness of grant disbursements and the level of monitoring.

Several measures can be taken to enhance the effectiveness of social development programs. One of the most innovative ideas is to utilise digital connectivity. By using more digital payment methods, things will become clearer, stipend and Allowance payments will be processed more quickly, scams will be less likely to occur, and money will reach the intended recipients on time. Better tracking is also needed to ensure that people who receive help from the program follow the program's rules, such as attending prenatal care visits and school regularly. The program will work more effectively and efficiently if it has robust tracking and compliance tools in place. Additionally, these programs will have a greater impact if they are more closely aligned with broader health and education policies. When national health and education policies are combined with social empowerment programs, these programs can help people in numerous ways, addressing multiple aspects of poverty and injustice simultaneously.

To sum up, programs like the MAP and PESP, which empower people, are crucial for addressing Bangladesh's fundamental problems and promoting long-term growth. The primary objectives of these programs are to enhance health, education, and financial stability, as well as to provide immediate financial assistance. If they want to reach their full potential, they need to fix problems with management speed, scope, and targeting. Bangladesh can continue to support its most vulnerable citizens and foster a more equitable and inclusive society by leveraging digital tools, enhancing tracking systems, and ensuring that national policies are implemented effectively.

The SSN programs in Bangladesh are crucial to the country's broader efforts to combat poverty, injustice, and inadequate social safety. These programs, such as job creation, food security, and social empowerment, are crucial for alleviating current suffering, preventing future problems, and ultimately strengthening society and the economy in the long run. Some problems, such as administrative delays, focused inefficiency, and limited resources (Samahar 2024), hinder the full effectiveness of these efforts. These problems need to be addressed by combining digital tools, maintaining closer oversight, and strengthening targeting systems. By overcoming these challenges, Bangladesh can strengthen its social safety net and ensure that low-income people have access to the necessary tools and opportunities for a safer and more secure future.

## 4 Fiscal Allocation and Policy Priorities

During the fiscal year 2023–2024, the Bangladeshi government allocated 16.58% of its national budget, equivalent to 2.55% of the country's GDP, for the SSN. This division demonstrates that the government is committed to eradicating poverty and assisting those in need. Still, not all SSN projects are getting the same amount of money. Most of the money goes to cash transfer programs because they help lift people out of poverty. Eliminating poverty should be the most important priority, but disparities in how resources are allocated could render the social safety net less effective overall. Focusing resources on certain areas could hinder the overall goal of comprehensive social aid because other important parts of the safety net may not receive sufficient funding.

In Bangladesh, SSN programs have a significant impact, as they cover approximately 25% of the population. Asma et al. (2023) state that these programs benefit people who are vulnerable due to their age, gender, health condition, or socioeconomic status. For example, the OAA has made it easier for seniors to maintain financial stability, reducing their likelihood of falling into poverty as they age. In comparison, the VGD program has done a commendable job of empowering women, enabling them to earn a living, and improving their social and economic status. In addition to reducing poverty, these programs also contribute to broader community goals, such as promoting gender equality, social inclusion, and the overall well-being and happiness of disadvantaged groups. Inequalities in society can be lessened by SSN programs, which give needy people a way to survive by offering a safety net.

The SSN scheme has benefits, but implementing it is challenging due to ongoing issues. Targeting has one major drawback: people sometimes exclude or include certain others by mistake. The programs are less equitable as a result of this issue, as some eligible people may not receive the aid to which they are entitled. In contrast, others who do not meet the criteria could be mistakenly viewed as recipients. Benefits are not distributed quickly and properly when managerial issues arise. If money is delayed or records are kept manually, beneficiaries may not receive their benefits when they need them most. These shortcomings reduce the likelihood that the programs will effectively alleviate poverty, thereby diminishing their overall utility.

SSN programs also struggle to succeed because they lack sufficient resources. A significant portion of the national budget is allocated to these projects, but the benefits achieved per person by some programs are still insufficient to reduce poverty rates significantly. With the help of the safety net, this limit makes it hard for some recipients to meet their basic needs. Finally, the differences between regions exacerbate the problems that SSN efforts already face. Infrastructure and transportation gaps, especially between cities and rural areas, make it harder for some people to get services than others. People in rural areas who are the most in need are often not helped because there is a lack of infrastructure or logistical assistance. This leaves gaps in program coverage and effectiveness (Sarwar et al. 2023). Finally, problems need to be addressed in targeting, administrative efficiency, resource availability, and regional access, despite the allocation of funds to SSN programs in Bangladesh, which suggests that the country is genuinely committed to ending poverty. Suppose the government wants to maximise the benefits of SSN programs without having to address these issues. In that case, it needs to focus on improving targeting, strengthening administration, and ensuring that resources are shared fairly across areas.

## 5 Moving Towards Digitalisation

The Bangladeshi government has made significant progress in digitising various aspects of its social safety system. This is because they recognise that managing SSN systems is becoming increasingly challenging. The new technology is designed to promote transparency and honesty, reduce cheating, simplify access to benefits, and reach a broader audience of those who need it.

Face recognition software is one of the most effective digital options available. The government has promised that benefits will only be given to approved people who use biometric information, such as fingerprints and facial recognition. This will reduce scams and abuse. According to Sarwar et al. (2023), programs such as the OAA and Widows Allowance now utilise biometric technologies to ensure that only qualified people receive benefits and that funds are not distributed to those who do not meet the eligibility criteria. Electronic funds transfers (EFTs) are another important part of going digital. A significant portion of Social Security payments was once distributed by hand, either through bank transfers or in cash.

In many cases, this led to loss, delays, and an increased likelihood of cheating. With EFTs, the government has made this process easier by allowing people to receive their money immediately in their bank or mobile account. Using digital records to track and confirm transactions reduces the work required to transfer money and makes the distribution of funds more transparent (Ingram 2021).

The goal of digitisation has also been to make it easier to identify and target vulnerable groups. With the help of GIS and advanced data analytics, the government can more effectively identify areas and individuals in need of social security assistance. Asma et al. (2023) note that this data-driven approach facilitates the identification of recipients, thereby reducing errors in both inclusion and exclusion. Mobile money services, such as bKash and Rocket, have made it much easier to send digital money to areas that lack access to traditional banking services. Beneficiaries have easily accessed their benefits, thanks to these platforms, particularly those residing in rural or remote areas. This has saved them time and effort by eliminating the need to visit banks or post offices that are far away. According to Sarwar et al. (2023), this is what most programs for women and the elderly, who often struggle with mobility and transportation, typically rely on.

Better supervision and accountability have also resulted from the inclusion of digital means. Better regulating the flow of money, keeping track of when payments are due, and identifying regions where the system is stalling are all advantages of digital systems for the government. Furthermore, allowing those who benefit to register grievances or delays ensures that problems are quickly addressed and reduces the likelihood of dubious behaviour. Digital solutions can either help or weaken the public service (Uddin and Kaiser 2021). Still, these developments demonstrate that the digitisation process remains challenging. Due to the digital divide, some vulnerable groups, particularly those in rural and isolated areas, face challenges in being included. If the recipients lack cell phones or mobile banking apps, digital transfers may not be as successful as they could be. In areas lacking sufficient digital infrastructure, Sarwar et al. (2023) also advise against relying on standard digital solutions. Bangladesh's decision to digitise its SSN systems, however, is a crucial first step towards more efficient and scalable social safety systems. Digital tools have the potential to transform the functioning of social safety networks as they expand, making them more accessible, versatile, and user-friendly for those who need them.

Among the most comprehensive social safety net initiatives in South Asia are those found in Bangladesh. These programs help a broad spectrum of at-risk people, alleviate poverty, and advance social inclusion and participation. Currently underway are 113 initiatives that demonstrate the government's commitment to enhancing social safety. Still, dealing with inaccuracies, administrative delays, and a dearth of resources is difficult. Ongoing adjustments will be required to help SSN initiatives maximise their effectiveness and guarantee they assist those in need. For instance, the government needs to improve, and digital technology must be more widely accessible.

## 6 Integration of Digital Cash Transfers in SSN Programs

Adding digital cash payments to Bangladesh's SSN programs is a significant change in how the government gives out and manages social benefits. Handheld cash transfer systems have long been plagued by issues such as slowness, fraud, and exclusion of certain people. This method aims to fix those issues. Some programs, such as the OAA and the Widow's Allowance, demonstrate how digital payment methods can simplify the process of paying people through social security. Examining the systems, methods, and tools employed in these projects helps people understand their power to transform and the challenges they present in maintaining them.

### *6.1 Infrastructure Supporting Digital Integration*

A robust system is necessary for digital cash exchanges to function effectively. Utilising MFS, banking networks, and digital identification tools, the Government of Bangladesh (GoB) has established a robust system. Mobile banking services have been at the forefront of this change. Leading companies, such as bKash, Nagad, and Rocket, collaborate with government agencies to ensure that funds reach the intended recipients without any issues. By 2023, over 80% of SSN users are expected to receive payments through MFS systems, making them significantly less reliant on cash (Gob 2023b). These systems make it easy to receive information, track payments in real-time, and conduct business remotely.

Another very important player is the financial sector. With the rise of agent banking, financial services can now reach groups that previously lacked access to them. As part of the Bangladesh Bank's Financial Inclusion Strategy, people who qualify can open simple bank accounts with just a few pieces of identification. Furthermore, the accuracy of beneficiary identification is ensured through a linkage with the National Identity Card (NID) database, thereby eliminating duplication and fake claims (Ubah et al. 2023). To facilitate digital payments, the GoB has made it easier to connect to the internet. Due to the Digital Bangladesh Initiative, it is now easier for people in rural areas to connect to 4G networks. Local union digital centres that are already set up also help users sign up, track payments, and settle disputes.

### 6.2 *Operational Processes for Digital Payments*

Digital cash transfers are implemented using a methodical approach that makes the process easier for both the sender and the recipient of the money. People seeking assistance must first register with their local government, where their information is verified and recorded for future reference. This information is compared to the NID database to ensure that the qualifying requirements are met and that errors are minimised. Biometric verification has been added to pilot sites to enhance the accuracy of recipient records further. The recipients are added to the system once they are confirmed, and the funds are sent directly to their MFS wallets or bank accounts. Payments are made instantly each month, and SMS messages are sent to remind people to make their payments. Switching to digital payments has significantly reduced fund delivery delays and leaks (Uddin 2013). Monitoring and reporting are very important to the system's success. Digital screens display real-time information on payments, enabling lawmakers to monitor progress and remove roadblocks. Regular checks, backed by data analytics, ensure that fund applications are open and transparent. Grievance redressal systems enable people to report problems and receive prompt responses. They can be accessed through mobile apps or helplines.

### 6.3 *Technological Tools and Innovations*

Digital money exchanges have been successful, largely due to the adoption of new technologies. Mobile apps designed specifically for people with SSNs provide access to support services, enable them to track their payments, and allow them to update their personal information. People who are not very good with computers can use these apps because they have easy displays and options for local languages. Some projects that aim to make things more open have experimented with blockchain technology. Blockchain uses a record of events that cannot be altered to ensure that money is sent directly to the intended recipients without passing through intermediaries. Similarly, artificial intelligence (AI) systems analyse transaction data to identify anomalies, such as exit trends that may indicate fraud or system issues (Hussain et al. 2022). Automated feedback systems provide lawmakers with a comprehensive view of a program's effectiveness. To help people make informed choices based on facts, these systems collect data on factors such as beneficiary comments, demographic coverage, and payment rates.

### 6.4 *Impact of Digital Integration*

Adding digital payment methods has made it much easier to get the Old Age Allowance and the Allowance for Widows. Gains in speed are some of the most impressive achievements. According to the Bangladesh Bureau of Statistics (2023), digital technologies have reduced transaction times by 40%, allowing people who need money to access it more quickly. Transparency has also improved, as the elimination of middlemen has reduced cheating and ensured that funds reach their intended recipients. A study by Ubah et al. (2023) found that 15% less money has been lost since digital payments started to be used. Another significant benefit is access. Thanks to rural banking systems and MFS, those in remote regions find it simpler to be compensated. Gelb et al. (2023) reported that the majority of rural users said they had less difficulty obtaining their benefits using digital techniques than they did with handwritten methods. Moreover, people who use these digital networks have grown stronger, especially women. The Allowance for Widows initiative has empowered women to be more financially independent, thereby giving them greater decision-making authority over their homes and families. The Old Age Allowance has also stabilised seniors' financial situations, so they need less help from their families.

### 6.5 *Challenges in Digital Integration*

Though digital cash transactions have been somewhat successful, they also have several problems. Recipients—especially older adults and rural women—often have less technological familiarity than others, which presents one of the most serious challenges. Many people struggle with using their phones or understanding how to use electronic payment systems. This problem is exacerbated in some areas, where reliable internet and cell phone access remain scarce. Errors in the NID database or an inability to obtain the necessary data can also lead to exclusion; those who do not meet the evidence requirements risk being removed from the system. The MFS platform system failure, which disrupts payment plans and annoys customers, is one of the technical issues. Adding digital cash payments to Bangladesh's Social Safety Net programs, especially for the Old Age

Allowance and the Widows Allowance, is a significant step towards making the nation safer. The government is now more transparent, accessible, and efficient, thanks to contemporary infrastructure and technology. To preserve these benefits, we must also address issues such as system resilience, poor connectivity, and digital literacy. The way governments create and improve social safety nets over time can be beneficial to nations seeking to strengthen them.

## 7 Challenges and Opportunities in Digital Implementation

Digital technology should be integrated into Bangladesh's social security programs, particularly the Old Age Allowance and the Allowance for Widows, to modernise these services. This part examines both sides of this change and the ways they can be improved to make things more open, efficient, and pleasant. They happen because of how it is used.

### *7.1 Challenges in Digital Implementation*

The social safety net program would be able to help a much greater number of people and function more efficiently if digital currency transfer mechanisms were established. Although digital technology is still evolving rapidly in the US, certain issues persist that hinder the efficiency of these systems. Access to and usage of internet platforms present more challenges for some, including older people and women living in rural areas, thereby increasing these difficulties. Improving the online money transfer tool requires solutions to these primary problems.

**First**, not everyone has ready access to technology; hence, digital cash transfer systems have among their main drawbacks. Many people who receive the Old Age Allowance and other social safety nets live in remote and distant areas, often lacking essential services such as reliable mobile phone and internet access (Hussain et al. 2022). The digital divide between rural and urban areas makes it more difficult for digital services to reach a large audience. It also increases the likelihood that low-income people will be excluded from these important projects. Additionally, many older people lack access to cell phones or digital payment systems, which are the primary means of utilising the Old Age Allowance. Bangladesh's social security programs, particularly the Old Age Allowance and Allowance for

Widows, need to adopt digital technology to become more modern. This section provides an in-depth overview of both aspects of this change and discusses ways to enhance openness, efficiency, and user experience. These problems happen because of how it is used.

**The second** major problem with digital cash payments that hinders their effectiveness is that people lack proficiency in using technology. Most older people and women are unfamiliar with using apps or digital payment systems (Hossain et al. 2023), whereas younger users are more accustomed to digital processes. Many people believe that mistakes occur frequently in digital transactions, which can lead to confusion and leave the system vulnerable to abuse. Because of this, they often rely on middlemen to assist them with deals, which can lead to problems and leave them vulnerable to exploitation. To ensure that everyone who benefits from digital currency transfer systems maximises their benefits, it is crucial to close the gaps in digital literacy through targeted training programs and support.

**Third**, there are several issues with the stability and reliability of technology. The reliability of the technology used is the most significant factor affecting the effectiveness of digital cash transfer methods. Beneficiaries may not trust the system due to computer downtime, system failures, and errors in payment handling (Ubah et al., 202). People who receive digital payments are more severely affected when payments are late. They may need to visit mobile money providers or bank branches more frequently. People are annoyed by these problems, and they make the program less effective because it cannot fulfil its main job of providing quick cash assistance to those in need.

**Fourth**, problems with identity checks persist, making it difficult for digital money exchanges to operate smoothly. Many digital systems utilise national or biometric identification systems to verify the identity of users. However, mistakes in these systems and old information for rural recipients could make it harder for them to get funds. Because they are older, the biometric data of older adults may not match up as well, which makes identification more challenging and can cause delays or rejections in benefit distribution (Raihan et al. 2021). This issue underscores the necessity for ongoing updates to identity verification methods and stricter policies to ensure that everyone, particularly the elderly, can exercise their rights without undue delay.

**Fifth**, cultural and gender differences make it more challenging for digital money transfers to function effectively. In some places, cultural norms and traditional gender roles make it more challenging for women to utilise technology. The Allowance for Widows program is mostly for weak women, but many of them still cannot use cell phones or handle their own money. Women face greater challenges accessing digital services due to their gender and geographical location (Choudhury et al. 2019). This is especially true in rural and conservative areas. They perpetuate economic and social inequality. To ensure that digital currency exchanges are accessible to everyone, regardless of their gender or financial situation, it is crucial to address cultural and gender-related issues.

### 7.2 Opportunities in Digital Implementation

Digitising SSNs can make it easier and more effective to provide help. By switching from traditional methods to digital platforms, the government can streamline administrative tasks, increase transparency, and ensure that benefits reach the intended recipients with minimal delays and costs. The move to digital also opens up more possibilities for financial inclusion, allowing people to use formal financial systems. Although there are some challenges, the benefits that come with going digital are very promising for SSN projects in Bangladesh.

**First:** One of the best things about going digital is that it makes things run more smoothly. Hand-delivering money is time-consuming and expensive, so automating the routine tasks of the SSN program saves a significant amount of both time and money. Digital payments have made it faster to send money for programs like the Old Age Allowance. This means that users can get their benefits more quickly. Working time has been reduced by up to 30% compared to previous methods, representing a significant improvement. Those who receive it benefit from its speed because it allows them to receive assistance more rapidly and frees up resources that can be utilised to enhance the program.

**Second**, digital tools contribute to increased accountability and transparency. Fraud and financial loss are less likely to occur when technology facilitates the clear and transparent sharing of funds. Digital platforms help eliminate the need for brokers by enabling people to send money directly to one another. Brokers could bring fraud or waste. The government can also monitor and oversee the system through real-time transaction tracking, ensuring that money reaches the intended recipients on time and that the system operates transparently and fairly (Uddin and Kaiser 2021).

**Third**, one of the best things about digitising SSN systems is that it may help reduce costs. Regular cash transfer methods have little impact because they incur significant administrative and organisational costs, such as the physical delivery of the money. With the help of modern tools, these costs can go down. Because they are fast and can reach a larger audience, digital cash payments, such as bank transfers or mobile money, are a more cost-effective way to distribute SSN programs nationwide. Hossain et al. (2023) state that this method is less costly than other methods. If costs were lower, more money could be used to improve results or serve more people through the programs.

**Fourth**, digital tools for transferring money are a terrific way to help more people access funds. Through traditional banks, people can access their mobile money wallets or bank accounts via these digital platforms. As a result, they can now handle their money more effectively. This is particularly crucial for women in rural and underdeveloped areas, as they often face obstacles when attempting to access banking services. People can become more involved in the market and gradually increase their families' financial stability by learning about different financial systems (Beck et al. 2007).

Some benefits contribute to the economy's growth in both the short and long term. In the short term, it is easier to get loans and find other ways to save money. Digital systems are useful because they can be modified and adapted as needed. SSN programs can quickly adjust to new situations or higher demand because digital platforms can be scaled up or down rapidly. Digital cash transfers made it easier for the government to quickly send money to those who needed it the most during the COVID-19 pandemic. This showed that people could change. The rapid responses of digital systems to disasters underscore their flexibility, which is crucial for ensuring that aid projects can meet users' needs swiftly and efficiently (Zimmerman et al. 2020). Ultimately, scanning the systems Bangladesh's SSN programs use to disperse money could help social services. Some issues, including people not understanding how to properly utilise technology, having inadequate access to it, and depending on it too much, have to be fixed. At any rate, greater speed, openness, and economic equality have great benefits. By leveraging these advantages and removing obstacles that hinder development, Bangladesh can strengthen its social safety net. This will ensure that people on the outside receive regular and necessary assistance.

## 8 Conclusion

Fighting poverty and injustice depends on Bangladesh's social safety net initiatives as well as on safeguarding the most vulnerable people. These programs significantly address present issues for future social development and resilience. They accomplish this by giving projects top priority, such as ensuring employment, improving food security, and enhancing community empowerment. These programs make a significant difference, but because the system is not functioning well enough, they have yet to reach their full potential. One reason is a lack of sufficient funding. To ensure SSN runs more smoothly and helps more people in the future, we need to utilise digital tools to track programs and refine our goals. By addressing these issues, Bangladesh can continue to strengthen its social safety net and provide low-income people with the necessary tools and opportunities for a safer and more equitable future.

## References

Ahmed, I., Jahan, N., and Zohura, F. (2014). Social safety net programme as a mean to alleviate poverty in Bangladesh. *Developing Country Studies, 4*(17), 46–54.

Anwar, R., and Cho, Y. (2019). *Employment generation program for the poorest Bangladesh: Program brief (English)*. Washington, D.C.: World Bank Group.

Asma, K. M., Misu, F., and Islam, M. A. (2023). The impact of social safety net programs on poverty, food security, and standard of living in Bangladesh. *The International Journal of Community and Social Development, 5*(1), 71–96.

Bangladesh Bureau of Educational Information and Statistics (BANBEIS). (2023). *Bangladesh education statistics 2023*. Dhaka: Ministry of Education, Government of Bangladesh.

Bangladesh Bureau of Statistics. (2023). *Statistical yearbook Bangladesh 2023*. Dhaka: Statistics & Informatics Division (SID), Ministry of Planning, Government of Bangladesh.

Beck, T., Demirgüç-Kunt, A., and Levine, R. (2007). Finance, inequality, and the poor. *Journal of Economic Growth, 12*(1), 27–49.

Choudhury, R., Khan, A., and Rahman, S. (2019). Gender dynamics in digital transformation. *Bangladesh Development Studies*.

Finance Division. (2023). *Budget speech 2023–24*. Ministry of Finance, Government of Bangladesh.

Gelb, A., Mukherjee, A., and Webster, B. (2023). *Can Digital G2P Payments Increase Financial Inclusion and Empower Women? Evidence from PESP in Bangladesh*. CGD Policy Paper 284, Centre for Global Development.

https://www.cgdev.org/publication/can-digital-g2p-payments-increase-financial-inclusion-and-empower-women-evidence-pesp
Government of Bangladesh. (2005). *Bangladesh: Poverty reduction strategy paper (PRSP).* Dhaka: Planning Commission.
Government of Bangladesh. (2015). *National social security strategy (NSSS) of Bangladesh.* Dhaka: Planning Commission.
Government of Bangladesh. (2023a). *Boyoshko Bhata (Old Age Allowance).* Dhaka: Directorate of Social Service, Ministry of Social Welfare.
Government of Bangladesh. (2023b). *Social security programs: 2023–2024.* Ministry of Social Welfare.
Hossain, B., Fatima, M. J., Muzykant, V. L., Hoesin, C. F. I. S., and Md Nahiduzzaman. (2023). An overview of digital media literacy in Digital Bangladesh. *Journal Cita Hukum (Indonesian Law Journal), 11*(2), 267–288.
Hussain, A. A., Emon, M. A., Tanna, T. A., Emon, R. I., and Onik, M. M. H. (2022). A systematic literature review of blockchain technology adoption in Bangladesh. *Annals of Emerging Technologies in Computing (AETiC), 6*(1), 1–31.
Ingram, G. (2021). Bridging the global digital divide: A platform to advance digital development in low- and middle-income economies. *Brookings Global Working Paper #157.* Global Economy and Development Program at Brookings.
Khuda, B. E. (2011). Social safety net programs in Bangladesh: A review. *The Bangladesh Development Studies, 34*(2), 87–108.
Ministry of Women and Children Affairs. (2023). *Maternity allowance programme (MAP).* Dhaka: Government of Bangladesh.
Rahman, H. Z., and Choudhury, L. I. (2012). *Social safety nets in Bangladesh: Ground realities and policy challenges (Vol. 2).* Power and Participation Research Centre (PPRC) and UNDP.
Raihan, S., Uddin, M., and Ahmed, S. (2021). Dynamics of youth and gender divide in technology in Bangladesh. *South Asia Economic Journal, 22*(2), 205–232.
Samahar - Multidisciplinary Research and Development Foundation. (2024). *Vulnerable group development program.* Available at: https://www.samahar.net.bd/completed-project/vulnerable-group-development-program (Accessed 6 December 2024).
Sarwar, M. B., Diepeveen, S., and Moreno, D. B. (2023). Cash transfers and digital financial inclusion: Regional evidence from Asia Pacific with a focus on Bangladesh, Cambodia, and Nepal. *ODI Report.* Overseas Development Institute (ODI), London.
Ubah, T. U., Mukherjee, A., Webster, B., Cunningham, W., and Marin, G. (2023). Delivering digital G2P payments to urban informal populations: Lessons and future policy implications from COVID-19 responses. *Regional Study Paper No. P169171.* Washington, DC: The World Bank.

Uddin, M. A. (2013). Social safety nets in Bangladesh: An analysis of impact of old age allowance program. *Unpublished Master's Dissertation*. Institute of Governance Studies (IGS), Brac University, Dhaka.

Uddin, N., and Kaiser, Z. R. M. A. (2021). Accelerating employability through social safety net in rural Bangladesh: Employment generation programme for the poorest. *The International Journal of Community and Social Development, 3*(3), 236–254.

World Health Organization (WHO). (2020). *Maternal health in South Asia: Progress and challenges*. Geneva: WHO.

Zimmerman, J. M., May, M., Kellison, E., and Klugman, J. (2020). Digital cash transfers in times of COVID-19: Opportunities and considerations for women's inclusion and empowerment (English). Washington, DC: World Bank Group.

# Measuring Success: Evaluating the Effectiveness of Digital Cash Transfers in Bangladesh's Social Safety Net Programs

**Abstract** There are several important measures used in this chapter to show how well digital cash transfers work in Bangladesh's Social Safety Net (SSN) schemes. These include how happy program participants are with the ease of use, reliability, accessibility, and timeliness of the programs. They also include how efficient the programs' administration is, such as the amount of time and money saved by reducing transaction costs, travel expenses, and administrative overhead. The report examines how technology has made it easier for underserved areas to access services and achieve better outcomes. To achieve this, it utilises a combination of data from SSN users, Union Parishad (UP) officials, and other key sources. Not only did the data show significant jumps in beneficiary happiness, but they also showed notable jumps in economic stability, financial freedom, and beneficiaries' ability to get to the services they need. There are also problems with technology, and people in distant places do not always have access to the internet. The final section of the chapter provides valuable tips for enhancing the digital money transfer system to ensure it works effectively for everyone, lasts a long time, and adheres to best practices worldwide.

**Keywords** Digital cash transfers • Social Safety Net programs • Bangladesh • Effectiveness evaluation • Beneficiary satisfaction • Financial inclusion



P. K. Panday, A. H. M. K. Ahsan, *Digital Revolution for the Vulnerable*, https://doi.org/10.1007/978-981-95-7980-8_4

## 1 Introduction

Bangladesh's Social Safety Net (SSN) programs have taken a significant step towards modernising their social safety net services by digitising the ways they give out cash. The real test of any change is how well it meets the needs of beneficiaries, makes things easier for administrators, and cuts costs. This chapter examines three key aspects of effectiveness: ensuring beneficiaries are satisfied, ensuring administrative processes are efficient, and reducing transaction costs. This chapter uses many factors to see if digital cash transfers have lived up to their promise of improving service delivery and the lives of vulnerable groups. These factors include how easy they are to use, how reliable they are, how much time they save, how simple the processes are, and how much money they save. Based on the primary objectives of the study, this research seeks to address a fundamental question: Has automation ensured that cash transfers in Bangladesh's SSN systems operate effectively?

## 2 Beneficiary Satisfaction: Ease of Use and Accessibility of Digital Platforms

The primary factor determining the success of digital cash transfer methods is the recipient's satisfaction. This happiness is based on how easy and accessible digital platforms are, which directly affects how quickly beneficiaries can receive their allowances. This part examines the experiences of individuals who obtained an SSN and the opinions of Union Parishad (UP) officials regarding the usefulness of digital platforms. Looking at things from different points of view helps us identify ways to improve the design and operation of digital systems, as well as the differences between how users and administrators perceive them. Triangulation using secondary data and literature supports the discussion and provides a picture of the challenges and achievements in digitising cash transfers.

### *2.1 Ease of Use and Accessibility*

Cash transfer systems' digitisation seeks to streamline procedures and improve beneficiary accessibility—many may have little digital literacy or technological knowledge. To judge how well digitisation projects are working, we need to know how easy it is for beneficiaries and UP representatives to use these technologies. Table 1 shows how both groups feel

**Table 1** Level of challenges in using the digital platform for receiving allowances

| *SSN beneficiaries* | *Total* | *UP functionaries* | *Total* |
|---|---|---|---|
| Options | 100 (100%) | Options | 20 (100%) |
| Very difficult | 00 (00%) | Very difficult | 00 (00%) |
| Difficult | 00 (00%) | Difficult | 01 (5%) |
| Neutral | 00 (00%) | Neutral | 01 (5%) |
| Easy | 48 (48%) | Easy | 08 (40%) |
| Very easy | 52 (52%) | Very easy | 10 (50%) |

Source: Field Data (2024)

about how hard it is to use the digital platform to acquire allowances. The findings suggested that 100% of all SSN beneficiaries found the digital platform either "Very Easy" (52%) or "Easy" (48%). This extremely favourable reaction points to the platform's design with user-friendliness in mind, therefore serving a demographic typically including elderly persons and those with less formal education. A female SSN beneficiary from a remote location, aged 65, shared her experience by saying, "*Before the digitalised system, I had to go for hours to collect my allowance. The money now appears in my mobile phone account with only a few taps on my cell phone. It is quite simple*!" (Interview Data 2024). Conversely, another SSN recipient with a primary education background said, "*I never used a phone before, but the agent showed me how to check my balance. I feel secure now applying the system*" (Interview Data 2024). The lack of any answers suggesting a challenge ("Very Difficult" or "Difficult") is a clear sign of the platform's success in attending to user demands. This is consistent with the global best practices in digital financial services, where low technological requirements and easy interfaces are prioritised to guarantee access for underprivileged groups (World Bank 2024).

With 88% of UP officials judging the system as either "Easy" (40%) or "Very Easy," they essentially reflected the favourable experiences of recipients. A tiny percentage of UP officials did, however, report minor challenges; 5% said the system was "Difficult," and another 5% said it was "Neutral." A UP Secretary said, "*Most recipients adjust fast, but elderly folks in isolated communities often suffer cell network troubles. To help them, we have begun planning community meetings*" (Interview Data 2024). According to a female UP Member, "*the system runs well. However, in some locations, inadequate internet access causes disruptions in transfer during the rainy season*" (Interview Data 2018). These answers could represent unique events in which recipients encountered particular challenges, including poor internet availability, absence of mobile device access, or platform navigation challenges. Being closer to the ground, UP officials are more likely to be aware of such localised challenges, which might not be immediately apparent from total findings (Sarwar et al. 2023).

Beneficiaries' positive comments align with the findings of earlier research on digital financial services in low-income communities. For instance, the simplicity and ease of use of mobile money systems like M-Pesa in Kenya have helped them to be widely adopted even among those with little digital literacy (World Bank 2020a). One Upazila Nirbahi Officer (UNO) said, "*The digital platform has drastically lowered corruption. Payments are transparent, and beneficiaries are free of middlemen now*" (KII 2024). On the other hand, a development practitioner said, "*While the system is user-friendly, we need more localised training programs for women and elderly beneficiaries to bridge the digital literacy gap*" (KII 2024). However, the little issues brought up by UP officials draw attention to Bangladesh's ongoing digital divide—especially in rural and isolated areas. Studies have revealed that lack of knowledge, insufficient training, and poor infrastructure—among other factors—cause extra challenges for elderly persons, women, and persons with disabilities using digital services (Government of Bangladesh 2022). These findings show how important it is to keep an eye on marginalised groups and give them treatments that are specifically designed to meet their needs. All respondents reported having good experiences, and the findings on ease of use and accessibility indicate that digital platforms are meeting the needs of SSN recipients. This success shows how well a design that is easy for people to use works and how important it is to keep things simple when digitising. However, the problems that UP officials identified suggest that issues such as slow internet connections or a lack of mobile devices in certain areas can still hinder digital cash transfers.

### 2.2 Timeliness and Reliability of Digital Payments

When it comes to digital cash transfer methods, reliability and timeliness are what make recipients happy. Payment delays or mistakes can hurt trust in the system and make it harder for it to meet the needs of disadvantaged groups. In this part, we look into how satisfied SSN users are with digital payments and what UP officials think about how reliable and on-time they are. Examining various viewpoints helps us evaluate how much payment procedures have been enhanced by digital technology and points out areas needing more development. Triangulation using secondary data and literature from Bangladesh and other countries supports the discussion and provides a picture of the challenges and achievements in guaranteeing accurate and timely payments.

The finding (Table 2) suggested that most SSN beneficiaries were happy with the payment timeliness, as 36% said they were "Satisfied," and 61% said they were "Very Satisfied." Just 3% of respondents reported having no opinion, and none expressed unhappiness (i.e., "Very Dissatisfied" or "Dissatisfied"). This significant satisfaction shows that the digital system has effectively guaranteed timely payments, improving over conventional cash transfer systems that often suffer delays and inefficiencies. One beneficiary observed, "*I used to wait weeks to receive my money, but now it comes on time every month. It has changed my life quite a bit*" (Interview Data 2024). Beneficiaries' enthusiastic comments highlight how well digitalisation simplifies payment methods and improves user experience.

This result makes sense, given experiences from elsewhere. For cash transfers, M-Pesa, for instance, considerably shortened payment delays and raised recipient satisfaction in Kenya (Jack and Suri 2011). In India, the Direct Benefit Transfer (DBT) system has also been praised for its ability to send payments directly to recipients' bank accounts, thereby reducing leaks and delays (Muralidharan et al. 2016). These examples demonstrate how digital technologies used globally can enhance the reliability and timeliness of social safety net transfers. While 38% of respondents called the system "Reliable" and 56% said it was "Very Reliable," UP officials also said they had much faith in how quickly and reliably digital

**Table 2** Level of satisfaction about timeliness of payments made through the digital system

| *SSN beneficiaries* | *Total* | *UP functionaries* | *Total* |
|---|---|---|---|
| Options | 100 (100%) | Options | 20 (100%) |
| Very dissatisfied | 00 (00%) | Very unreliable | 01 (5%) |
| Dissatisfied | 00 (00%) | Unreliable | 00 (00%) |
| Neutral | 03 (3%) | Neutral | 00 (00%) |
| Satisfied | 36 (36%) | Reliable | 06 (40%) |
| Very satisfied | 61 (61%) | Very reliable | 09 (55%) |

Source: Field Data (2024)

payments would be processed. Six per cent of people who answered said the system was "Very Unreliable," which could mean that there were a few computer issues or delays. A UP official said, "*The system works well most of the time, but sometimes it does not, especially during busy times or when there are network problems*" (Interview Data 2024). These replies highlight the importance of monitoring the system and making improvements to prevent any potential issues from developing. UP officials are well-positioned to notice and address problems like these, as they are intimately involved in the implementation process. This ensures that the system remains reliable for all beneficiaries (Sarwar et al. 2023). The minor issues that our authorities have brought to light are identical to those that occur in other regions. Digital currency transfers in Nigeria, for instance, encountered issues including network outages and delays in checking the recipient, which occasionally prohibited payments from getting through (Aker et al. 2016). The Benazir Income Support Program (BISP) in Pakistan also experienced trouble registering IDs, which occasionally made things take longer (Nayab and Farooq 2014). These stories highlight how crucial it is to have robust infrastructure and take proactive actions to make sure that digital systems work.

The Deputy Director of Local Governance (DDLG), Upazila Nirbahi Officers (UNOs), Local Government Experts, and Development Practitioners were among the key informants who provided valuable insights into the challenges and successes of the digital payment system. Emphasising the need for coordination among stakeholders, the DDLG of one district said, "*The Local Government Division, banks, mobile financial service businesses, and UP authorities all need to work together precisely for the digital payment system to succeed. Any disruption in this procedure might cause delays*" (KII 2024). Likewise, a UNO underlined the necessity of capacity building, saying, "*We showed UP representatives and receivers how to use the digital system, but we still need help with technical issues and making sure everything works well*" (KII 2024).

Experts in local government said that while the digital system has made things more open, data quality and links are still big problems. One expert said, "*The digital system is a huge step forward, but we need to guarantee that beneficiary data is routinely updated and that there is dependable internet access in remote locations. Without these, the system cannot run as it ought*" (KII 2024). Reflecting this attitude, practitioners underlined the significance of early actions to close gaps. One practitioner said, "*We have seen fantastic development, but the system is not flawless. Maintaining the dependability of digital payments depends on regular audits, feedback systems, and infrastructure investments*" (KII 2024).

The significant pleasure among recipients corresponds with global data on the advantages of digitising cash transfers. Studies have indicated, for instance, that digital solutions may considerably lower payment delays and increase transparency—especially in low-income environments where conventional approaches are prone to inefficiencies (World Bank 2020b). However, the minor concerns expressed by UP officials align with findings from other settings, where administrative delays, technological problems, and connection challenges occasionally disrupt payment procedures (Government of Bangladesh 2022). These challenges highlight how important strong infrastructure is and how proactive steps are needed to guarantee the dependability of digital systems. Apart from the examples from Kenya, India, Nigeria, and Pakistan, data from Brazil's Bolsa Família program emphasises the need to include digital systems with robust administrative systems. The program's use of a centralised database and real-time monitoring—which reduces delays and guarantees accountability—has helped it make timely payments (Lindert et al. 2007). Bangladesh can use these ideas to keep making its digital cash flow systems better.

The finding on timeliness and reliability shows how well digital technologies ensure regular and on-time payments. This is shown by the fact that users are happy with the service, and UP officials trust it. This achievement demonstrates how digitisation can completely transform processes, making SSN programs more effective and payment systems more streamlined. Still, some of the problems that UP officials brought up tell us that the system needs to keep getting better so that any gaps can be filled and it works all the time.

### 2.3 Role of Digital Systems in Reducing Access Challenges

Reducing access challenges for recipients—such as extensive travel distances, waiting times, and bureaucratic obstacles—is one of the main objectives of digitising cash transfer systems. SSN projects utilise digital platforms to enhance the user-friendliness, efficiency, and accessibility of financial transfers. Based on responses from UP officials and beneficiary accounts, this section investigates how digital systems have successfully reduced access challenges. The study offers practical ideas for further improvement and emphasises the achievements and constraints of digitisation in tackling these problems. Triangulation using secondary data and literature from Bangladesh and other nations helps enhance the discussion by showing how digital systems could improve access.

With 33% of respondents saying their access issues were "Greatly" and 64% expressing they were "Completely" reduced, the data (Table 3) shows that most beneficiaries—97%—believe digital systems have greatly lessened their access challenges. Just 3% of respondents said that challenges were "somewhat," and none said that digital systems had no effect ("Not at all" or "A little"). This response emphasises how digitalisation has transformed cash transfers into more convenient and quicker tools. Notably, the decrease in travel and waiting times has benefited many beneficiaries, many of whom are older or people with restricted mobility (World Bank 2024).

While commenting on the role of the digital system in reducing access challenges, one SSN recipient said, "*I had to go to the UP office and wait in huge crowds to get my payment before the digital system. The money now shows right in my mobile account. Given my trouble travelling long distances, it saves me time and effort*" (Interview Data 2024). Another recipient stated, "*I no longer worry about missing work or spending money on transport to collect my payment. The digital system makes Everything much easier*" (Interview Data 2024).

The findings of the study align well with the experiences of other countries. For instance, especially in rural regions, M-Pesa for financial transfers considerably lessened the need for recipients to travel long distances to get payments in Kenya (Jack and Suri 2011). In India, the Direct Benefit Transfer (DBT) system has also been praised for its ability to directly

**Table 3** Role of digital systems in reducing access challenges

| *Role of digital systems in reducing access challenges* | | *Challenges faced by beneficiaries in accessing digital cash transfers* | |
|---|---|---|---|
| *SSN beneficiaries* | *Total* | *UP functionaries* | *Total* |
| Options | 100 (100%) | Options | 20 (100%) |
| Not at all | 00 (00%) | Very often | 00 (00%) |
| A little | 00 (00%) | Often | 02 (10%) |
| Somewhat | 03 (3%) | Occasionally | 00 (00%) |
| Greatly | 33 (33%) | Rarely | 09 (45%) |
| Completely | 64 (64%) | Never | 09 (45%) |

Source: Field Data (2024)

transfer benefits to recipients' bank accounts, thereby eliminating intermediaries and reducing waiting periods (Muralidharan et al. 2016). These illustrations highlight how digital platforms might improve accessibility globally and address access issues.

In response to the question relating to challenges faced by the beneficiaries in accessing digital cash transfers, the UP representatives echoed a similar response, saying that recipients hardly had challenges obtaining digital cash transfers. Among the respondents, 45% said that the recipients "Rarely" faced problems in assessing digital cash transfers, and another 45% indicated that they "Never" faced problems in assessing digital cash transfers. However, a tiny percentage (10%) said that they experience "often," which might indicate localised concerns such as network connectivity issues, lack of access to mobile devices, or trouble navigating the digital platform. A UP secretary said, "*Most beneficiaries are delighted with the digital system, but others in distant locations have challenges owing to inadequate network connection. Sometimes they have to go to other towns to get cell networks, negating the goal of less travel*" (Interview Data 2024). Another UP Chairman pointed out, "*Older recipients sometimes have trouble utilising cell phones. Their handling of the system depends on seeking help from others*" (Interview Data 2024). These answers underline the need to remove certain obstacles so that every beneficiary can fully use digital systems.

Key informants offered more analysis of the achievements and challenges of digital systems in lowering access restrictions. Emphasising diversity, the DDLG said, "*While the digital system has been a game-changer for many, we must guarantee that no one is left behind. This implies attending to the requirements of people living in rural regions and those less tech-savvy*" (KII 2024). Emphasising the need for awareness programs, a UNO said, "*Many beneficiaries, especially in rural regions, are not entirely aware of how the digital system works. We must run additional outreach initiatives and training courses to remedy this disparity*" (KII 2024).

Underlining the importance of infrastructure development, one local government expert said, "Reliable internet and mobile networks define the success of the digital system. Without these, even the best-made systems would fall short in delivering" (KII 2024). On the other hand, a development practitioner stated, "*We have seen great improvement, but there is still work to be done. For instance, some recipients cannot pay the fees connected with mobile banking or may not have access to cell phones. These problems must be resolved to guarantee universal access*" (KII 2024).

The minor issues UP officials brought up contradict observations from other nations. For example, periodic access was hindered in Nigeria when digital cash transfers were implemented due to network issues and delays in beneficiary verification (Aker et al. 2016). In Pakistan, the BISP also encountered issues with biometric verification, resulting in delays in some cases (Nayab and Farooq 2014). These examples show how important it is to have a strong infrastructure and move quickly to make sure that everyone can use digital systems.

The fact that receivers were very happy with the money transfers aligns with data from around the world on the benefits of digitising cash payments. Studies have shown, for example, that digital technologies can greatly reduce access problems by cutting down on the need for travel and making government procedures more efficient (World Bank 2020b). However, the small concerns raised by UP officials are similar to those found by researchers in Bangladesh, where access is sometimes hindered by administrative delays, technical issues, and connectivity problems (Government of Bangladesh 2022). These problems show how important it is to have strong infrastructure and strict rules that make sure digital systems are always available.

In addition to the examples from Pakistan, data from Brazil's Bolsa Família program also shows how important it is to include digital systems with strong management tools. A central database and real-time tracking, which cut down on delays and made sure that everyone was responsible, have helped lower access problems (Lindert et al. 2007). Bangladesh can use what it has learnt as it continues to make its digital money transfer methods better. By looking at how satisfied beneficiaries are, we can see how much digitising cash transfer systems has changed Bangladesh's SSN schemes. Beneficiaries mostly have good experiences with how easy, quick, and reliable digital platforms are. They also say that they make access problems like travel times and government hurdles a lot easier to deal with. These accomplishments show how digital technologies might make it easier and faster to send money, especially to groups that are not as fortunate.

# 3 Streamlining Efficiency: Administrative Gains from Digital Cash Transfers

Getting cash transfer systems digitalised is meant to make them more efficient by lowering costs, making processes easier, and shortening processing times. This is because effective SSN programs depend on efficient administration. This part rates the management efficiency of digital cash transfers by looking at how quickly payments are made, how easy the system is to use, and how much it costs. This part looks at the good and bad things about digitisation in making administrative work easier, looking at the views of both receivers and UP officials. The findings provide valuable insights that can assist in ensuring the full utilisation of the benefits of digitalisation and enhancing the effectiveness of SSN operations.

## *3.1 Timeliness of Receiving Payments Through Digital Platforms*

Timeliness is a key measure of how well an administration works in cash transfer systems. Delays in payments might make the SSN program less successful and put participants in a tough financial situation. The goal of digitising cash transfer systems is to speed up processing times and make sure that payments are delivered on time. This section examines the speed at which funds provided through digital methods are received, based on statements from beneficiaries and UP officials. We can see how much digitalisation has accelerated and facilitated cash transfers by examining multiple perspectives and identifying areas that require further attention.

With 49% indicating they are "Shorter" and another 49% reporting they are "Much Shorter," the data (Table 4) shows that the great majority of beneficiaries—98%—said payments were received more promptly through the digital system than under the prior method. Just 2% of respondents said payments took "Longer," and none said they were "Much Longer" or "About the same." This favourable response emphasises how well digitisation has cut processing times and guaranteed accurate payment delivery. For vulnerable groups, who usually depend on these payments for their basic requirements, the drop in delays is especially noteworthy.

While commenting on the timeliness, one SSN recipient said, "*Before, I had to wait weeks to receive my money, and occasionally, it would never come on time. I get my money on the same monthly date using the digital*

**Table 4** Timeliness of receiving payment through digital cash transfer platform

| *SSN beneficiaries* | *Total* | *UP functionaries* | *Total* |
|---|---|---|---|
| Options | 100 (100%) | Options | 20 (100%) |
| Much longer | 00 (00%) | Not at all | 00 (00%) |
| Longer | 02 (2%) | To a small extent | 00 (00%) |
| About the same | 00 (00%) | To some extent | 02 (10%) |
| Shorter | 49 (49%) | To a greater extent | 10 (50%) |
| Much shorter | 49 (49%) | Completely | 08 (40%) |

Source: Field Data (2024)

*method. For my family, this is quite relieving*" (Interview Data 2024). On the other hand, another recipient said, "*Everything is faster because of the computerised system. Delays and missed payments are no longer causes of concern for me. It has changed my life*" (Interview Data 2024). These findings align well with the experiences of other countries. By removing intermediaries and simplifying administrative procedures, the Direct Benefit Transfer (DBT) system has, for instance, significantly lowered payment delays in India (Muralidharan et al. 2016). In Kenya, the launch of M-Pesa for financial transfers has also enabled recipients—even in remote areas—to receive immediate payments (Jack and Suri 2011). These cases highlight how digital technologies might improve the timeliness of cash transfers globally.

The majority of the UP representatives expressed their views positively while commenting on the timeliness of the cash transfer. Among the respondents, 50% of UP representatives said that digitisation has "to a greater extent," and 40% thought it has "completely" ensured timeliness in the cash transfer. Only 10% of respondents believed the influence was restricted "To some extent," and none claimed no benefit ("Not at least" or "To a small extent"). These answers underline the advantages of digitisation in the case of ensuring administrative efficiency, which has simplified procedures and cut the cash transfer time needed. Nonetheless, the little challenges brought up by certain UP officials point to possible opportunities for development, especially in terms of localised problems such as technological faults or connection problems. While commenting on the timeliness, one UP secretary stated, "*Most beneficiaries receive their payments on time, but occasionally there are delays owing to network problems or system faults*" (Interview Data 2024). On the other hand, one UP chairman said, "*The digital system has made our work much easier, but we still face challenges during peak times when the system slows down. Sometimes, this causes delays for a few beneficiaries' payments*" (Interview Data 2024). These issues must be resolved to ensure that everyone's equitable gain is achieved.

On the other hand, the DDLG said, "*The digital system has significantly reduced payment delays, but its success depends on the seamless collaboration between banks, mobile financial service providers, and local government offices. Any disruption in this chain will cause delays*" (KII 2024). One UNO stated, "We have seen great improvements in timeliness, but we need real-time monitoring to identify and resolve issues as soon as they arise" (KII 2024). Conversely, one development practitioner who emphasised the importance of infrastructure upgrades mentioned, "While the digital system has been instrumental, we still face challenges in remote areas where network connectivity is poor. Thus, there is a need to work on strengthening infrastructure to ensure that every beneficiary gets their payments on time" (KII 2024).

What UP officials and key informants say agrees with what other countries have found. In Nigeria, for example, digital cash transfers faced issues such as network failures and delays in verifying the recipient, which sometimes slowed down payment operations (Aker et al. 2016). The BISP in Pakistan also had problems with ID registration, which sometimes caused delays (Nayab and Farooq 2014). These examples show that to make sure that digital money transfers happen on time, we need strong systems and strong acts. The large number of happy beneficiaries and positive statements from UP officials align with findings from around the world on the benefits of digitising cash transfers. For example, studies have shown that digital solutions can significantly reduce working times and clarify processes, especially in low-income areas where traditional methods often fail (World Bank 2020a). However, the small worries that UP officials raised are similar to what other places have found: sometimes governmental delays, technological issues, and link problems make it hard to pay (Government of Bangladesh 2022). The Bolsa Família program in Brazil shows how important it is to include digital tools with strong management frameworks. A central database and real-time tracking help the program cut down on delays and make sure that everyone is held accountable, which helps to explain why it works so well at reducing payment delays (Lindert et al. 2007). These lessons are especially useful for Bangladesh as it works to improve its digital cash transfer networks.

The timing study shows how well digital technologies have cut down on payment delays and made sure that cash transfers are delivered quickly. The favourable response from SSN recipients and the high degree of confidence displayed by UP officials make this evident. This result indicates that digitisation can transform processes by improving the overall functionality of SSN systems and simplifying administrative duties. However, the minor concerns that UP authorities raised indicate that we still have work to do to eliminate these gaps and ensure that everyone can benefit from digitisation. Policymakers should apply the best practices from throughout the world, make things clearer, and strengthen the technical infrastructure to build on the benefits of automation and make sure that digital cash transfer systems continue to be dependable and successful for supporting impoverished populations.

### 3.2 *Simplification of Procedures Through Digital Cash Transfers*

Cash transfer systems' digitisation seeks to streamline administrative tasks, lowering the complexity and bureaucratic obstacles related to manual operations. Simplified processes not only increase the general experience for administrators and recipients but also help to improve the efficiency of service delivery. Based on responses from SSN recipients and UP officials, this section examines the extent to which digital solutions have streamlined cash transfer receipt and distribution processes. From these points of view, we have evaluated the effectiveness of digitisation in simplifying procedures, pinpointing areas for development, and investigating the reasons behind particular differences between the reactions of beneficiaries and UP officials.

With 29% of respondents stating that the procedures for obtaining digital cash transfers are "Simple" and 70% saying they are "Very Simple," the data (Table 5) indicate that most beneficiaries—99%—perceive the procedures as simpler than those for manual transactions. Just 1% of respondents said they had no opinion, and none said the processes were "Very complex" or "Complex." This mostly favourable response emphasises how well digitisation has lowered administrative obstacles and simplified the cash transfer receiving procedure. Vulnerable groups significantly benefit from simplifying processes as they can find the complexity of manual systems difficult (World Bank, 2020b). One SSN recipient said, "*Before I had to visit several places and complete many documents to get my money.*

**Table 5** Level of procedural simplification of digitalised cash transfer system compared to manual process

| *SSN beneficiaries* | *Total (n = 100)* | *UP functionaries* | *Total (n = 20)* |
|---|---|---|---|
| Options | 100 (100%) | Options | 20 (100%) |
| Very complex | 00 (00%) | Very complex | 00 (00%) |
| Complex | 00 (00%) | Complex | 00 (00%) |
| Neutral | 01 (1%) | Neutral | 01 (5%) |
| Simple | 29 (29%) | Simple | 09 (45%) |
| Very simple | 70 (70%) | Very simple | 10 (50%) |

Source: Field Data (2024)

*Right now, I use my cell phone to handle everything. It is far faster and easier*" (Interview Data 2024). Another recipient said, "*The paperwork and long lines used to irritate me. The computerised system has simplified things so intensely. I just checked my phone, and the money is there*" (Interview Data 2024). This finding aligns with the experiences of other countries. For instance, by cutting intermediaries and streamlining documentation, the Direct Benefit Transfer (DBT) system has significantly streamlined processes in India, therefore facilitating beneficiary access to their accounts (Muralidharan et al. 2016). In Kenya, the launch of M-Pesa for cash transfers has simplified procedures so recipients may get money with little effort (Jack and Suri 2011). These illustrations highlight how digital technologies might streamline administrative processes globally.

Conversely, UP officials noted procedural simplifications as 45% of respondents said the digital method was "Simple," compared to 50% who said it was "Very Simple." Only 5% said they had no opinion, and none said the processes were "Very complex" or "Complex." These answers underline the advantages associated with the administrative efficiency of digitalisation, which has simplified procedures and lessened the stress of the administrators. Nonetheless, the indifferent answers of a small number of UP officials point to possible opportunities for development, especially concerning localised problems such as technological challenges or connection concerns (Sarwar et al. 2023). A UP chairman clarified, "*Our work has been considerably simpler due to the computerised system. Manual computations and mountains of documentation are no longer issues we must cope with. However, occasionally, especially during upgrades or network issues, we encounter problems with the system" (Interview Data 2024)*. Another UP member stated, "*Most beneficiaries find the system extremely straightforward. However, we occasionally have to help individuals unfamiliar with mobile banking. This can occupy time*" (Interview Data 2024).

Although most beneficiaries and UP officials agree that digital technology has streamlined processes, their answers differ somewhat. For example, compared to UP officials (50%), a more significant percentage of beneficiaries—70%—rated the operations as "Very Simple." On the other hand, compared to beneficiaries (1%), a somewhat more significant share of UP officials (5%) stated a neutral position. Their jobs and experiences help explain these differences. Beneficiaries primarily engage with the digital system's straightforward and understandable end-user interface. Their satisfactory comments show how well the user-friendly design has made the procedure available even to people with low digital literacy. While commenting on the ease of the system, one SSN recipient said, "*I was worried I would not understand the digital system, but it is quite easy to use. Just following the directions on my phone, everything goes well*" (Interview Data 2024). Conversely, UP officials participate in the operational and administrative facets of the system. Their indifferent answers might reflect technological problems, poor connection, or backend system management obstacles. Although not directly observable to beneficiaries, these challenges can compromise the general system's efficiency. A UP secretary said, "The system is fantastic when it works, but we need improved training and help to address technological challenges. Sometimes, we must depend on outside IT help, which might slow the process" (Interview Data 2024). These differences underline the need to take administrator and user points of view into account when assessing the performance of digital systems. Beneficiaries may find the system relatively simple to use, but managers may encounter practical issues that need to be addressed to ensure the system operates effectively in the long term.

The study of procedural reduction focuses on how effectively digital technologies facilitate the removal of bureaucratic barriers and simplify processes. This is clear from the positive feedback from recipients and the high level of trust among UP officials. Still, the fact that their answers were different shows how important it is to look at digital systems from both the administrator's and user's points of view when judging their success. People who use the system think it is fairly easy to use. However, UP representatives may encounter practical problems that need to be addressed for the system to function effectively in the long term.

### *3.3 Cost Efficiency of Digital Cash Transfers*

Cost efficiency is a good way to measure how well digital cash transfer systems work because it has a direct effect on how long and how big the SSN programs can be. Digitalisation tries to make the most of the resources that are available to those who need them by cutting down on operations and management costs and reducing waste and inefficiency. This section looks into what recipients and UP officials said about how cost-effective digital cash payments were. Comparing different points of view helps us figure out how much money digitisation has saved and shows us where more work needs to be done. Additionally, the differences in responses between UP officials and recipients were discussed, highlighting the disparities in their situations and perspectives.

The available data (Table 6) suggested that 100% of all SSN beneficiaries saw the digital cash transfer system as cost-effective. Among the respondents, 27% described it as "Efficient," and 73% as "Very Efficient." Of the respondents, none identified the system as "Very efficient," "Inefficient," or "Neutral." This overwhelmingly positive feedback emphasises how well digitisation has lowered recipient costs by removing intermediaries' fees, lowering travel expenditures, and minimising bureaucratic overhead. The significant degree of satisfaction reflects the real advantages of digital technologies in enabling vulnerable groups to afford and receive more reasonably priced cash transfers. One SSN recipient said, "*Before, I had to pay for transportation to pick up my payment, and occasionally I had to pay bribes to middlemen. The money now appears straight in my cell account; therefore, I can spend nothing further. For my family, it is quite relieving*" (Interview Data 2024). Another SSN recipient said, "*The*

**Table 6** Level of cost efficiency of digital cash transfer system compared to manual process

| *SSN beneficiaries* | *Total (n = 100)* | *UP functionaries* | *Total (n = 20)* |
|---|---|---|---|
| Options | 100 (100%) | Options | 20 (100%) |
| Very inefficient | 00 (00%) | Very inefficient | 00 (00%) |
| Inefficient | 00 (00%) | Inefficient | 00 (00%) |
| Neutral | 00 (00%) | Neutral | 00 (00%) |
| Efficient | 27 (27%) | Efficient | 12 (60%) |
| Very efficient | 73 (73%) | Very efficient | 08 (40%) |

Source: Field Data (2024)

*computerised method has saved me time and money. Long travels to the UP office and hidden costs are no longer of concern to me. It has changed my life*" (Interview Data 2024).

With 60% of UP officials identifying the digital system as "Efficient" and 40% as "Very Efficient," the representatives indicated great cost efficiency. Not one respondent described the procedure as "Very efficient," "Inefficient," or "Neutral." These answers highlight the administrative cost reductions achieved through digitisation, which have lowered operational overhead and increased overall SSN program efficiency. However, the somewhat lower percentage of UP officials evaluating the system as "Very Efficient" (40%) compared to beneficiaries (73%) suggests that administrators may be more aware of the residual costs and challenges associated with sustaining digital systems. A UP secretary said, "*The digital system has reduced costs for beneficiaries. However, we still have to invest in maintaining the system, training staff, and resolving technical issues. Although not often apparent to recipients, these expenses are vital for maintaining the system's operation*" (Interview Data 2024). One UP member said, "*While the system is cost-efficient overall, we need more infrastructure and technical support funding to ensure its long-term sustainability*" (Interview Data 2024).

Although UP officials and recipients agree that digital systems are cost-effective, their answers noticeably differ. Compared to UP officials (40%), 73% of the SSN recipients reported that the system was "Very Efficient." On the other hand, more UP representatives (60%) described the system as "Efficient" than as "Very Efficient." Their responsibilities and perspectives help explain these variances. Mostly, beneficiaries of digital systems see immediate cost reductions, including lower travel expenditures and the removal of middleman fees. Their mostly favourable comments capture the real advantages they get from digitalisation. For instance, one SSN recipient said, " *I spent a lot of money on fees and travel. Everything is done now using my phone, and I save a lot. It is a gift for those like myself who have a limited income*" (Interview Data 2024).

Conversely, UP officials deal with the administrative and operational sides of the system. Their more modest comments might reflect an understanding of the expenses of preserving digital infrastructure, like technical support, platform maintenance, and training. Although not readily visible to consumers, these expenses are crucial for the long-term viability of digital systems. One UP chairman said, "*We see the benefits of the digital system, but we also know the costs involved in keeping it running smoothly. Saving money is only one aspect; another is investing in the system's future*" (Interview Data 2024). These differences highlight the importance of considering both administrator and user perspectives to evaluate the cost-effectiveness of digital systems. Although recipients save much money, managers must deal with continuous running expenses to guarantee the system's viability.

The highly satisfactory response of the SSN recipients and the favourable comments from UP officials align well with the study result on the cost-effectiveness of digital cash transfers in different countries. For example, studies have shown that digital systems may save much money on administrative and operational costs, especially in countries where traditional methods are not very effective (World Bank 2024). Data from Brazil's Bolsa Família program also demonstrate the importance of combining digital technology with sound financial management (Lindert et al. 2007). Research on the success of digital cash transfer systems shows that SSN beneficiaries and UP authorities have observed significant improvements in speed, convenience of use, and cost-effectiveness. Most beneficiaries like the system since it is quick, easy to use, and cheap. This illustrates how technology has altered their life. However, the fact that recipients and UP officials gave different replies shows that managers are more concerned with commercial considerations like technological challenges and continuing expenditures. At the same time, those who get the money are more interested in the evident benefits of lower expenses and fewer delays. These realisations show how crucial it is to solve problems with the backend so that digital systems may flourish and survive for a long time.

## 4 Reducing Transaction Costs: The Impact of Digital Cash Transfers

For a long time, it has been tougher to deliver SSN services to more people due to transaction expenses, such as agent fees, trip costs, and administrative overhead. People assumed that digitising ways to distribute money would cut these expenses and make sure that more resources got to the correct people immediately. This part examines how digital solutions can help minimise transaction costs by eliminating agency fees, reducing travel and administrative expenses, and lowering the costs of running a business. This section presents a detailed picture of the merits and downsides of cutting transaction costs by digitising them. It does this by looking at them from the points of view of SSN recipients, UP authorities, and relevant sources. The findings provide us with valuable information that we can use to enhance SSN systems and make them more accessible and useful.

### 4.1 *Elimination of Intermediary Fees*

Beneficiaries of the SSN programs have always found intermediary fees a significant hardship, limiting the quantity of cash transfers that reach intended receivers. By allowing direct payments to recipients' accounts, digitising cash transfer systems seeks to eradicate these costs. Based on responses from UP officials and recipients, this section looks at how well digital solutions have eliminated middleman costs. Supporting and contextualising these viewpoints, insights from KIIs help to provide a more profound knowledge of the challenges and successes in this area.

With 40% of respondents indicating a "Significant" reduction and 58% claiming that costs have been "Completely" reduced, the data (Table 7) shows that most beneficiaries—98% feel that digital systems have either considerably cut or reduced intermediary fees. Only 3% of respondents reported a modest impact ("A little" or "Somewhat"), and none claimed no reduction at all ("Not at all"). This overwhelmingly favourable response emphasises how well digitisation has guaranteed that more financial transfers reach recipients directly, free from intermediate costs. One SSN recipient said, "*Before, I had to pay middlemen some of my money to get it. I now have the whole amount in my account with the digital system. It is very comfortable for someone like me who depends on every take*" (Interview Data 2024). Another SSN recipient said, "*The digital system has prevented the corruption we used to confront. Nobody may now cut from my pawet. It is*

**Table 7** Contribution of digital cash transfer system in eliminating intermediary fees

| *SSN beneficiaries* | *Total* | *UP functionaries* | *Total* |
|---|---|---|---|
| Options | 100 (100%) | Options | 20 (100%) |
| Not at all | 00 (00%) | Not at all | 00 (00%) |
| A little | 01 (1%) | A little | 00 (00%) |
| Somewhat | 02 (2%) | Somewhat | 00 (00%) |
| Significantly | 40 (40%) | Significantly | 06 (30%) |
| Completely | 58 (58%) | Completely | 14 (70%) |

Source: Field Data (2024)

*entirely mine, and it will significantly impact my family*" (Interview Data 2024). Important insights into these findings came from key informants. The DDLG said, "*The digital system has been a game-changer in minimising corruption and ensuring that money reaches recipients immediately. Their faith in the system has been much enhanced as beneficiaries no longer have to pay middlemen to obtain their rights*" (KII 2024). This realisation highlights how radically digitisation is changing beneficiary experiences.

The findings corroborate the findings of other studies. For instance, by allowing direct transfers to recipients' bank accounts, the Direct Benefit Transfer (DBT) system has drastically cut intermediary costs in India (Muralidharan et al. 2016). In Kenya, the launch of M-Pesa for cash transfers has also replaced middlemen, guaranteeing that recipients get their payments as a whole (Jack and Suri 2011). These illustrations highlight how global digital systems can lower transaction costs.

On the other hand, 30% of UP officials said the impact was "significant," while 70% said the elimination of middleman fees was "complete." None of the respondents thought the impact was modest, as nobody responded in the category of "Not at all," "A little," or "Somewhat." These answers underline the administrative efficiency benefits of digitisation, which have simplified procedures and lessened the load of intermediate costs on recipients. The somewhat lower proportion of UP representatives rating the impact as "Significantly" (30%) compared to beneficiaries (40%) suggests that administrators may be more aware of residual challenges, such as ensuring compliance and preventing informal fees in specific contexts (Sarwar et al. 2023). A UP member said, "*Middlemen find it much more challenging to profit from beneficiaries due to the computerised method. Although most contributions go directly to the recipients, we occasionally hear complaints about illegal fees in outlying locations" (Interview Data 2024).* One UP chair said, "*Once the digital system was implemented, corruption dropped dramatically. Transparency gains significantly when beneficiaries receive their entire payouts*" (Interview Data 2024).

Although the system has largely eliminated official intermediary fees, one UNO official stated, "*We must remain vigilant to prevent informal fees from creeping back into the system, especially in remote areas where monitoring is challenging*" (KII 2024). This finding emphasises the importance of ongoing monitoring and capacity-building to maintain the improvements attained by digitisation, as they correspond with the few issues expressed by beneficiaries and UP officials. On the other hand, one local government expert stated, "*The success of digitisation in lowering transaction costs depends on continuous monitoring and capacity-building at the local level. UP authorities have a big role to play in making sure the system stays open and works well*" (KII 2024). This perspective underscores the necessity for financial support for training and helps for local management to ensure the effective use of digital technologies.

The high level of satisfaction among recipients and the positive feedback from UP authorities are in line with what other studies have found throughout the world. Studies have shown, for example, that digital solutions can significantly reduce costs for intermediaries and clarify processes, especially in developing countries (World Bank 2020b). The data from Brazil's Bolsa Família program shows how crucial it is to have robust control structures in digital systems. The program has been able to minimise transaction costs by using a central database and real-time tracking to cut down on waste and make sure people are held accountable (Lindert et al. 2007). These lessons are particularly helpful for Bangladesh as it seeks to improve its digital cash transfer networks. The study of intermediary fees shows how successfully digital technologies cut transaction costs. This is seen from the overwhelmingly positive feedback from users and the trust of UP authorities. However, the expertise of key informants reminds us that we need to continue addressing issues to resolve the remaining problems and ensure that everyone who benefits from digitisation receives the benefits.

### 4.2 Reduction in Travel and Documentation Costs

For those who live in rural or poor areas, travel and administrative costs have long been a big problem for people who utilise the SSN program. By cutting the need for actual travel and streamlining documentation requirements, the digitisation of cash transfer systems seeks to lower these expenses. Based on responses from SSN beneficiaries and UP officials, this section investigates how digital solutions have lowered travel and paperwork expenses. Using insights from interviews and KIIs, these points of view are supported and contextualised to provide a better understanding of the challenges and successes in this area.

With 36% of respondents indicating a "Significantly" reduction and 61% claiming that costs have been "Completely" reduced, the data (Table 8) shows that most beneficiaries—97%—believe that digital systems have significantly lowered or reduced travel and paperwork expenses. Just

**Table 8** Contribution of digital cash transfer system in eliminating travel and documentation costs

| *SSN beneficiaries* | *Total (n = 100)* | *UP functionaries* | *Total (n = 20)* |
|---|---|---|---|
| Options | 100 (100%) | Options | 20 (100%) |
| Not at all | 00 (00%) | Not at all | 00 (00%) |
| A little | 00 (00%) | A little | 00 (00%) |
| Somewhat | 03 (3%) | Somewhat | 00 (00%) |
| Significantly | 36 (36%) | Significantly | 09 (45%) |
| Completely | 61 (61%) | Completely | 11 (55%) |

Source: Field Data (2024)

3% of respondents said the impact was modest ("Somewhat"), and none said there was no change at all ("Not at all" or "A little"). Particularly for individuals in distant locations who previously had to travel great distances to obtain their payments, this overwhelmingly favourable response emphasises the achievement of digitisation in lowering recipients' financial and logistical loads. One SSN recipient said, "*Before, I had to spend much money commuting and taking time off work to collect my payout. I have it right now, straight on my phone. It has saved me much time and money and eliminated my need to worry about losing records*" (Interview Data 2024). This quotation captures the clear advantages of digitisation for consumers, especially in lessening conventional cash flow methods' logistical and financial costs.

Important feedback on these findings also came from key informants. For instance, the DDLG stated, "*The digital system has been transforming to eliminate the need for beneficiaries to travel to UPs or government offices. They have saved money and time, particularly important for women with caregiving duties and elderly persons*" (KII 2024). This realisation emphasises the clear advantages of digitalisation for underprivileged groups. This result aligns with the findings of similar studies carried out in other countries. For instance, by allowing direct transfers to recipients' bank accounts, the Direct Benefit Transfer (DBT) system has significantly lowered travel and verification expenses in India (Muralidharan et al. 2016). In Kenya, the launch of M-Pesa for cash transfers has also reduced the need for recipients to visit payment facilities, guaranteeing them easy access to their money (Jack and Suri 2011). These illustrations highlight how global digital systems can lower transaction costs.

With 45% of UP officials characterising the impact as "Significantly" and 55% as "Complete," they also claimed notable progress in lowering travel and paperwork costs. None of the respondents thought the impact was modest in the form of Not at all, "A little," or "Somewhat". The somewhat lower number of UP representatives assessing the impact as "Significantly" (45%) compared to beneficiaries (36%) suggests that administrators may be more aware of lingering challenges, including ensuring all beneficiaries have access to digital services (Sarwar et al. 2023). A female member of the UP said, "*For most beneficiaries, the digital system has made a significant impact. However, we still notice specific issues in distant places where people lack access to cell phones or stable internet. We must close these inequities if everyone gains fairly*" (Interview Data 2024). This quotation emphasises the need to remove local obstacles to guarantee the inclusion of digital networks. On the other hand, one UNO said, "*While the system has eliminated the need for travel and documentation, some beneficiaries in remote areas still face challenges due to limited access to mobile devices or internet connectivity. Dealing with these obstacles will help to guarantee that everyone can benefit from digitalisation*" (KII 2024). One local government expert noted, "*Digitalisation can help cut down on travel and paperwork costs, but only if it is watched all the time. People learn new talents in their own area*" (KII 2024). UP authorities play a crucial role in ensuring that the system is user-friendly and operates smoothly for everyone. This perspective underscores the necessity of offering training and assistance to local employees to guarantee the proper utilisation of digital technologies. The high level of enjoyment among beneficiaries and the good comments from UP authorities are in line with what studies have shown about the benefits of digitising cash transfers throughout the world. For instance, research has demonstrated that digital technology may significantly reduce travel and writing expenses by minimising the necessity for in-person meetings and streamlining administrative activities (World Bank 2020c).

The findings for travel and administrative costs suggest that digital techniques make things easier for recipients in terms of both financial and practical considerations. The good response from beneficiaries and the high level of confidence among UP authorities back this up. Nevertheless, the replies from important sources show that more has to be done to solve the problems that remain and make sure that everyone can benefit from becoming digital.

### 4.3 Reduction in Administrative Overhead

Implementing the SSN program has always been challenging due to factors such as paperwork, office visits, and manual record-keeping. By automating procedures, reducing documentation, and simplifying administrative tasks, the digitisation of cash transfer systems aims to lower this cost. Based on responses from SSN recipients, UP officials, and KIIs, this section examines how effectively digital systems have reduced administrative overhead. With 46% of respondents indicating a "Significantly" reduction and 50% claiming that overhead has been "Completely" reduced, the data (Table 9) shows that a great majority of beneficiaries—96%—believe that digital systems have significantly lowered or eliminated administrative overhead. Only 4% of respondents reported a modest effect ("A little" or "Somewhat"), and none indicated that there was no decrease at all ("Not at all"). This overwhelmingly favourable response emphasises how well digitisation minimises the bureaucratic load on beneficiaries by lowering the requirement for office visits and paperwork. A SSN recipient said, "*Before, I had to visit many places and present mounds of documentation simply to obtain my payout. Everything is done now using my phone. It is much simpler, and I am not worried about losing records or standing in huge queues*" (Interview Data 2024). This response captures the real advantages of digitisation for beneficiaries, especially in lessening the administrative load connected with conventional cash transfer methods. Key informants expressed similar views in this regard. One UNO mentioned, "*Because of the digital method, beneficiaries do not have to go to government buildings or turn in paper forms as often. This saves time and makes it easier for our workers to handle paperwork*" (KII 2024). This type

**Table 9** Contribution of digital cash transfer system in reducing administrative overhead

| *SSN beneficiaries* | *Total* | *UP functionaries* | *Total* |
|---|---|---|---|
| Options | 100 (100%) | Options | 20 (100%) |
| Not at all | 00 (00%) | Not at all | 00 (00%) |
| A little | 03 (3%) | A little | 00 (00%) |
| Somewhat | 01 (1%) | Somewhat | 00 (00%) |
| Significantly | 46 (46%) | Significantly | 09 (45%) |
| Completely | 50 (50%) | Completely | 11 (55%) |

Source: Field Data (2024)

of answer highlights the two benefits of technology for both managers and users.

The study findings are more likely to be true because they are similar to what other studies have found. For example, India's Direct Benefit Transfer (DBT) system has greatly reduced the cost of running the government by automating tasks and getting rid of the need to keep records by hand (Muralidharan et al. 2016). Also, the start of M-Pesa for sending money has made routine tasks easier in Kenya, making service delivery faster and better (Jack and Suri 2011). These pictures show how digital systems can help cut down on costs for running governments around the world.

Forty-five per cent of UP officials said the effect was "Significantly," and 55% said it was "Completely." UP officials also said they had done a great job of lowering management costs. None of the people who answered "Not at all," "A little," or "Somewhat" thought the effect was small. It is clear from these answers that technology has made the UP officials work more efficiently by streamlining processes and making officials more accountable. Clarifying the advantages of digital cash transfers, one chairman of the UP said, "*Even though the digital system has made our job a lot easier, we still need to do some things by hand sometimes, like when users are having trouble with digital proof or paperwork. To automate the method, we need to close these holes*" (Interview Data 2024). This response from the UP official emphasises the need to tackle the remaining issues to guarantee the long-term viability of digital systems. One development practitioner said, "*Even though the system has cut down on administrative work a lot, some things still need to be done by hand, especially when beneficiaries are having trouble with digital proof or paperwork*" (KII 2024). This idea shows how important it is to keep integrating and automating systems, since it fits with the small problems that UP officials and recipients have brought up. The study's findings support those of Lindert et al. (2007), who said that data from Brazil's Bolsa Família program stresses the need for strong digital systems with strong control structures. A central database and real-time tracking used by the program have helped lower management costs by cutting down on waste and making sure that people are held accountable. These lessons are especially useful for Bangladesh as it works to improve its digital cash transfer networks. Based on the high level of trust among UP officials and the large number of positive comments from recipients, the study of administrative waste shows how well digital methods work at removing bureaucratic barriers and speeding up processes.

### 4.4 Effectiveness of Digitised Cash Transfers in Meeting Beneficiaries' Needs

The capacity of digitised cash transfer systems to efficiently satisfy beneficiary demands defines their final degree of success. Based on beneficiary responses, this section assesses the general efficiency of digital cash transfers in satisfying the social and financial needs of the recipients. By looking at things from their points of view, we can tell if digitalisation has succeeded in its goal of making SSN services more accessible, reliable, and powerful. On the other hand, key sources give information that helps put these points of view in context and gives a better picture of the difficulties and successes in meeting the needs of recipients.

With 71% of respondents stating that the system is "Effective" and 26% saying it is "Very Effective," the data (Table 10) indicate that most beneficiaries—97%—believe digital cash transfer systems meet their needs. Just 3% of respondents said they were impartial, and none said the system was "Very Ineffective" or "Ineffective." Particularly for underprivileged groups that depend on cash transfers for their necessities, this overwhelmingly favourable response highlights how much digitisation has improved the accessibility, dependability, and effectiveness of cash transfers. While commenting on this issue, one SSN beneficiary said, "*The digital method has made it much easier to get my payments on time. For us, it has been important*" (Interview Data 2024). A similar response has been expressed by one UNO, who stated, "*The digital system has revolutionised how recipients obtain their payments. It has guaranteed that money reaches people most in need in addition to accelerating and guaranteeing the dependability of the procedure*" (KII 2024). Particularly in guaranteeing quick and consistent access to cash transfers, these responses highlight the apparent advantages of digitisation for beneficiaries.

**Table 10** Level of effectiveness of digitised cash transfer system in meeting needs

| *SSN beneficiaries* | *Total* |
|---|---|
| Options | 100 (100%) |
| Very ineffective | 00 (00%) |
| Ineffective | 00 (00%) |
| Neutral | 03 (3%) |
| Effective | 71 (71%) |
| Very effective | 26 (26%) |

Source: Field Data (2024)

A member of the UP said, "*The digital system has been a game-changer for most beneficiaries, but we still need to address challenges in remote areas where access to mobile phones and internet connectivity is limited. Our first concern is ensuring the system will help everyone*" (Interview Data 2024). Conversely, a development practitioner said, "*While the system has been essentially effective, there are still areas where improvements are needed, particularly in ensuring that all beneficiaries, including those in remote areas, can access digital services without additional burdens*" (KII 2024). This understanding highlights the importance of continually improving system accessibility and inclusion, as it aligns with the few problems that recipients have mentioned. The study's findings align with those of other studies conducted in various parts of the world. For example, the Direct Benefit Transfer (DBT) system has made cash transfers in India a lot more efficient by making sure that payments are made on time and in an open way (Muralidharan et al. 2016). M-Pesa, a mobile money transfer service, has also made social safety net services in Kenya more accessible and reliable, especially in rural areas (Jack and Suri 2011).

The high level of happiness among receivers is in line with data from around the world about the benefits of digitising cash exchanges. For example, studies have shown that digital systems can make cash payments much more efficient by making them clearer, cutting down on delays, and preventing leaks (GSMA 2020). In other countries, however, technical problems and access limitations sometimes render the benefits of digitisation less useful (UNDP 2023)—important informants raised these issues. The Prospera program in Mexico stresses the importance of combining strong government frameworks with digital technology (Levy 2006). These problems show how important strong infrastructure and strict rules are for making sure that digital systems are reliable and easy to use.

## 5 Impact of Digitised Cash Transfers on Livelihood Improvement

By providing people with regular and timely financial support, SSN services aim to enhance their quality of life. Employing transparent and effective money transfer, the digitisation of cash transfer systems seeks to improve this impact. Based on responses from beneficiaries, UP officials

**Table 11** Contribution of digital cash transfer system in improving livelihoods

| *SSN beneficiaries* | *Total* | *UP functionaries* | *Total* |
|---|---|---|---|
| Options | 100 (100%) | Options | 20 (100%) |
| Very ineffective | 00 (00%) | Very ineffective | 00 (00%) |
| Ineffective | 01 (1%) | Ineffective | 00 (00%) |
| Neutral | 03 (3%) | Neutral | 00 (00%) |
| Effective | 44 (44%) | Effective | 10 (50%) |
| Very effective | 52 (52%) | Very effective | 10 (50%) |

Source: Field Data (2024)

and key informants, this section assesses how well digital cash transfers enhance recipients' general quality of living. With 44% of respondents saying the system is "Effective" and 52% saying it is "Very Effective," the data (Table 11) shows that most beneficiaries—96%—think digital cash transfer systems have successfully enhanced their livelihoods. Just 4% of respondents said they were indifferent or negative ("Neutral," "Ineffective," or "Very Ineffective"). This overwhelmingly favourable response emphasises how well digitisation has improved recipients' financial stability and general well-being, particularly for underprivileged groups that depend on these payments for their fundamental necessities. While commenting on this, one recipient remarked, "*The digital cash transfer system has been a lifeline for my family. Timeliness in payments has allowed me to create a small business and invest in my children's education. It provides hope for a brighter future*" (Interview Data 2024). This comment highlights how digitisation really does improve people's lives by boosting their standards of living and making their lives more stable and prosperous.

The key informants of the study provided important insights into this finding. One UNO observed, for instance, "*Not only has the digital system made sure that payments are paid on time, but it has also given recipients greater control over their money, which makes them less susceptible and improves their quality of life*" (KII 2024). This understanding shows how fundamentally technology is altering the lives of beneficiaries. Tests done in other regions of the world have reached the same conclusion. The Direct Benefit Transfer (DBT) system in India, for instance, has considerably improved the lives of its users by making sure that payments are sent on time and in a straightforward way. This has made it possible for people to put money into things like health, education, and small companies

(Muralidharan et al. 2016; Ahluwalia and Bhatti 2017). M-Pesa's debut for cash payments in Kenya has also made it simpler for individuals in rural areas to receive money and use banking services (Jack and Suri 2011; Mathew 2021). These photographs show how individuals all across the world are using contemporary tools to make their lives better.

Half of the UP authorities claimed the system was "Effective," while the other half said it was "Very Effective." They did see progress in making people's lives better through digital currency payments. No one who answered thought the method was "Very Ineffective," "Ineffective," or "Neutral." Because of these answers, it is clear that digitisation helps people stay healthy and safe financially. Still, the fact that the number of responses was similar between "Effective" and "Very Effective" suggests that even if the system has worked, there is still room for improvement to make it even more powerful. One UP secretary said, "*The digital method has made a big change in the quality of life for those who benefit, especially those who live in rural areas. With their income, many people have started small businesses or fixed up their homes. To help them make the most of these opportunities, we need to give them more training and help*" (Interview Data 2024). This quote emphasises the importance of collaborating on various projects to enhance the impact of digital money transfers on people's lives.

Although the system has been mainly successful in enhancing livelihoods, a development practitioner underlined, "*There are still some places that need focused help, especially to make sure that people who get payments can use them to build long-term businesses*" (KII 2024). This response emphasises the importance of complementing initiatives supporting livelihood diversification and economic empowerment in line with the viewpoints of UP officials. On the other hand, one local government expert said, "*If technology is to help people make better livings, it needs to be constantly supervised, and local communities need to be given the tools they need to use it. UP officials play a key role in making sure that the system stays sensitive to the needs of all beneficiaries*" (Interview Data 2024). This point of view emphasises the importance of providing training and support to local workers to ensure that digital technology is utilised effectively.

The large number of happy recipients and positive words from UP officials are in line with what studies have found about the benefits of digitising cash transfers. Studies have shown that digital systems can make people's lives a lot better by making it easier for them to get credit, lowering poverty, and investing in their own people (GSMA 2020). Still, the few problems that key sources brought up are similar to what other countries have found: the benefits of digitalisation are often harmed by limited entry and job opportunities (UNDP 2023). These difficulties highlight how crucial it is to have strong infrastructure and other policies that work together to make sure that income gains last. The research on the impacts of digitalised currency transfer systems examines their enhancement of user experiences, since the majority of users exhibited positivity and considerable trust in UP authorities. However, the knowledge of crucial informants reminds us that we need to keep working on things to fix the problems that are still there and make sure that everyone who benefits from digitisation gets the advantages.

## 5.1 *Impact of Digitisation on Household Expense Management*

By guaranteeing prompt and consistent access to money, the digitisation of cash transfer systems can significantly increase beneficiaries' capacity to manage household spending. Effective management of home spending is essential for users of Bangladesh's SSN programs to satisfy necessities and raise the general quality of living. Based on the responses of the SSN beneficiaries, this section examines how digitisation affects beneficiaries' capacity to control household costs. Through an analysis of several perspectives, the section aims to assess the extent to which digitisation has enhanced financial management and identify areas requiring further improvement.

The study findings suggest that most SSN recipients believe digitising helps them control home spending better. Table 12 shows that 24% of recipients viewed the impact as "Very Positive," and 65% said it is "Positive." Only 11% of respondents said they had challenges; 7% said the impact was "negative" and 4% were indifferent. None of the recipients

**Table 12** Impact of digitisation on ability to manage household expenses

| *Indicator* | *SSN beneficiaries (n = 100) (%)* |
|---|---|
| Very negatively | 0 |
| Negatively | 7 |
| Neutral | 4 |
| Positively | 65 |
| Very positively | 24 |

Source: Field Data

said their influence is “Very Negative.” One SSN beneficiary said, “*I have been able to better budget for household spending since the payments began arriving digitally. Delays and lost money are no longer concerns for me*” (Interview Data 2024). One SSN recipient from a rural region pointed out, “*The digital system has made it easier to budget and save. I can now save money for food, school, and health care in a smarter way*” (Interview Data 2024). Key informants provided additional suggestions on how technology could enhance the management of finances. A social welfare officer said, “*Digitalisation has made sure that payments are always on time and has given people the tools they need to handle their own money. This has an immediate influence on how well they can pay their bills and improve their quality of life*” (KII 2024). Likewise, a development practitioner underlined, “*Digitisation has made it easier for people to prepare for their family's requirements and has made it less stressful to find money by offering them easy access to monies*” (KII 2024). These findings are consistent with global research on the impact of digital financial services on personal money management. For instance, Jack and Suri's (2011) study reveals that individuals are better off financially when they use digital cash because it helps them save and spend their money more wisely. Research by the World Bank (2020b) shows that monthly payments help people keep track of their expenditures and make long-term investments in their health and happiness. These links show that technology has transformed the power to improve lives and manage money better.

The research that looks at how technology changes family spending control highlights how it helps people become more financially stable and improves their quality of life. The positive comments from SSN users indicate that digitisation effectively ensures people have reliable and quick access to money, which facilitates spending and planning. However, the few problems that a very small number of users brought up show how important it is to keep improving things to get rid of delays and make sure that everyone can fully benefit from digital cash transfers. By fixing these problems and making the system better, Bangladesh can help SSN users learn how to handle their money better, which will improve their general quality of life.

### 5.2 *Financial Independence: Empowering Beneficiaries Through Digital Cash Transfers*

One important thing that effective digital cash transfer systems must do is give recipients financial freedom. This means that they should be able to handle their money on their own and make smart choices about their family's needs. In Bangladesh, SSN programs try to help groups that are not getting enough help. Digitising cash transfers can give users more power by giving them quick and direct access to money. In this part, we look at how much the digital cash transfer system has given SSN users more financial freedom by looking at their answers. By analysing several points of view, an attempt is made to evaluate how digitisation influences financial empowerment and points out areas requiring more development.

Table 13 suggests that most SSN users believe the digital cash transfer system improves their financial freedom. The data shows that 33% of recipients expressed "Strongly Agree," and 57% of beneficiaries expressed "Agree" that they have become more financially independent. With 3% "Disagreeing" and 7% remaining indifferent, just a tiny percentage (10%) indicates low influence. Not one among the recipients "Strongly Disagree." *While discussing the issues, one recipient said, "The digital system has given me financial control. I may choose how to spend the money for my family's requirements instead of depending on others to access my payments"* (Interview Data 2024). Another beneficiary said, "*Direct access to my money has given me more confidence and independence. I can now make plans without having to worry about agents or delays*" (Interview Data 2024). The key informant also gave more information about how automation might help people become financially free. One social welfare officer engaged in the deployment of digital cash transfers said, "*Digitisation has given people more power by giving them direct access to their money. Their*

**Table 13** Experiencing financial independence as a result of the digital cash transfer system

| *Indicator* | *SSN beneficiaries (%)* |
|---|---|
| Strongly disagree | 0 |
| Disagree | 3 |
| Neutral | 7 |
| Agree | 57 |
| Strongly agree | 33 |

Source: Field Data (2024)

*overall sense of independence, worth, and financial freedom has improved*" (KII 2024). Likewise, a development practitioner noted: "*One of the best things about digital payments is that they do not withhold money. The method empowers individuals in the long run and breaks the cycle of dependency by allowing them to manage their own finances*" (KII 2024).

The findings align with research examining the impact of digital financial services on financial independence. For instance, Aker et al. (2016) and Ahmad et al. (2020) found that digital currency payments help people become more financially independent by giving them direct access to funds and making them less reliant on middlemen. World Bank (2024) research found that digitisation has made individuals financially independent. This is especially crucial for women and underprivileged groups, who often face greater challenges in accessing financial services. These links indicate that modifying how digital cash exchanges function can help people get out of debt.

Looking at financial freedom makes digital cash payments even more important for Bangladesh's SSN recipients. Beneficiaries' mostly positive comments show how well the system helps them handle their money and make smart choices about their family needs by giving them direct and timely access to money. However, the few problems that a very small number of users brought up indicate that we need to continue working to eliminate obstacles that hinder financial independence, such as a lack of computer literacy and limited access to cell phones. Bangladesh could give SSN users even more financial freedom by making the system stronger and filling in these gaps. This would improve their long-term stability and quality of life.

### 5.3 *Access to Essential Services: Enhancing Well-Being Through Digital Cash Transfers*

Most of the time, basic services like schooling and healthcare are very important for people's general health and quality of life. Digitising cash payments could make it easier for people in the SSN program to get services by making sure they always have access to money. Based on the responses of SSN beneficiaries, this section investigates how the digital cash transfer system affects beneficiaries' access to essential services. By analysing several perspectives, an attempt is made to evaluate the degree to which digitisation enhances access to education and healthcare, and to identify areas that require further development.

**Table 14** Contribution of digital systems in accessing essential services

| *Indicator* | *SSN beneficiaries (%)* |
|---|---|
| Very negatively | 0 |
| Negatively | 3 |
| Neutral | 1 |
| Positively | 64 |
| Very positively | 32 |

Source: Field Data (2024)

Table 14 suggests that most SSN users believe the digital cash transfer system improves access to necessary services. The data shows that whereas 32% of recipients viewed the impact as "Very Positive," 64% of them said it is "Positive." Only 4% of respondents said they have challenges; 3% said the impact is "Negative," and 1% stayed indifferent. Not one of the beneficiaries noted a "Very Negative" impact. One SSN recipient said, "*The digital system has simplified paying for school fees and healthcare. My family may now get these services as needed since I no longer worry about delays or lost money*" (Interview Data 2024). Another beneficiary from the rural areas stated, "*Having timely access to funds has allowed me to prioritise my children's education and ensure they attend school regularly*" (Interview Data 2024).

Key informants offered more analysis on how digitisation may help to increase access to necessary services. One social welfare worker who was in charge of giving out digital cash transfers remarked, "*Digitisation has not only made sure that payments are made on time, but it has also helped people better manage their money for things like schooling and health care. This has a direct impact on their quality of life*" (KII 2024). In the same way, a development practitioner said, "*The digital system has made it easier for people with low incomes to get important services by giving them stable access to funds*" (KII 2024). These findings are consistent with prior research examining the impact of digital financial services on access to essential services. For instance, Muralidharan et al. (2016) found that digital currency payments help people manage their money better, which makes it simpler for them to seek medical treatment and attend school. The World Bank's (2019) study also found that regular and continuous payments make it simpler for people to invest in their long-term health and education. These links show how technology has changed power, making it simpler for individuals to get the help they need.

The research that looks at how digitalisation impacts access to fundamental services highlights how vital it is for enhancing people's well-being and quality of life. The good feedback from SSN receivers indicates how effectively the digital cash transfer system works to make sure individuals can obtain money swiftly and reliably. This allows them to allocate more funds to areas such as healthcare and education. However, the few difficulties that a very small number of people raised illustrate the importance of continually improving the system to prevent delays and ensure that everyone can fully benefit from digital currency transfers. By strengthening the system and filling in these gaps, Bangladesh can make it easier for people to access essential services. This will improve the overall quality of life for SSN recipients.

### 5.4 *Social Inclusion and Empowerment: Transforming Lives Through Digital Cash Transfers*

When digital cash transfer systems work well, they lead to important findings like more social inclusion and strength, which encourage people to be more involved in their communities and make smarter choices about their lives. Digitising cash payments could give poor people in Bangladesh more power and include them in society. This is because SSN programs are meant to help these groups by giving them quick access to money. Based on what SSN recipients said, this part looks into how the digital cash transfer method makes them more socially included or gives them more power. By analysing different points of view, the section seeks to evaluate the transforming effect of digitisation on social inclusion and empowerment and points out areas needing more work.

Table 15 suggests that most SSN recipients believed the digital cash transfer system improved their sense of social inclusion and

**Table 15** Contribution of digital cash transfer system in feeling empowered

| *Indicator* | *SSN beneficiaries (%)* |
|---|---|
| Not at all | 0 |
| A little | 1 |
| Somewhat | 27 |
| Significantly | 43 |
| Completely | 29 |

Source: Field Data (2024)

empowerment. The table shows that whereas 29% of recipients characterised the impact as "Complete," 43% of beneficiaries felt "Significantly" more included or empowered. Just 1% felt "A little" more involved or influential; 27% reported feeling "Somewhat" more included or empowered. None of the beneficiaries felt "Not at least" more included or powerful. One SSN recipient said, "*I feel dignity and freedom due to the digital system. I feel more assured in handling family demands and am free from depending on others to access my payments*" (Interview Data 2024). Another recipient said, "*Having direct access to my payments has helped me to feel more involved with my community. I can now help make choices that affect my family and make sure we are safe*" (Interview Data 2024).

Key informants commented on how digitisation has helped people come together and made them stronger. One Social Welfare official in charge of giving out digital currency remarked, "*Digitisation has not only made it easier for people to get money, but it has also given them more power by letting them control their resources. This makes them feel less independent and less like they belong*" (KII 2024). A development practitioner also said, "*Social inclusion and empowerment are two important benefits of digital cash transfers. This strategy fosters enduring resilience by empowering individuals with financial autonomy and eliminating obstacles*" (KII 2024).

Researchers have investigated the influence of digital financial services on social engagement and autonomy across different regions globally, and their conclusions are consistent with these findings. Aker et al. (2016) conducted a study demonstrating that digital currency payments enhance social engagement by providing individuals direct access to funds and reducing their dependence on middlemen. In this vein, a 2019 study by the World Bank demonstrates that digitalisation has a significant impact on equality, especially for women and low-income individuals who face greater difficulties accessing financial services. These links explain how altering the way people send and receive digital money might help them get along better and give them more power.

The finding on social inclusion and empowerment shows how important digital currency transfers are for making a difference in the lives of SSN users in Bangladesh. Most of the positive remarks from beneficiaries indicate that the system provides individuals with direct and rapid access to money. This helps them get more active in their communities and make sensible choices about their lives. However, the few concerns that some users brought up illustrate that we still have work to do to get rid of things that come in the way of freedom, including not knowing how to utilise technology or having access to cell phones. Bangladesh could enhance the system and address these gaps to enable SSN users to be more actively involved in their communities and offer them greater autonomy. This would also make their lives better and help them be stronger in the long run.

### 5.5 *Contribution of the Digital Cash Transfer System in Bringing Change in Economic Stability*

Switching to digital cash transfers has been a huge step towards making the SSN program better all over the world. These systems leverage technology to work better, waste less, and make sure that money goes to the correct people on time. This section examines the impact of digital cash transfers on the financial well-being of SSN receivers, utilising first-hand data collected from beneficiaries. Most individuals who received digital currency transfers reported that their financial situations became more stable after the shift, as shown in Table 16. Twenty-four per cent of the 100 persons who replied said that their financial security had changed a lot, while 72% said it had become better. Less than 3% of the people who got the message indicated their financial security had changed substantially, and none said it had changed a lot.

The findings align with other research findings on the benefits of using digital technologies for international money transfers. For instance, World Bank (2024) research found that digital payment systems in Sub-Saharan Africa lowered transaction costs by 80% and sped up the distribution of cash. This made it easier for low-income people to receive financial services and keep their money steady. Research by the World Bank (2020b) on digitising government-to-person (G2P) payments in India, on the

**Table 16** Changes in economic stability among SSN beneficiaries

| *Options* | *Number of beneficiaries* | *Percentage (%)* |
|---|---|---|
| Significant decrease | 00 | 00 |
| Decrease | 00 | 00 |
| No change | 03 | 3 |
| Increase | 72 | 72 |
| Significant increase | 24 | 24 |
| **Total** | **100** | **100** |

Source: Field Data (2024)

other hand, revealed that people who got the payments had greater access to financial services and saved 30% more. These findings support the poll findings by demonstrating the significant impact of digital cash payments on maintaining economic stability.

The receivers' mostly positive views of the digital cash transfer systems demonstrate how effectively they address economic problems. Digital technologies make sure that money gets to the right people quickly by cutting out middlemen and reducing delays. This lets people meet their basic needs and invest in businesses that make money. One SSN beneficiary said, "*Now that the money goes straight to my phone bank, I do not have to drive far or wait in line. Because this saved me time and money, I can now help my family*" (Interview Data 2024). Another recipient stated, "*It used to be hard for me to save money, but now it is easy for me to set aside some of my cash transfer for small businesses or situations*" (Interview Data 2024). Digital payments, mobile banking, and other financial services have also made it easier for people to save, trade, and manage their money. Another respondent said, "*After getting paid digitally, I opened a mobile bank account. I can now get loans to help my little shop grow*" (Interview Data 2024). The fact that there were no negative responses to the poll reinforces the point that these systems are reliable and accessible to everyone. Ultimately, the digital cash transfer method has been crucial in stabilising the finances of SSN users. The findings of the survey demonstrate that digitising cash transfer programs makes them more helpful and helps people get their finances in order.

In Bangladesh's attempts to enhance the lives of SSN beneficiaries, going digital with cash transfers is a game-changer. The fact that 96% of respondents said they had better jobs and that the majority of the remarks from recipients were favourable shows how well digital methods operate for offering regular and timely cash support. These findings are even more supported by what UP authorities and key informants have said about how important digitisation is for lowering risks and increasing long-term resilience. India's Direct Benefit Transfer (DBT) and Kenya's M-Pesa are two projects that have shown time and time again how important it is to combine digital technologies with specific actions and teach people new skills.

## 6 Overall Effectiveness of Digitised Cash Transfer Systems: The Perspective of UP Functionaries

The overall success of digitalised currency transfer mechanisms is a major measure of how effectively they satisfy the aims of SSN activities. This section looks at how UP authorities thought digital currency transfers worked in general, with an emphasis on how they might make things faster, clearer, and better for the people who would benefit from them. From a managerial point of view, examining their replies helps us identify the advantages and disadvantages of becoming digital. The study result (Table 17) shows that all UP officials (100%) thought that digital methods of sending money were useful. Seventy per cent of people said the method was "Effective," and 30% said it was "Very Effective." Not a single person who answered said the method was "Very Ineffective," "Ineffective," or "Neutral." It is clear from this positive reaction that digitisation has made cash transfer systems more effective, clear, and useful in general. The high level of trust among UP officials comes from their own experience with the administrative benefits of digitisation, such as faster working times, less paperwork, and more responsibility.

Service recipients also offered an insightful analysis of the efficiency of digital cash transfer systems. One recipient, for instance, said, "*Before the electronic system, we had to wait hours in long lines and often had to wait to get our funds. The process is much faster, and it is easy to get our money back*" (Interview Data 2024). Another beneficiary said, "*We are getting our funds on time more often now that everything is done digitally. This has*

**Table 17** Level of overall effectiveness of digitised cash transfer systems

| *UP functionaries* | |
|---|---|
| *Options* | *Total*<br>*20 (100%)* |
| Very ineffective | 00 (00%) |
| Ineffective | 00 (00%) |
| Neutral | 00 (00%) |
| Effective | 14 (70%) |
| Very effective | 06 (30%) |

Source: Field Data (2024)

*helped us better plan our spending*" (Interview Data 2024). These answers stress the real benefits of digitisation for receivers, mainly reliability and ease. Key sources gave us useful information. For instance, one UNO said, "*The digital method has changed how we keep track of money exchanges. In addition to making things easier for administrators, it has also made things more accountable and clearer so that money goes to the right people*" (Interview Data 2024). This understanding shows how deeply digitisation is changing the way government works. On the other hand, one development practitioner said, "*It has mostly worked, but there are still some things that need to be fixed. For example, making sure that all beneficiaries, even those in remote places, can easily receive digital services is something that needs work*" (KII 2024). This insight underscores the need for ongoing improvement in system usability and inclusivity, which aligns with the views of UP officials.

Studies done in other places have come to the same conclusions as this one. India's Direct Benefit Transfer (DBT) system is one example. It has made cash transfers clearer and more efficient, leading to faster and more reliable payments (Muralidharan et al. 2016). People in Kenya may now obtain money more easily through M-Pesa's cash transfer service. This has also made it easier for firms to transact business (Jack and Suri 2011). The examples below show how global digital technology may make money transfer schemes work better. The fact that UP authorities are so happy is in keeping with what other research across the world has revealed concerning the benefits of making cash payments digital. According to research (GSMA 2020), digital solutions might make currency transfer processes significantly more efficient, transparent, and useful overall. That is because they reduce leaks and delays, which makes everyone more accountable. Still, the little problems that key informants brought up are similar to what has been seen in other places, where technological problems and access constraints often make the advantages of digitisation less clear (UNDP 2023). These challenges highlight how crucial it is to have robust infrastructure and stringent standards to make sure that digital systems are dependable and easy to use. The study's findings on the general utility of digitalised cash transfer systems, supported by predominantly favourable input from UP authorities, suggest that these technologies effectively enhance efficiency, transparency, and beneficiary outcomes. However, the important sources and service providers that have informed us show that we need to continue improving to address any remaining difficulties and ensure that everyone can benefit from digitisation.

## 7 Conclusion

When examining the effectiveness of Bangladesh's SSN digital cash transfer systems, we can identify both areas that require improvement and notable successes. From many points of view, including speed, ease of use, lower transaction costs, and overall impact on people's ability to make a living, digitising cash payments has been a game-changer. People who get an SSN and people who work for UP are both very happy with the system because it cuts down on delays, gets rid of middleman fees, and makes routine tasks easier. These findings demonstrate that digital technologies can be utilised globally to enhance the accessibility, efficiency, and transparency of social safety net programs. Still, the information from KIIs and the open-ended answers from service users make it clear that much work needs to be done. The method has mostly worked, but there are still problems like broken technology, limited access in rural areas, and the need to keep building up people's skills. These problems align with what global studies have consistently shown: a lack of infrastructure and digital knowledge has hindered digitisation from reaching its full potential.

Finally, making cash payments digital has made it much simpler for social safety net programs to run in Bangladesh. This is excellent for both the individuals who get services and the people who give them. The system holds considerable promise as a vehicle for long-term prosperity, as it can enhance financial independence, economic stability, and access to essential services. However, there are still issues that need to be addressed to ensure the system remains open, functional, and able to meet the demands of everyone involved. Bangladesh can continue to lead the way in harnessing digital innovation to enhance social safety nets by building on its existing efforts, adopting best practices from around the world, and supporting targeted initiatives. The beneficiaries' thoughts and the information gained from this study are significant reminders of how digital systems may change things and how they need to keep getting better so that no one is left behind.

## References

Ahluwalia, H. S., and Bhatti, K. K. (2017). Financial inclusion: Unshackle the impediments to growth. *International Journal of Innovative Research and Development, 6*(1), 82–87.

Ahmad, A. H., Green, C., and Jiang, F. (2020). Mobile money, financial inclusion and development: A review with reference to African experience. *Journal of Economic Surveys, 34*(4), 753–792.

Aker, J. C., Boumnijel, R., McClelland, A., and Tierney, N. (2016). Payment mechanisms and anti-poverty programs: Evidence from a mobile money cash transfer experiment in Niger. *Economic Development and Cultural Change, 65*(1), 1–37.

Global System for Mobile Communications (GSMA). (2020). *The mobile economy 2020.* London: GSMA.

Government of Bangladesh. (2022). *Action plan for implementation of National Social Security Strategy (NSSS) of Bangladesh.* Cabinet Division.

Jack, W., and Suri, T. (2011). Mobile money: The economics of M-PESA (Working Paper No. 16721). *National Bureau of Economic Research.* https://doi.org/10.3386/w16721

Levy, S. (2006). *Progress against poverty: Sustaining Mexico's Progresa-Oportunidades Program.* Brookings Institution Press.

Lindert, K., Linder, A., Hobbs, J. A., and Brière, B. D. L. (2007). *The nuts and bolts of Brazil's Bolsa Família program: Implementing conditional cash transfers in a decentralized context* (Social Protection Discussion Paper No. 0709). World Bank.

Mathew, V. (2021). Prospects, challenges, and opportunities of digital financial services in developing countries. In T. Esakki (Ed.), *Managerial issues in digital transformation of global modern corporations* (pp. 69–88). IGI Global. https://doi.org/10.4018/978-1-7998-2402-2.ch006

Muralidharan, K., Niehaus, P., and Sukhtankar, S. (2016). Building state capacity: Evidence from biometric smartcards in India. *American Economic Review, 106*(10), 2895–2929.

Nayab, D. E., and Farooq, S. (2014). Effectiveness of cash transfer programmes for household welfare in Pakistan: The case of the Benazir Income Support Programme. *The Pakistan Development Review, 53*(2), 45–174.

Sarwar, M. B., Diepeveen, S., and Moreno, D. B. (2023). Cash transfers and digital financial inclusion: Regional evidence from Asia Pacific with a focus on Bangladesh, Cambodia, and Nepal. *ODI Report.* Overseas Development Institute (ODI).

United Nations Development Programme (UNDP). (2023). *From vision to action: Explaining UNDP's digital transformation framework.* Concept Note. UNDP.

World Bank. (2019). *Social safety nets in Bangladesh help reduce poverty and improve human capital.* World Bank Group.

World Bank. (2020a). *Digital Financial Services.* Washington, DC: World Bank.

World Bank. (2020b). *Improving the transparency and efficiency of safety nets for the most vulnerable in Bangladesh.* World Bank Group.

World Bank. (2020c). *Electronic payments acceptance incentives: Literature review and country examples.* World Bank Group.

World Bank. (2024). *Bangladesh—Cash Transfer Modernization Project: Improving transparency and efficiency of safety nets.* World Bank Group.

# Enablers and Challenges: Key Determinants Shaping Digital Cash Transfers in Bangladesh's Social Safety Net Programs

**Abstract** This chapter looks at how Bangladesh's Social Safety Net (SSN) programs use digital cash transfers and how technology infrastructure, digital skills, government processes, and socioeconomic variables affect their success. Digital access is based on technical infrastructure, which includes having a cell phone, being able to get online, and making sure the platform is strong. However, there are problems, including poor connections and technical issues. People need to be digitally literate in order to have the abilities they need to use digital platforms. On the other hand, women and elderly persons are usually not as good at using computers as younger people are. This highlights how crucial it is to deliver personalised training and make sure digital tools are simple to use. People in rural locations do not trust the government as much as they should, but they do trust it because it is transparent, accountable, and supports good policies. A person's socioeconomic situation, gender roles, and where they reside have a big impact on their access. People who reside in distant areas, women, and families with low incomes have it the worst. We need to enhance infrastructure, train more people how to use technology, empower governance, and eliminate social inequality so that everyone can utilise digital cash transfers fairly, quickly, and easily. Ultimately, this will enable all individuals who receive money to do so safely and independently.



P. K. Panday, A. H. M. K. Ahsan, *Digital Revolution for the Vulnerable*, https://doi.org/10.1007/978-981-95-7980-8_5

**Keywords** Digital cash transfers • Social Safety Net programs • Bangladesh • Digital literacy • Technology infrastructure • Governance

## 1 Introduction

Digitising financial transfers in Bangladesh's Social Safety Net (SSN) programs is a significant step forward for everyone who wants to make social safety nets more visible, efficient, and transparent. These digital systems may not work exactly as planned, but several factors can affect their performance. This chapter discusses the most important aspects of sending money online. These are things like technical infrastructure, digital skills, governing systems, and social and economic issues. The chapter gives a detailed picture of the things that help individuals achieve and the things that inhibit them from progressing by looking at these problems. Digital cash transfer systems need a strong technological base, a mobile device, and an internet connection to work well. Even the most complicated systems need a strong basis to perform successfully. Digital literacy, which includes fundamental digital skills, programs to promote awareness, and tests of how easy it is to use digital services, is crucial to make sure that everyone can utilise these services. Governance tools, such as frameworks for accountability, transparency, and policy support, are particularly essential since they have a significant impact on how well the system operates and how fair it is. Ultimately, factors such as wealth, gender roles, and geography highlight the necessary steps to ensure everyone is treated equally and has access. This chapter looks at how these factors affect how well digital money works in this situation.

## 2 Technological Infrastructure: The Foundation of Digital Cash Transfers

Digital cash transfer systems operate because of the technology that underpins them. It makes it easy to transmit money to other individuals. Digital cash transfers in Bangladesh's SSN programs can only work if people can readily access and trust essential technological tools, such as a reliable platform, a mobile phone, and internet access. Even the best-designed programs can fail if the infrastructure is not solid. This stops individuals from obtaining their money and hurts the program's overall aims. This section speaks about how the structure of technology influences how successfully digital cash transactions function. It looks at how many people can use digital services, especially in rural and distant places where individuals can connect to the internet and use cell phones. It also examines how stable and reliable digital platforms are, paying special attention to problems caused by technology, system failures, and hackers. This section examines Bangladesh's technology infrastructure to find out what works well and what does not. It will also come up with suggestions for making the digital ecosystem stronger and more transparent for everyone. This section highlights the importance of investing in technological infrastructure to ensure that digital cash transfer systems operate efficiently and remain stable over time.

## 2.1 Mobile Phone Ownership: A Gateway to Digital Inclusion

One of the most significant factors influencing access to digital cash transfer systems is whether someone owns a mobile phone, which is the primary means by which people interact with digital platforms. How well digital cash transfers work depends a lot on how many people own them and what kinds of devices are available in Bangladesh, where cell phones are quickly becoming essential for both contact and business. This section talks about what Union Parishad (UP) officials said about how common it is for SSN users to own mobile phones, what kinds of phones they own, and how easy it is for them to get mobile phones. By looking at these issues, the section tries to figure out how much having a cell phone either helps or hurts digital inclusion and access to money transfers.

The data (Table 1) reveals significant gaps in the number of cell phones owned by individuals who obtain an SSN, which supports the usability problems that UP officials have identified. Table 1 shows that just 33% of SSN recipients have mobile phones, while 67% do not. Beneficiaries without mobile phones cannot directly utilise digital cash transfer systems, so this low ownership percentage shows a significant obstacle to digital inclusion. Of those who own mobile phones, 100% utilise feature phones, and thus, none use smartphones. Although inexpensive and popular, feature phones lack smartphone capabilities, limiting users' ability to fully utilise digital services such as internet platforms or mobile banking applications.

The viewpoints of UP officials help to frame these findings further. Table 1 reveals that 55% of UP officials consider mobile devices "Accessible" for beneficiaries in their areas of accountability; 35% consider them "Very Accessible." On the other hand, a small percentage (10%) said they have

**Table 1** Mobile phone ownership

| *Indicator* | *SSN beneficiaries* | *UP functionaries* |
|---|---|---|
| Mobile phone ownership | 33% own mobile phones | – |
| Type of mobile phone | 100% feature phones | – |
| Accessibility of mobile devices | – | 55% accessible, 35% very accessible, 5% inaccessible, 5% neutral |

Source: Field Data (2024)

problems, while 5% called mobile devices "inaccessible" and 5% stayed indifferent. One UP chairman said, "*Many beneficiaries still depend on shared devices or cannot afford their own, even if mobile phones are growing more prevalent*" (Interview Data 2024). This reduces their capacity to use digital payments on their own.

These findings align with global research findings on the impact of mobile phone ownership on digital financial inclusion. For example, research in Sub-Saharan Africa has revealed that low mobile phone ownership, especially among women and in rural areas, is a significant obstacle to using digital financial services (GSMA 2020). Similarly, in India, the lack of smartphone ownership has been identified as a significant barrier to the implementation of digital welfare initiatives (Muralidharan et al. 2016). These similarities highlight the need to close mobile phone ownership disparities to guarantee the inclusiveness of digital cash transfer mechanisms. The mobile phone ownership findings show notable obstacles to digital inclusion among SSN recipients in Bangladesh. Only 33% of recipients have mobile phones—all of which are feature phones—so they are still cut off from direct access to digital payment transfer systems. Although UP officials stated that mobile devices are quite accessible, the use of shared or borrowed phones, as well as the absence of smartphones, restricts the ability and independence of users of digital services.

## 2.2 *Internet Connectivity: The Lifeline of Digital Cash Transfers*

Effective digital cash transfer systems rely on consistent internet connectivity, enabling real-time access to financial services and facilitating smooth transactions. The effectiveness of digital platforms delivering SSN payments in Bangladesh, where they are being utilised increasingly, is greatly influenced by the quality and dependability of internet access. Reported by both SSN recipients and UP officials, this section investigates the consistency of internet access in the research locations. An attempt is made to evaluate the degree to which internet connection either facilitates or impedes the execution of digitised cash transfers by analysing these viewpoints.

Though their answers show significant differences, the research finding shows that most SSN recipients and UP officials view internet connection as dependable. Table 2 shows that while 8% of SSN recipients assess it as "Very Reliable," 88% characterise the internet connection as "Reliable." Four per cent of recipients stayed indifferent, and none said "Very Unreliable" or "Unreliable." This significant degree of dependability shows the increasing prevalence of internet services in many areas of Bangladesh, especially in metropolitan and semi-urban areas. On the other hand, UP officials offer a somewhat more nuanced perspective. A tiny percentage (10%) said they have problems, 5% called it "Unreliable," and 5% stayed indifferent. While commenting on this, a UP member said, "*Internet connectivity is usually good, but there are still areas where the network is weak or unstable, especially during bad weather, which can annoy recipients and cause payment delays*" (Interview Data 2024).

Key informants provided more in-depth analysis on the challenges of ensuring a consistent internet connection. A social welfare official working on digital cash transfers said, "*Although we have made great strides in increasing internet access, the connection quality in rural and isolated locations is still uneven. This significantly hinders our ability to guarantee that all recipients may obtain digital payments without delays*" (KII 2024). A development worker underlined in the same way, "*Digital financial transfers depend on internet access, which is its backbone. Even the most*

**Table 2** Level of reliability of internet connectivity

| *Indicator* | *SSN beneficiaries (%)* | *UP functionaries (%)* |
|---|---|---|
| Very unreliable | 0 | 0 |
| Unreliable | 0 | 5 |
| Neutral | 4 | 5 |
| Reliable | 88 | 70 |
| Very reliable | 8 | 20 |

Source: Field Data (2024)

*well-designed systems might fail to provide their intended advantages without consistent access*" (KII 2024).

These findings support studies from around the world that suggest digital cash transfer systems should be connected to the internet at all times. In Sub-Saharan Africa, a bad internet link, especially in rural areas, is a big reason why people cannot use mobile money services (GSMA 2020). In India, too, an unstable internet link has been named as a major problem with digital aid programs, leading to delays and wasted time (Mathew 2021). These connections show how important a strong internet infrastructure is for making sure that digital money transfer methods work. The fact that the internet service was found to be reliable shows how important it is for digital money transfers in Bangladesh. Most people who obtained an SSN and UP officials stated that they had a steady internet connection. However, problems in rural and remote areas make it clear that more needs to be done to improve access to healthcare. To make digital money transfer systems more reliable, we need to first improve the internet infrastructure, especially in places that do not have a lot of it, and then make sure that the networks stay stable even when bad things happen. Bangladesh can make sure that everyone has equal access to digital financial services by fixing these gaps. This way, people can use these services from anywhere.

### 2.3 Platform Stability: Ensuring Seamless Access to Digital Payments

To make sure that consumers can always use financial transfer systems, there needs to be stable digital platforms and internet connections. In Bangladesh, where more and more people are using digital monies to pay for SSN services, the stability of these platforms has a direct effect on how people see the system and how much they trust it. This section looks at how stable digital platforms and internet connectivity are based on what SSN beneficiaries and UP authorities said. We try to figure out how stable a platform affects the ease and reliability of digital cash transfers by looking from different points of view.

Though their views differ significantly, the research shows that SSN recipients and UP officials view digital platforms and internet access as stable. Table 3 shows that 36% of SSN recipients regarded internet connection as "Very Stable," while 58% called it "Stable." Of them, 1% said it is "Unstable," 5% remained indifferent, and 6% reported problems. This significant degree of consistency shows the increasing dependability of digital platforms and internet services in various areas of Bangladesh. On the other hand, UP officials provide a far more conservative view. A tiny percentage (15%) said they have problems; 5% called platforms "Very Unstable," 5% called them "Unstable," and 5% stayed neutral. While 60% identified digital platforms as "Stable" and 25% called them "Very Stable." A UP official from a remote location observed, "*Generally speaking, the platforms are stable; yet, especially during high usage times, there are sporadic problems. This might annoy recipients and cause payment delays*" (Interview Data 2024).

Compared to UP officials, SSN recipients said they are more satisfied with platform stability. Though just 85% of UP officials agreed, 94% of recipients called the connection "Stable" or "Very Stable." While UP officials are more conscious of systematic problems, this disparity might result from recipients' lack of exposure to backend technological concerns. Compared to just 1% of beneficiaries, UP officials are more inclined to express instability, with 10% characterising systems as "Unstable" or "Very Unstable." This implies that although beneficiaries have seamless access, administrators are more sensitive to the technological and operational issues that might compromise the system. Key informants offered more information on these differences. One UNO said, "*Beneficiaries usually encounter the system's front-end, which is meant to be user-friendly. On the other hand, administrators handle the backend, where technical problems and connection concerns are more obvious*" (KII 2024). On the other hand, a development worker underlined, "*Platform stability is crucial for guaranteeing that beneficiaries can access their payments without delays. Even small changes can be important, especially for communities that are weak and rely on these supports to meet their basic needs*" (KII 2024).

**Table 3** Level of stability of internet connectivity for accessing payment platform

| *Indicator* | *SSN beneficiaries (%)* | *UP functionaries (%)* |
|---|---|---|
| Very unstable | 0 | 5 |
| Unstable | 1 | 5 |
| Neutral | 5 | 5 |
| Stable | 58 | 60 |
| Very stable | 36 | 25 |

Source: Field Data (2024)

The findings of this study are consistent with those of other studies conducted in various countries. In Sub-Saharan Africa, for example, unstable digital systems have been named as a big reason why people cannot use mobile money services, especially in rural areas (GSMA 2020). India has also noted that difficulties with technology in digital assistance systems pose significant challenges, slowing down processes and reducing efficiency (Muralidharan et al. 2016). These linkages demonstrate the importance of having a robust digital infrastructure to ensure that cash transfer techniques are effective.

### 2.4 *Transaction Stability: Ensuring Smooth Digital Payments*

Digital payment sites need to be stable throughout transactions for cash transfer systems to be dependable and trustworthy. A permanent place for people who receive benefits from Bangladesh's SSN programs makes it easy and quick to make payments, which are often necessary to meet necessities. This section analyses how stable digital payment methods are during agreements based on what SSN receivers say. It works out how transaction stability affects the efficiency of digital money transfers by looking at things from multiple angles. The findings show that most people who received an SSN thought the digital payment system was stable while they were using it. As Table 4 reveals, 71% of those who benefited thought the platform was "Stable," and 28% thought it was "Very Stable." Only 1% of those who answered were not sure, and none of them said "Very Unstable" or "Unstable." This remarkable degree of stability shows the strength of the digital payment system in enabling seamless transactions for beneficiaries. While commenting on this, one SSN recipient said, "*I have never had any problems getting my money. The system runs well every month, and I receive my money on schedule*" (Interview Data 2024).

**Table 4** Level of stability of digital payment platform during transactions

| *Indicator* | *SSN beneficiaries (n = 100) (%)* |
|---|---|
| Very unstable | 0 |
| Unstable | 0 |
| Neutral | 1 |
| Stable | 71 |
| Very stable | 28 |

Source: Field Data (2024)

Another recipient said, "*The connection is quite dependable. I need not stress transaction glitches or delays*" (Interview Data 2024).

Key informants, however, provided additional background information to support these findings. A Social Welfare Officer associated with the disbursement of digital cash transfers said, "*Although the platform is usually stable, especially during high transaction volumes, there are occasional technical issues. Though uncommon, these problems might interfere with payments for some recipients*" (KII 2024). A development worker also underlined, "*Stable transactions are important for building trust in the system. Even small problems can make people less likely to trust each other, especially in poor communities that count on these funds to stay alive*" (KII 2024). Another study on the digital cash transfer system in Bangladesh has found the same things. Rashid's (2020) research suggests that while digital cash transfer systems have significantly improved transaction efficiency, they continue to experience sporadic technical difficulties, particularly in remote regions with unreliable internet connectivity. Research by the World Bank (2024) shows that platform stability is even more important for making sure that digital payment transfer systems work well. It indicates that even little difficulties can have a major impact on how happy and confident the people who face them are.

The discourse on transaction security highlights the importance of ensuring that digital cash payments in Bangladesh are always safe and easy. The digital payment system is very robust because 99% of those who got an SSN called it "Stable" or "Very Stable." However, the fact that important sources are worried about random technological problems shows how important it is to keep an eye on the platform and make it work better, especially when there are many transactions. Bangladesh can make its digital cash transfer systems more reliable and trustworthy by fixing these little difficulties. This would make sure that everyone who gets money can get it without any complications.

When attention is paid to factors such as who has mobile phones, the speed of the internet, and the stability of the platform, it has become evident how much these aspects affect the effectiveness of digital cash transfer services in Bangladesh. Access to cell phones and the internet has gotten a lot better, but there are still some problems, especially in rural and isolated places. Most people who acquired an SSN reported they had solid digital platforms and a dependable internet connection. This demonstrates that attempts to digitise payment systems are successful. However, difficulties such as poor connectivity in disadvantaged regions, unpredictable tech glitches, and a lack of smartphone ownership indicate that coordinated efforts are necessary. UP leaders and key sources, on the other hand, have given considerable thought to the real-world problems that arise from maintaining a robust IT infrastructure. They stressed the need to take care of behind-the-scenes problems to make sure that service delivery goes smoothly. Bangladesh can close the digital divide and make sure that everyone, regardless of wealth, has equal access to digital financial services by making it easier for people to connect to the internet, lowering the cost of smartphones, and making platforms more reliable. These changes are necessary to build trust in the system, make beneficiaries happier, and ensure the sustainability of SSN programs.

## 3 Digital Literacy: Empowering Beneficiaries for Inclusive Access

Digital literacy, or the ability to use digital networks safely and on your own, is an important part of digital cash transfer systems that work well. The operating success of digital technologies has a significant impact on how well they work to send SSN payments to people in Bangladesh. This section discusses three important topics: basic digital skills, methods for improving understanding, and evaluations of usefulness. It also examines how learning about technology can enable people to send and receive digital cash. This section examines how digital literacy impacts individuals, highlighting areas that require improvement to ensure everyone has equal access to digital banking services.

### *3.1 Basic Digital Skills: The Foundation of Digital Inclusion*

Users need to have some basic technical abilities in order to utilise digital payment systems and start cash transfers on their own. The level of basic digital skills of people who receive SSN payments through digital systems in Bangladesh has a big impact on how well those systems work. This is because more and more people are using these platforms to receive SSN payments. Based on what recipients and UP staff said, this section talks about the basic computer skills that SSN recipients should have. The section evaluates the degree to which basic digital skills either facilitate or impede access to digital financial transfers, employing analysis of various viewpoints and highlighting areas for development.

The research demonstrates that SSN beneficiaries possess significantly different basic digital skills. Most of them indicated that they are unfamiliar with digital cash transfer methods. Table 5 reveals that 52% of those who got an SSN thought their basic digital abilities were "Very Poor," and 8% said they were "Poor." Of the 37% who said they have "Good" or "Very Good" skills, 17% said their skills are "Good" and 20% said their skills are "Very Good." Three per cent stayed neutral. Beneficiaries with inadequate digital skills could find it challenging to negotiate digital platforms independently. Hence, this low degree of digital literacy is a significant obstacle to digital inclusion. UP officials offered a comparable but rather more critical viewpoint. Table 5 shows that 35% of recipients ranked their basic literacy skills as "Very Poor," and 25% rated them as "Poor." Of the 40%, 20% said their skills are "Good" and 20% said they are "Very Good." A UP secretary from a remote region stated, *"Many beneficiaries, especially elderly persons and women, struggle with simple chores like logging in to the platform or entering their PIN. Often, they require help, which might postpone payments*" (Interview Data 2024).

Key informants offered more analysis on these issues. A social welfare officer engaged in the execution of digital cash transfers said, "*Although we have advanced in digitising payments, the absence of fundamental digital skills among recipients continues to be a significant obstacle. Many depend on local agents or family members to conduct transactions, compromising the system's efficiency*" (Interview Data 2024). A development worker underlined similarly: "*Digital literacy is the basis of financial inclusion. No matter how well-designed the system is, people lacking fundamental abilities cannot wholly benefit from digital cash transfers*" (Interview Data 2024).

These findings are consistent with research on digital literacy in Bangladesh and other nations. For instance, IFC (2017) research shows that in rural Bangladesh, especially among women and older people, low technical skills constitute a significant obstacle to using digital financial

**Table 5** Level of basic skills in using digital payment systems

| *Indicator* | *SSN beneficiaries (%)* | *UP functionaries (%)* |
|---|---|---|
| Very poor | 52 | 35 |
| Poor | 8 | 25 |
| Neutral | 3 | 0 |
| Good | 17 | 20 |
| Very good | 20 | 20 |

Source: Field Data (2024)

services. Also, research in India has shown that digital aid programs do not work as well when individuals do not know how to use technology, which leads to delays and waste (Muralidharan et al. 2016). These links show how important it is to close the digital knowledge gap so that everyone can use digital tools for financial tasks.

The findings on crucial digital skills illustrate how necessary they are to make sure that everyone in Bangladesh can take part in the social safety net activities. Many folks with SSNs and UP representatives say they do not know how to use digital payment methods. Still, the fact that a smaller proportion of people felt the same way shows that things may get better. To address these issues, we need to implement measures such as creating training programs for digital literacy, simplifying user interfaces, and establishing community-based support networks to help people effectively utilise digital platforms. Bangladesh could teach everyone, regardless of age or gender, basic computer skills so that they can manage their own payments. This would help people get the most out of technology.

### 3.2 *Awareness Campaigns: Bridging the Digital Literacy Gap*

People who get digital cash transfers need to know how to utilise them responsibly; thus, they require training and awareness initiatives. In Bangladesh, where digital platforms are more commonly used for SSN payments, the availability and efficacy of these programs are crucial in ensuring that recipients can easily and confidently receive their payments. This section discusses the participation of SSN recipients in awareness campaigns and training, as well as the efforts of UP members to undertake additional activities. The numbers demonstrate that there is a considerable disparity between persons who receive an SSN and people who take part in training and learning programs. Table 6 shows that only 33% of the people who got the money stated they had taken part in training or awareness efforts on how to use digital cash transfer systems. The other 67% said they had not. People who do not have enough training could find it hard to use internet platforms on their own. So, this low proportion of participation shows that there is a big problem with digital inclusion.

On the other hand, UP officials said they are far more involved in running awareness programs. Table 6 indicates that 90% of UP officials have run awareness programs to enhance recipients' knowledge of digital cash transfers, while just 10% said they have not. A UP chairman from a remote

**Table 6** Receipt of training on using the digital payment system

| *Indicator* | *SSN beneficiaries (%) (receipt of training)* | *UP functionaries (%) (organised training)* |
|---|---|---|
| Yes | 33 | 90 |
| No | 67 | 10 |

Source: Field Data (2024)

location said, "*We often organise awareness events to assist recipients in knowing how to operate the digital cash transfers system. Still, reaching everyone, particularly in rural regions, is difficult*" (Interview Data 2024).

Key informants offered more analysis of these differences. One UNO said, "*Although awareness campaigns are significant, resource limitations and logistical issues frequently limit their reach and impact. Many recipients, especially in rural regions, are still ignorant of the training options accessible to them*" (KII 2024). A local government expert underlined in the same way that "*Awareness campaigns are the first step towards teaching people how to use technology. However, in order for people to use what they learn, they need to be given real training and ongoing support*" (KII 2024).

These findings are in line with studies of programs in Bangladesh and other countries that teach people how to use technology. Aziz and Naima (2020) found that awareness activities had made individuals more aware of digital payment methods. However, their effects are typically restricted because not enough people become involved, and not enough follow-up help is available. According to research conducted in India, specialised training classes may help people learn more about technology and utilise digital banking services more effectively (Mathew 2021). These connections show that more needs to be done to teach people how to make digital cash transfer sites more accessible to everyone.

The education and training programs have demonstrated their importance in helping Bangladeshi SSN users improve their technology skills. Officials from UP state that they are involved in several awareness-raising projects. Still, the low participation rate shows that these projects need to be more detailed and transparent to everyone. To make sure that everyone has the skills and trust to use digital payment systems on their own, more training programs and hands-on help will be needed, especially in remote and rural places. By fixing these problems, Bangladesh can make its digital cash transfer services more useful and easier for everyone to use. This will make sure that the most vulnerable people benefit from being online.

### 3.3 *Effectiveness of Awareness Campaigns: Measuring Impact on Digital Literacy*

How well outreach programs work is a significant part of how well they can close the digital literacy gap and give people the confidence to use digital payment systems. These campaigns directly affect the outcome of digitisation initiatives in Bangladesh, as digital platforms are often employed to provide SSN payments. Based on the responses of SSN recipients and UP officials, this section looks at the perceived effectiveness of awareness programs in enhancing beneficiaries' knowledge of digital cash transfers. Although their views varied significantly, the research shows that most SSN recipients and UP officials find awareness programs to be successful. Table 7 shows that although 21% of SSN beneficiaries rated the awareness initiatives as "Effective," 79% identified them as "Very Effective." None of the recipients said the initiatives are "Very Ineffective," "Ineffective," or "Neutral." This clear response shows how well awareness initiatives have helped recipients grasp digital cash transfers.

However, UP officials offered a somewhat more nuanced viewpoint. Although a tiny percentage (22%) remained "neutral," 55% considered the efforts "Effective," and 23% considered them "Very Effective." None of the UP officials said the campaigns are "Very Ineffective" or "Ineffective." A UP member from a remote location said, "*The campaigns have been beneficial, but their influence changes depending on the audience. Older recipients and those with little education often require more individualised assistance to understand the ideas*" (Interview Data 2024).

**Table 7** Level of effectiveness of campaigns

| *Indicator* | *SSN beneficiaries (%) (n = 33 who responded positively)* | *UP functionaries (%) (n = 18 who responded positively)* |
|---|---|---|
| Very ineffective | 0 | 0 |
| Ineffective | 0 | 0 |
| Neutral | 0 | 22 |
| Effective | 21 | 55 |
| Very effective | 79 | 23 |

Source: Field Data (2024)

Key informants offered more analysis on how well awareness campaigns worked. A social welfare officer associated with the disbursement of digital cash transfers said, "*Beneficiaries have benefited greatly from awareness campaigns in terms of trust and understanding. However, adding more engaging and practical components, such as hands-on training courses, may improve their effectiveness*" (KII 2024). A development worker emphasised that "*Although the campaigns have raised awareness, their long-term effect relies on follow-up support and ongoing interaction with beneficiaries*" (KII 2024).

These findings are consistent with earlier research regarding the efficacy of digital literacy initiatives in comparable contexts. The research conducted by Zainudeen and Ratnadiwakara (2011) demonstrates that awareness initiatives are most effective when they incorporate practical examples and address the specific needs of the target audience. Chibesa and Mwange (2025) conducted research that demonstrates that persons aiming to improve their digital literacy necessitate coaching during their learning process. These links show how important it is to keep refining awareness initiatives so that they operate as well as they can. The findings of the awareness campaign indicate that it had a substantial impact on educating people in Bangladesh on how to use digital cash transfers. People who got SSNs said favourable things about the programs, which suggests that they worked to make people trust digital payment systems. On the other hand, UP authorities and important sources are more circumspect. This shows that the strategy and implementation of awareness efforts need to improve.

## *3.4 User-Friendliness of Digital Payment Systems: Enhancing Accessibility for Beneficiaries*

Beneficiaries will be able to easily access, believe, and move around digital cash transfer systems if they are user-friendly. The way digital tools for SSN payouts are made and used in Bangladesh has a big effect on how happy and confident beneficiaries are. This section talks about what SSN recipients said about how easy they thought digital payment methods were to use. By looking at things from different points of view and finding ways to make the system better for users, this section tries to figure out how the design helps or hurts accessibility. Among SSN recipients, the finding shows varied views on the user-friendliness of digital payment methods. Table 8 shows that 35% of beneficiaries found the system "Friendly," 31% found it "Very Friendly." Many recipients, meanwhile, said they have problems; 23% called the system "Unfriendly," and 4% called it "Very Unfriendly." Of the recipients, 8% also remained neutral. This varied response emphasises the necessity of changing the design and operation of digital payment systems to guarantee their accessibility to all users, including those with low digital literacy. One SSN recipient said, "*The system is easy to use once you get the hang of it, but it can be confusing at first, especially for someone unfamiliar with digital platforms*" (Interview Data 2024). Another rural area recipient said, "*I find it hard to manage the system alone. Often, I require assistance from a neighbour or my son to finish transactions*" (Interview Data 2024).

Key informants offered more analysis on these issues. One UNO said, "*Though some recipients, especially older adults and those with less knowledge, may find certain aspects difficult, the system is meant to be user-friendly. Reducing the interface and offering more logical direction can assist in solving these problems*" (KII 2024). A development worker underlined in the same way, "*User-friendliness is crucial to ensure that recipients can access their payments freely. Even small design changes can have a big effect on how well it works and how happy people are*" (Interview Data 2024).

These findings support a study that examines the usefulness of digital banking systems in various situations. For example, Donner and Tellez's (2008) study emphasises the importance of mobile banking services being easy to use, especially for individuals with low incomes and limited technical knowledge. A study by the Consultative Group to Assist the Poor (CGAP 2016) also shows that digital payment systems need to be easier for people to use, with clear instructions and simple displays. These connections demonstrate the importance of continually improving system design to ensure it is accessible to everyone and easy to use. Researchers found that making digital payment systems easy to use is very important for making them available to everyone. Most people who got an SSN said the system was "Friendly" or "Very Friendly," but many of those who said

**Table 8** User-friendliness of digital payment system

| *Indicator* | *SSN beneficiaries (n = 100) (%)* |
|---|---|
| Very unfriendly | 4 |
| Unfriendly | 23 |
| Neutral | 8 |
| Friendly | 35 |
| Very friendly | 31 |

Source: Field Data (2024)

they were having problems stressed the need for changes to the way it works and how it is designed. Lessening the interface, giving clear instructions, and letting users input can help make the system easier to use and make sure that even people who are not very good with computers can figure it out on their own.

### 3.5 *Beneficiary Feedback: Enhancing Usability Through User Input*

Beneficiaries can help make digital payment systems easier to use and more useful by giving their feedback. Finding out how often recipients give comments and what is done with that information can help find ways to make things better for users in Bangladesh, where digital platforms are being used more and more to send SSN payments. Based on the answers from UP representatives, this section examines how often recipients mention the ease of use of digital systems. This section examines the role of feedback in driving system changes from various perspectives and provides strategies to encourage users to become more involved.

Though there is an opportunity for improvement in promoting more consistent input, the data shows that comments from UP officials on the usability of digital platforms are given at different frequencies. Table 9 indicates that although 25% said input is given "Occasionally," 40% of UP representatives said beneficiaries give comments "Often." Many UP officials, however, pointed out that input is lacking, while 25% said beneficiaries "Never" give comments, and 10% said it is given "Rarely." None of the respondents said that feedback is given "Very Often." A UP chairman from a rural region said, "*Beneficiaries sometimes tell us about their experiences and challenges, but this input is often informal and infrequent. We require better-organised systems to gather and respond to their comments*" (Interview Data 2024). A female member of the UP said, "*Beneficiaries'*

**Table 9** Frequency of providing feedback by beneficiaries on the utility of the digital platform

| *Indicator* | *UP functionaries (%)* |
|---|---|
| Never | 25 |
| Rarely | 10 |
| Occasionally | 25 |
| Often | 40 |
| Very often | 0 |

Source: Field Data (2024)

*feedback is quite useful when they give it. Their recommendations, for instance, have guided us in streamlining some procedures and enhancing the system's usability*" (Interview Data 2024).

Key informants provided a deeper understanding of the need for beneficiary input. A social welfare officer executing digital cash transfers said, "*Identifying weakness and enhancing the system depends on beneficiary feedback. Many recipients, nevertheless, lack knowledge on how to offer official comments or may not feel empowered to do so*" (KII 2024). A development worker underlined in the same way that "*Establishing avenues for consistent and organised input may assist in guaranteeing the system changes to fit the demands of its users. This is especially crucial for vulnerable people with specific challenges accessing digital platforms*" (KII 2024). These findings match up with studies that looked at how people enter information into digital cash transfer methods. For example, Batista and Vicente (2023) study stresses how important it is to get regular feedback from users in order to make digital services easier to use and to encourage more people to use them, especially in low-income areas. The study by Goel and Agrasen (2024) shows how important it is to create feedback systems that everyone can use so that everyone's voice is heard and acted upon, especially the voices of underrepresented groups. These connections indicate that Bangladesh's digital cash transfer tools need to improve their ability to gather and utilise feedback from beneficiaries. The input from users highlights the importance of making digital payment systems in Bangladesh easier to use and more user-friendly. Many UP officials claimed that people send comments "often" or "sometimes." The fact that input is not supplied in other circumstances indicates how crucial it is to have tools that are better arranged and easier to discover to get people to participate often. Establishing formal channels for feedback, enhancing awareness of the significance of user input, and ensuring the utilisation of feedback may all contribute to the enhancement of the system's design and usability.

Digital literacy, which includes fundamental digital abilities, attempts to enhance awareness, simplicity of use, and feedback from recipients, is vital for ensuring that digital cash transfer systems in Bangladesh operate. Beneficiaries have learnt how to utilise digital platforms, but there are still challenges. This is especially true for the elderly, women, and people living in rural regions. Not many people know how to use computers effectively, and there are diverse opinions about what user-friendliness should entail. This highlights the importance of collaboration in enhancing digital literacy and ensuring that everyone can receive their payments safely and conveniently. People who receive digital financial transfers now understand them better due to initiatives aimed at promoting awareness. However, more interactive and hands-on training programs might help them reach and touch even more people. Also, the fact that beneficiaries do not give feedback very often shows that systems need to be better managed to collect and act on user input, making sure that the system changes to meet the needs of the users. In the end, digital literacy is not just about teaching people how to use digital tools; it is also about building their trust in the system.

## 4 Governance Mechanisms: Ensuring Transparency and Accountability in Digital Cash Transfers

Transparency, accountability, and trust in the distribution of SSN payments are built on top of effective digital cash transfer systems and government processes. In Bangladesh, where digital tools are being used more and more to run SSN operations, the legitimacy and effectiveness of the system are closely linked to how strong the government structures are. This section discusses three important things: pushing for policy, being transparent, and having ways to be held accountable. It also discusses how government systems facilitate the transfer of digital money. This part looks at these parts to see how governance systems improve the usefulness of digital money transfers and find places that need more work to make sure that everyone gets fair and on-time service. The first section discusses how clear digital money transfer methods are. It emphasises how easy it is for the receiver to get information and how clear the process is for them. After that, it looks at the financial processes that were put in place to keep an eye on and fix problems like fraud, delays, and technology problems. It examines how government assistance can create optimal conditions for digital cash transfers to operate effectively.

### *4.1 Transparency in Digital Cash Transfers: Building Trust Through Transparent Processes*

Transparency is crucial for digital cash transfer systems to function effectively, as it enables receivers to understand precisely what is happening with their funds and how they are being managed. Since digital platforms are being increasingly used to spread SSN payments, the level of Transparency in Bangladesh has a direct impact on the level of trust and satisfaction among beneficiaries. Based on what SSN receivers and UP officials said, this section examines how transparent the digital cash transfer system is perceived to be. This section looks at different points of view to see how much transparency improves the trustworthiness of digital money transfers. It also points out areas that need more work to make sure that processes are transparent and accountable.

The findings show that most SSN recipients and UP officials believe the digital cash transfer system is transparent. This shows that the system works well at making information clear and easy to find. Table 10 shows that 53% of people who got an SSN thought the process was "Completely Transparent," while 45% thought it was "Highly Transparent." Only 2% of the recipients reported "little transparency." Another 1% said it was "slightly transparent," and the last 1% said it was "moderately transparent." No one who got the information said that the process was "Not Transparent at All." UP officials also provided a similar viewpoint, as 50% identified the system as "Highly Transparent," and 50% called it "Completely Transparent." None of the UP officials described the level of transparency as "Not Transparent at All," "Slightly Transparent," or "Moderately Transparent." While commenting on the degree of transparency, one UP chairman said, "*The digital system has made the payment process much more transparent. Real-time payment tracking by beneficiaries has considerably lowered grievances and misconceptions*" (Interview Data 2024).

On the other hand, key informants offered more understanding of the need for transparency. One social welfare officer said, "*Transparency is essential to building trust in the system. Providing recipients with precise*

**Table 10** Level of transparency in the digital cash transfer process

| *Indicator* | *SSN beneficiaries (%)* | *UP functionaries (%)* |
|---|---|---|
| Not transparent at all | 0 | 0 |
| Slightly transparent | 1 | 0 |
| Moderately transparent | 1 | 0 |
| Highly transparent | 45 | 50 |
| Completely transparent | 53 | 50 |

Source: Field Data (2024)

*payment information will help them feel confident and safe utilising digital platforms*" (KII 2024). A development worker emphasised that "*transparency helps lower the risk of scams and mistakes, allowing those who benefit from the system to hold it accountable. This is especially important for poor groups that rely on these payments to meet their basic needs*" (KII 2024).

The findings align with prior studies examining the significance of transparency in digital money systems. Muralidharan et al. (2016) demonstrate that transparent methods significantly enhance the legitimacy and acceptance of digital aid projects, particularly in economically disadvantaged regions. Agostino et al. (2020) did a study that illustrates the importance of real-time tracking and transparent communication in fostering the trust and contentment of users using digital cash transfer platforms. These linkages illustrate the significance of upholding and augmenting transparency to guarantee the efficient functioning of digital money transfers in Bangladesh.

The research on transparency highlights its significance in establishing trust and credibility within Bangladesh's digital cash transfer mechanisms. The system's ability to provide clear and accessible information on payment alternatives is evidenced by the positive comments from SSN recipients and UP authorities, supported by significant sources. The minor concerns raised by certain recipients underscore the need to enhance transparency continually. Bangladesh may improve its digital money transfer systems by implementing real-time tracking, facilitating clear communication, and providing simple access to information. This method instils a sense of security and confidence in all recipients of funds about the use of these instruments.

### 4.2 *Accountability Mechanisms: Ensuring Responsiveness in Digital Cash Transfers*

Accountability measures need to be put in place to make sure that digital cash movement systems meet the needs and worries of users. How well digital methods for sending SSN payments work in Bangladesh depends on how confident and happy the receivers are with these services. In this part, we look at how SSN users and UP officials talked about accountability measures, such as ways to report problems and file complaints. This section looks at how accountability systems deal with problems in digital money transfers by comparing various points of view and finding methods to make them better, which will make them work better overall. Despite significant variations in their views, the finding shows that most SSN recipients and UP officials find accountability systems successful. Table 11 shows that 23% of SSN recipients assessed the systems as "Very Satisfactory," and 75% identified them as "Satisfactory." Of the beneficiaries, just 2% voiced worries; 1% called the systems "Dissatisfactory" and 1% stayed indifferent. None of the recipients claims to be "Very Dissatisfied."

UP officials offer a comparable but more cautious viewpoint. Table 11 shows that 50% identified accountability systems as "Effective," and 50% called them "Very Effective." None of the UP officials said the systems are "Very Ineffective," "Ineffective," or "Neutral." A UP member from a remote location said, "*In most situations, the grievance redressal mechanism functions effectively; nevertheless, sometimes it takes time to address more complex concerns. We must simplify the procedure to guarantee quicker replies*" (Interview Data 2024).

SSN recipients said they are more satisfied with accountability systems than UP representatives. Though 100% of UP officials agreed, 98% of beneficiaries characterise the systems as "Satisfactory" or "Very Satisfactory." While UP officials are more conscious of systematic issues, this disparity might result from recipients' limited exposure to backend operations. Concerning delays and process simplification, UP officials are more inclined to stress the need for accountability system changes. This implies that although recipients have seamless grievance redressal, administrators are more sensitive to operational issues that can compromise reactivity. Key informants offered more analysis of these differences. A social welfare officer said, "*Maintaining system credibility depends on accountability tools. Their effectiveness, however, relies on prompt replies and transparent engagement with recipients*" (KII 2024). A development worker emphasised that "*The method works pretty well most of the time, but it could*

**Table 11** Level of effectiveness of accountability mechanisms/structures

| *Indicator* | *SSN beneficiaries (%)* | *UP functionaries (%)* |
|---|---|---|
| Very dissatisfied/very ineffective | 0 | 0 |
| Dissatisfied/ineffective | 1 | 0 |
| Neutral | 1 | 0 |
| Satisfied/effective | 75 | 50 |
| Very satisfied/very effective | 23 | 50 |

Source: Field Data (2024)

*do a better job of dealing with difficult issues and making sure all complaints are taken care of quickly*" (KII 2024).

The findings align with those of other studies on the tools that enhance the accountability of digital banking systems. For example, a study by Muralidharan et al. (2016) shows that effective ways to handle complaints make people believe and be happy with digital welfare programs a lot more. The study by Agostino et al. (2020) shows how important it is for digital payment transfer networks to respond quickly and clearly to complaints in order to protect their reputation. These connections show how important it is for accountability systems to keep getting better so they work well and are flexible. Even though most SSN users and UP officials said they were very satisfied and successful, the differences in how they felt made it clear that the program needs to keep improving. Accountability systems could work even better if they dealt with delays, made procedures easier, and promised quick responses to complaints. By making these organisations stronger, Bangladesh could make sure that its digital money transfer systems work well and take into account the needs and concerns of all receivers.

### 4.3 *Policy Support: Enabling the Success of Digital Cash Transfers*

Digital cash transfer systems that work well depend on help from government policies, which create the laws and institutions needed to make sure they work. Since digital platforms are often used for SSN payments, Bangladesh's level of policy support has a direct impact on how well the system functions, its inclusivity, and its longevity. This section looks into how well people who receive SSNs and people who work for UP think that government policies are supporting digital cash transfers. The section seeks to evaluate the degree to which policy support helps digitised cash transfers and highlights opportunities for development employing an analysis of these viewpoints, thus strengthening the enabling environment.

Despite significant variations in their views, the finding suggests that most SSN recipients and UP officials view government policy support as substantial. Table 12 indicates that 33% of SSN recipients "Agreed" that the government offers adequate policy assistance, while 67% "Strongly Agreed." Reflecting great trust in the government's dedication to digital cash transfers, none of the recipients said they disagreed or stayed neutral. Conversely, the UP officials offered a somewhat more complex viewpoint.

Table 12 shows that 40% of respondents assess government policies as "Completely Supportive" and another 40% as "Highly Supportive." A tiny percentage (25%), on the other hand, identified the policies as "Moderately Supportive," while none said they were "Not Supportive at All" or "Slightly Supportive."

Compared to UP officials, SSN recipients have more trust in government policy support. Though 80% of UP representatives rated policies as "Highly Supportive" or "Completely Supportive," 100% of recipients "Agree" or "Strongly Agree" that the government provide adequate support. This disparity can result from beneficiaries' emphasis on the findings of policy assistance, such as prompt payments. In contrast, UP officials are more aware of the challenges in implementing similar policies. Specifically, regarding infrastructure and service delivery, UP officials are more inclined to stress the need for changes in policy implementation. This implies that although the policy framework is robust, its effectiveness relies on handling local practical issues.

Key informants offered more analysis on the function of policy assistance. One UNO said, "*Policy support has played a big role in ensuring cash transfers become digital. These rules need to be followed correctly, especially in places where things are not going well*" (KII 2024). On the other hand, a local government expert said, "*for creating a good setting, strong policy support is needed. But for it to work, problems with execution must be solved and broad agreement must be reached*" (KII 2024). Because of these findings, more research needs to be done on how government help affects digital banking systems. According to Muralidharan et al. (2016), strong regulatory systems make digital help projects more popular and useful. Agostino et al. (2020) stress how important it is to make sure that policies and the

**Table 12** Level of policy support from the government for digital cash transfers

| *SSN beneficiaries* | | *UP functionaries* | |
|---|---|---|---|
| *Indicator* | *Response (%)* | *Indicator* | *Response (%)* |
| Strongly disagree/ | 0 | Not supportive at all | 0 |
| Disagree | 0 | Slightly supportive | 0 |
| Neutral | 0 | Moderately supportive | 25 |
| Agree | 33 | Highly supportive | 40 |
| Strongly agree | 67 | Completely supportive | 40 |

Source: Field Data (2024)

ways they are put into action work together. The importance of following policies correctly to ensure that government aid is effective is emphasised by these connections. The policy's positive effects show how important it is to make it easier for digital money transfer services to grow in Bangladesh. The smart approach of UP officials shows how important it is to deal with problems linked to killings—mostly good comments from people who got an SSN show that the government is serious about going digital. More strict adherence to policies is needed, especially in rural and impoverished areas, and these policies must align with the current situations in those areas for government aid to be effective. If Bangladesh fixes these problems, it can make sure that its digital money transfer methods work well and that everyone can use them.

The study of governance mechanisms, including accounting systems, policy support, and transparency, demonstrates the importance of these factors in ensuring the proper functioning of Bangladesh's digital cash transfer systems. The positive response from SSN recipients and UP officials indicates that the system has built confidence, ensured timely payments, and created an optimal environment for digital transactions. However, the differing views of UP officials and critical sources indicate that we need to address implementation issues and ensure that our government mechanisms are robust and accessible to everyone.

## 5 Socioeconomic Factors: Shaping Access and Equity in Digital Cash Transfers

In countries like Bangladesh, where there are many people and limited resources, socioeconomic considerations have a significant impact on the effectiveness and efficiency of digital money transfer systems. People's income, gender roles, and where they reside have a big impact on how they utilise digital media, which in turn influences how they can get and spend SSN money. This section examines the influence of three primary social determinants on digital cash transfers: income levels, gender relations, and disparities in resource availability. By looking at these elements, the evaluator may find out how social issues impact access to digital payments. This will help policymakers make choices that encourage equitable distribution of services. We examine how people's financial resources influence their ability to utilise digital tools and services, such as cell phones and the internet, in this section. It examines how gender influences digital literacy and engagement, with a focus on the unique challenges faced by women. Finally, it discusses changes in geography and the issues that people in rural and disadvantaged areas confront. This section discusses how to ensure that digital money transfer techniques are both fair and user-friendly, as well as how to address social and economic challenges.

### 5.1 *Income Levels: Affordability and Access to Digital Services*

People in Bangladesh and other low-income nations have a hard time getting and using internet services, and how much money they make is a big part of it. People who get money from SSN programs may have problems sending money because utilising digital tools like mobile phones and the internet might be too expensive due to transaction costs. Based on the responses of SSN recipients and UP officials, this section explores the link between family income levels and the affordability of digital services. The section intends to evaluate the degree to which income levels either facilitate or impede access to digital cash transfers, employing these viewpoints and proposing ways to guarantee affordability for all recipients.

Though a tiny percentage struggled, the finding shows that most SSN recipients believed their family income was adequate for accessing digital services. Table 13 shows that 67% of SSN recipients considered their income "Sufficient," while 23% considered it "Very Sufficient." Of the 8% who said they have problems, 3% said their income is "Very Insufficient" and 5% said it is "Insufficient." The remaining 3% of recipients stayed neutral. This implies that although most recipients can pay for digital services, a small percentage struggle financially and have limited access.

UP officials provided a more measured view. Table 13 indicates that 40% considered the income levels of the SSN beneficiaries "Highly Sufficient" for accessing digital platforms, while 10% ranked them "Completely Sufficient." Of them, 50% said they have problems; 25% said their income is "Slightly Sufficient," and the other 25% said it is "Moderately Sufficient." None of the UP officials said the income levels of the beneficiaries are "Not Sufficient at All." While commenting on the income level of the SSN beneficiaries, a UP representative from a remote location said, "*Although many recipients can afford basic digital services, individuals with very low incomes frequently find it challenging to pay for*

**Table 13** Household income level and affordability of digital services

| *SSN beneficiaries* | | *UP functionaries* | |
|---|---|---|---|
| *Indicator* | *Responses (%)* | *Indicator* | *Responses (%)* |
| Very insufficient | 3 | Not sufficient at all | 0 |
| Insufficient | 5 | Slightly sufficient | 25 |
| Neutral | 3 | Moderately sufficient | 25 |
| Sufficient | 67 | Highly sufficient | 40 |
| Very sufficient | 23 | Completely sufficient | 10 |

Source: Field Data (2024)

*cell phones and internet access. This reduces their capacity to use digital platforms independently*" (Interview Data 2024).

Compared to UP officials, SSN beneficiaries said they are more confident in their capacity to pay for digital services. Though just 50% of UP officials agreed, 90% of recipients said their income is "Sufficient" or "Very Sufficient." Beneficiaries' emphasis on their immediate capacity to pay expenses may explain this disparity. On the other hand, UP officials are more aware of the significant financial challenges that low-income families face. Especially in rural and distant places, UP officials are more inclined to stress low-income people's financial challenges. This implies that, although most beneficiaries can afford digital services, targeted assistance is necessary to ensure that disadvantaged groups are not excluded from these services.

Key informants offered more analysis on how income levels affect access to digital services. A social welfare officer said that "*cost is a big problem for digital participation, especially for families with low incomes. This gap can be closed with low-cost options or funding that make sure everyone has access to digital platforms*" (KII 2024). A development worker said, "*How well people can use digital services is greatly affected by their income. To make sure that digital cash payments are fair and transparent to everyone, cost problems must first be fixed*" (KII 2024).

The statistics on how much money SSN holders in Bangladesh make indicate how this impacts their capacity to use digital services. Most of the people who obtained help indicated they had enough money to use digital tools, but the issues that low-income families are encountering illustrate how crucial it is to find the right answers. Community-based support networks, low-cost solutions, and subsidies can help reduce the price gap and ensure that everyone can access digital cash transfers, regardless of their income level. These findings are consistent with studies evaluating the cost-effectiveness of digital banking services for low-income persons. For example, GSMA's (2020) study shows that those with low incomes have a harder difficulty going online and utilising cell phones since they are so expensive. Muralidharan et al. (2016) conducted further research that illustrates the imperative of addressing cost-related challenges for the efficacy of digital aid efforts. These links show how important it is to help those with low incomes make better use of digital services.

### 5.2 *Gender Dynamics: Overcoming Barriers to Digital Inclusion*

Gender concerns play a significant role in determining who can use digital systems, especially in places where cultural norms and financial disparities hinder women's participation. In Bangladesh, where an increasing number of people are utilising digital platforms to send money, it is essential to understand how gender affects relationships to ensure that everyone can use digital financial transfers. This section examines how culture and gender issues affect SSN recipients' ability to access and use digital tools based on what they said to UP officials and KII. The section intends to evaluate the degree to which gender dynamics hinder digital inclusion, analysing various viewpoints and suggesting ways to advance gender equality in digital cash transfers. The findings show that a notable percentage of SSN recipients and UP representatives see gender dynamics as an obstacle to utilising and accessing digital technologies. Table 14 indicates that 32% of SSN recipients believed gender dynamics have a "Significant" effect on their usage of digital systems, while 27% said the effect is "Complete." Fifteen per cent also said a "Somewhat" effect, while 9% termed it "A little." Of beneficiaries, just 17% said gender dynamics have no impact on their access "At all." UP officials have a comparable but rather more complex viewpoint. Table 14 indicates that 20% believed the effect is "Completely," while 45% said gender dynamics affected access to digital cash transfers "To a greater extent." A small percentage (35%), on the other hand, reported less influence. Specifically, 5% said "Not at all," 20% said "To a small extent," and 10% said "To some extent."

Compared to UP representatives, SSN recipients are more likely to report notable or total effects of gender dynamics. Although only 65% of UP representatives shared the same view, 59% of recipients reported that the effect is "Significant" or "Complete." While UP officials could have a more general view of systematic challenges, this disparity could result from recipients' encounters with gender-based obstacles. Particularly in rural regions where conventional gender roles are more prominent, both recipients and UP officials stress the influence of cultural norms in forming gender dynamics. This implies that changing cultural views requires official actions and community involvement to remove gender-based impediments.

Key informants offered more analysis on how gender dynamics affect digital inclusion. One UNO said, "*Gender roles are a big problem when it comes to internet inclusion, especially for women who live in rural places. It is crucial to provide women with mobile phones and computer abilities so they may send and receive money the same way as men*" (KII 2024). A development worker said, "*Cultural conventions may make it hard for women to use digital technologies on their own. We need to focus on certain things, including initiatives to raise awareness in the community and workshops specifically for women, to get past these issues*" (KII 2024). These findings are consistent with findings from earlier research regarding the influence of gender on digital financial procedures. The GSMA (2020) research says that women in developing nations are substantially less likely to acquire mobile phones or utilise digital banking services due to social and cultural restrictions. Research by Agostino et al. (2020) indicates that policies and initiatives designed to foster digital equality should take gender into account. These links highlight how vital it is to fix problems that impact men and women in various ways so that everyone may use digital money transfer instruments equally. Most of the people who got the message and

**Table 14** Relation between cultural or gender dynamics and ability to access and use digital systems

| *SSN beneficiaries* | | *UP functionaries* | |
|---|---|---|---|
| *Indicator* | *Response (%)* | *Indicator* | *Response (%)* |
| Not at all | 17 | Not at all | 5 |
| A little | 9 | To a small extent | 20 |
| Somewhat | 15 | To some extent | 10 |
| Significantly/ | 32 | To a greater extent | 45 |
| Completely/ | 27 | Completely | 20 |

Source: Field Data (2024)

UP authorities assumed the consequences were huge or all-encompassing. Even so, the fact that they have diverse opinions illustrates that we need to work together to break down barriers based on gender. Women need to learn how to utilise technology and obtain mobile phones so that digital money transfers are more fair for both men and women. Communities should also try to modify the way things are done. Bangladesh can make sure that everyone can utilise its digital money transfer services fairly and easily by fixing these challenges. This would allow all recipients, regardless of their gender, to access their money independently and feel secure doing so.

### 5.3 *Regional Disparities: Bridging the Urban-Rural Divide in Digital Access*

Differences between regions, especially between cities and rural areas, have a big effect on how people use and benefit from digital cash payment systems. People living in rural areas of Bangladesh often face more challenges using digital platforms than those in cities, as services and resources are not distributed equally. Depending on the responses of SSN beneficiaries and UP officials, this section looks at the relative accessibility of digital payment systems in rural and urban settings. The section intends to evaluate how much geographical differences influence the execution of digitised cash transfers by analysing various viewpoints and suggesting ways to close the urban-rural gap.

The research shows that although most SSN recipients find digital payment systems accessible, there are significant variations in accessibility across rural and urban locations. Table 15 shows that 57% of SSN recipients found the sites "Accessible," and 32% found them "Very Accessible." Of them, 11% said they have problems, 4% said the sites are "Inaccessible," and 7% stayed indifferent. None of the recipients termed the sites "Very Inaccessible." UP officials, on the other hand, provided a more complex viewpoint. Table 15 indicates that 40% said geographical differences influence the execution of digitised cash transfers "To a greater extent," while 15% said "Completely." However, 45% said less impact, 35% said "Not at all," 5% said "To a small extent," and 5% said "To some extent." While commenting on the impact of regional variations, a UP chairman from a rural area said, "*Although digital platforms are usually available, beneficiaries in remote locations frequently struggle because of poor internet connection and limited access to mobile phones. Urban regions see fewer frequent problems*" (Interview Data 2024).

Compared to UP officials, SSN beneficiaries reported having more access. Though just 55% of UP officials agreed, 89% of recipients said the platforms are "Accessible" or "Very Accessible." While UP officials are more conscious of the systematic problems experienced in rural regions, beneficiaries' emphasis on immediate access to services may explain this discrepancy. UP officials are more inclined to emphasise the effects of regional inequalities, especially in remote areas with limited infrastructure and resources. This implies that, although most beneficiaries have access to digital platforms, targeted interventions are necessary to address the challenges faced by individuals in underprivileged areas.

Key informants offered more analysis of how geographical differences influence digital access. A social welfare officer said, "*Regional differences are a significant obstacle to digital inclusion, especially in rural and remote areas. To make sure that everyone can use digital media, we need to enhance infrastructure and make the internet available to more people*" (KII 2024). A local government expert said, "*One huge concern is that some rural locations do not have as good internet access as some urban areas. To fix these challenges, money and equipment need to be divided equally, especially in places that are not getting much aid*" (KII 2024). These findings are consistent with research examining the geographical variations in digital banking systems. According to the GSMA (2020) report, rural communities with low incomes typically have trouble getting access to cell phones and the internet. A World Bank (2019) research found that fixing regional inequality is also important for making sure that digital aid initiatives

**Table 15** Level of comparative accessibility of digital payment platforms between rural and urban areas

| *SSN beneficiaries* | | *UP functionaries* | |
|---|---|---|---|
| *Indicator* | *Response (%)* | *Indicator* | *Response (%)* |
| Very inaccessible | 0 | Not at all | 35 |
| Inaccessible | 4 | To a small extent | 5 |
| Neutral | 7 | To some extent | 5 |
| Accessible | 57 | To a greater extent | 40 |
| Very accessible | 32 | Completely | 15 |

Source: Field Data (2024)

work. These links highlight how crucial it is for individuals in cities and rural regions to work together to make sure that everyone can utilise digital cash payments.

The figures indicate that the various regions in Bangladesh have a significant impact on the digital payment options available. Most people with an SSN reported that their websites are straightforward to discover and utilise. People who live in rural or remote areas face challenges that highlight the differences in the requirements of urban and rural populations. It is necessary to enhance infrastructure, simplify internet access, and ensure that everyone can use mobile phones, allowing underprivileged areas to connect to the internet. Bangladesh must ensure that its digital cash trading systems are fair and transparent to everyone by addressing these issues. In this manner, everyone may get their money safely and on their own, no matter where they are.

## 6 Conclusion

This chapter closely looks at the main elements that affect how well digital cash transfer systems work in Bangladesh's SSN programs. Each factor has a big impact on how easy, quick, and inclusive digital money transfers are. The way these factors combine highlights both the successes and failures of digitisation efforts. Technology infrastructure is becoming the backbone of digital cash transfers. To make payments easy, users must own a cell phone, be connected to the internet, and have a stable platform. Infrastructure growth has made significant progress, but the fact that not many people own smartphones, internet access is not always equitable, and technology issues occur from time to time highlights the importance of continued investment and innovation.

Digital knowledge was emphasised as a key way to help everyone use technology. Basic digital literacy skills, efforts to raise knowledge, and designs that were easy for people to use were all necessary to give beneficiaries the tools they needed to use digital platforms successfully. Some groups, such as older adults and women, may struggle with using technology effectively. This shows how important it is to have specialised training programs and easier-to-use platforms so that everyone can get their payments on their own. It was found that governance tools, including transparency, accountability, and policy support, are necessary to build trust and confidence in digital cash transfer systems. Both receivers and managers praised how transparent and quick the system was, especially in remote areas.

However, we still need stronger mechanisms of accountability and improved policy implementation right soon. Access to digital media was greatly affected by things like money, gender roles, and where people live. Women, low-income families, and those who live in rural areas may face even more problems, such as cultural barriers, lack of money, and lack of infrastructure. To address these unfair situations, we must ensure that digital monetary transactions are fair and accessible to everyone.

The study shows how hard it is to develop digital money transfer systems in a country like Bangladesh that is diverse and has few resources. There has been significant progress, but the problems still require a comprehensive solution that incorporates new technology, programs to build capacity, strict regulations, and targeted social and economic initiatives aimed at specific groups. Bangladesh can make sure that its digital financial transfer networks are effective, trustworthy, and fair by putting these projects first. This lets people get to their funds whenever they choose and with confidence.

## References

Agostino, D., Saliterer, I., and Steccolini, I. (2020). Digitalisation, accounting and accountability: A literature review and reflections on future research in public services. *Financial Accountability & Management, 38*(2), 152–176. https://doi.org/10.1111/faam.12265

Aziz, A., and Naima, U. (2020). Rethinking digital financial inclusion: Evidence from Bangladesh. *Technology in Society, 64*, 1–10. https://doi.org/10.1016/j.techsoc.2020.101509

Batista, C., and Vicente, P. C. (2023). Introducing mobile money in rural Mozambique: Evidence from a field experiment. *NOVAFRICA Working Paper Series No. 1301*. Available at SSRN: https://ssrn.com/abstract=2384561 or https://doi.org/10.2139/ssrn.2384561

Chibesa, K., and Mwange, A. (2025). The role of digital financial literacy in enhancing financial inclusion among informal entrepreneurs in Zambia. *East African Finance Journal, 4*(1), 141–146.

Consultative Group to Assist the Poor (CGAP). (2016). *Digital financial services: Challenges and opportunities for emerging market banks* (Note 42). International Finance Corporation, The World Bank Group.

Donner, J., and Tellez, C. A. (2008). Mobile banking and economic development: Linking adoption, impact, and use. *Asian Journal of Communication, 18*(4), 318–332. https://doi.org/10.1080/01292980802344190

Global System for Mobile Communications (GSMA). (2020). *Connected women: The mobile gender gap report 2020.* GSM Association, London.

Goel, P., and Agrasen, M. (2024). Customer satisfaction improvement with feedback loops in financial services. *Journal of Emerging Technologies and Innovation Research (JETIR), 11*(5), q263–q274.

International Finance Corporation (IFC). (2017). *Digital financial services: Challenges and opportunities for emerging market banks.* The World Bank Group.

Mathew, V. (2021). Prospects, challenges, and opportunities of digital financial services in developing countries. In T. Esakki (Ed.), *Managerial issues in digital transformation of global modern corporations* (pp. 69–88). IGI Global. https://doi.org/10.4018/978-1-7998-2402-2.ch006

Muralidharan, K., Niehaus, P., and Sukhtankar, S. (2016). Building state capacity: Evidence from biometric smartcards in India. *American Economic Review, 106*(10), 2895–2929. https://doi.org/10.1257/aer.20141346

Rashid, M. H. (2020). Prospects of digital financial services in Bangladesh in the context of the Fourth Industrial Revolution. *Asian Journal of Social Sciences and Legal Studies, 2*(5), 88–95.

World Bank. (2019). *Social Safety Nets in Bangladesh Help Reduce Poverty and Improve Human Capital.* Washington, DC: World Bank Group.

World Bank. (2024). *Bangladesh - Cash Transfer Modernisation Project: Improving transparency and efficiency of safety nets.* World Bank Group. http://documents.worldbank.org/curated/en/099739201032424234

Zainudeen, A., and Ratnadiwakara, D. (2011). Are the poor stuck in voice? Conditions for adoption of more-than-voice mobile services. *Information Technologies & International Development, 7*(3), 45–59.

# Discussion: Integrating Findings with the Theoretical Framework

**Abstract** This chapter discusses a lot about how well digital cash transfers work in Social Safety Network (SSN) programs in Bangladesh. The chapter achieves this by combining research findings with data on how individuals use technology, interact with the government, and receive payments. The chapter argues that digital cash transfers have greatly improved access to financial services, governance, and service delivery. The Capability Approach by Sen, the Beneficial Governance Framework by the World Bank, the Technology Acceptance Model by Davis, and the Diffusion of Innovations Theory by Rogers, all help it achieve this. But it could be difficult to fully enjoy these benefits because of challenges like slow internet, not knowing how to use technology well, and social and cultural hurdles. The study reveals the interconnections among these three groups. They discuss how issues with infrastructure, social and cultural norms, and people who do not know how to use technology well might make digital cash transfers less effective. This chapter demonstrates to academicians, lawmakers, and professionals how they can enhance the sustainability, effectiveness, and accessibility of digital cash transfer systems by integrating these findings with a theoretical framework. This chapter is one way that automation might help individuals who are most at risk.

**Keywords** Digital cash transfers • Social Safety Net programs • Bangladesh • Theoretical framework • Financial inclusion • Digital literacy



P. K. Panday, A. H. M. K. Ahsan, *Digital Revolution for the Vulnerable*, https://doi.org/10.1007/978-981-95-7980-8_6

## 1 Introduction

This chapter looks at how well digital cash transfers work in Bangladesh's Social Safety Net (SSN) schemes. It does this by combining study findings with information about how people use technology, how governments run things, and how everyone can gain access to cash. Switching cash transfers to digital forms is a significant step forward in providing social support. Its objective is to address persistent issues such as scams, waste, and financial hardship. There have been important steps forward in lowering transaction costs, improving the effectiveness of management, and raising recipient satisfaction. Still, there are issues that need to be addressed, such as the need for better digital literacy training, occasional technical problems, and limited digital access in rural areas. This chapter thoroughly discusses the pros and cons of digital cash transfers using a theoretical framework. It also includes useful suggestions for making them work better.

The three main parts of the theory structure form the basis of this chapter. Every one of them offers a different view on how digital cash transfers work. Financial inclusion looks into how technology has made it easier for people to obtain access to capital and given them more power, especially those who were not able to use official financial institutions before. The study employs Sen's Capability Approach to examine how digital solutions can enhance people's capabilities by facilitating access to financial resources. However, the discussion highlights unequal access issues that need to be addressed if the benefits of technology are to be shared fairly, especially among less fortunate groups.

Second, governance examines how automation has made the sharing of SSN funds more effective, transparent, and accountable. The findings indicate that digital technologies have the potential to reduce corruption, eliminate intermediaries, and simplify routine tasks. These changes align with the World Bank's Effective Governance Framework, which identifies transparency and responsiveness as two key components of positive governance. The intermittent issues with technology and internet access, particularly in rural areas, underscore the necessity for increased infrastructure and capacity-building to guarantee the reliability of digital systems.

The study of digital adoption looks into how cultural and social norms, perceived usefulness, and digital skills affect how people accept and use digital platforms. Many users, especially women and older people, think that digital tools are simple to use, but the findings indicate that there are still big problems with usage. These findings support

Rogers' Diffusion of Innovations Theory and Davis's Technology Adoption Model, which argue that people accept new technologies based on how advantageous they seem, how easy they are to use, and how much time they have to try them out. To solve these problems, our main goals should be to improve people's digital skills and ensure that everyone, regardless of where they live or how much money they have, has access to digital tools.

By combining the findings with the theoretical framework, this chapter shows how digital solutions could improve SSN systems in areas with low income. The study suggests that digital cash transfers could change how social security is given out, but only if basic problems like poor digital literacy, insufficient infrastructure, and established cultural and societal norms are fixed. At the end of the chapter, there are practical suggestions for lawmakers and practitioners. It argues how important it is to have a complete plan that includes new technology, skill-building programs, and targeted interventions to make sure that the most disadvantaged groups benefit from digitisation. This chapter carefully examines how well digital cash transfers work in Bangladesh's SSN programs by combining theories of digital adoption, financial inclusion, and government with real-life examples. This chapter provides helpful tips to researchers, practitioners, and lawmakers aiming to improve the effectiveness of digital efforts in SSN.

## 2 Financial Inclusion: Expanding Access and Empowering Beneficiaries

The findings show that digital cash transfers have made it much easier for people in Bangladesh who use social security to receive money. Based on Sen's (1999) Capability Approach, the findings indicate that technology has improved users' skills by making it easier and faster to acquire money. Ninety-seven per cent of customers said that digital systems made it easier to acquire information, and 64% said that their problems were "completely" fixed ("Measuring Success: Evaluating the Effectiveness of Digital Cash Transfers in Bangladesh's Social Safety Net Programs" chapter, Sect. 2.3). This aligns with Sen's argument that poverty is more than just a loss of money; it is also a loss of skills and capabilities. Sen states that digital solutions can help close this gap. By allowing recipients to receive payments immediately, digital cash transfers have reduced the need for intermediaries, shortened delays, and given recipients greater control over their funds. Women and low-income families need this empowerment more than anyone else, as they have generally struggled to access formal banking institutions.

The study also revealed issues with financial participation, particularly for women and families with low incomes. For instance, only 33% of those who received the letter had cell phones, and none of them had computers ("Enablers and Challenges: Key Determinants Shaping Digital Cash Transfers in Bangladesh's Social Safety Net Programs" chapter, Sect. 2.1). This finding aligns with the findings of Beck et al. (2007) regarding systemic barriers, such as high transaction costs and limited infrastructure. The dearth of digital tools in many areas, particularly rural ones, emphasises how crucial it is to ensure that the most vulnerable people benefit from digital cash transfers. Beneficiaries who do not have smartphones or computers have a tougher time managing and collecting their money, which makes it harder for them to use digital platforms well. Because of variations in income and gender norms, the digital gap is bigger for women and those with low incomes.

These findings add to the growing body of literature from throughout the world that suggests technology may help those who are poor. GSMA (2020) states that digital cash transfers have changed throughout the years to make it simpler for people to receive money, especially for people in developing countries. People in rural areas and women still have trouble adopting digital technologies. When resources are few, analogous occurrences have taken place in many places. The researchers (Muralidharan et al. 2016) assert that the lack of cell phones and an inconsistent internet rendered the initiation of digital assistance initiatives in India unfeasible. These differences highlight how important it is to get rid of the structural hurdles that keep some customers from adopting electronic money transfer services. If these issues could be fixed, the most disadvantaged people would be able to use technology, which would make its advantages available to more than just the current users of digital tools.

Lawmakers should consider taking several initiatives to make it easier for people to send and receive digital money. First, giving low-income families free or cheap mobile phones is one way to lower prices and make sure that everyone can use important digital services. One way to do this is to engage with mobile network providers to give out phones that are cheaper or less expensive, especially to women and those who live in rural areas. Second, it is important to develop programs that teach people how to utilise digital networks safely. A lot of people, particularly women and older people, are projected to benefit from these programs. They also need to include activities that boost people's self-esteem and help them do better at what they do. Third, the government has to spend money on infrastructure to make sure that everyone can use digital services. This means building community centres where people can get help with digital tools, making networks more reliable, and making it easier for people to get online. These characteristics show how important it is for financial inclusion to have low prices and easy access.

Lawmakers should also consider how gender-inclusive laws may improve the experience of using institutions. Due to cultural norms and money problems, women in Bangladesh have a hard time using computers and the internet. Many women cannot be financially independent since they rely on male family members for help. We must address these challenges by improving women's access to the internet and cell phones and by creating training programs that are expressly geared to assist them in sharing information with others in their community. Bangladesh would make sure that everyone, no matter their gender or socioeconomic background, could use digital money by getting rid of these old and institutional impediments.

The numbers show that digital cash transfers are getting easier for SSN users in Bangladesh. Digital platforms have given people more power and made them less reliant on middlemen by giving them quick and direct access to finance. There is a need to fix problems like not having enough digital tools, not having enough digital skills, and not having equitable access to finance in order for the most disadvantaged populations to benefit from technology. The government could make the digital cash transfer system easier to use and fairer for everyone by solving problems like excessive charges, a lack of technical knowledge, and bad infrastructure. This makes sure that everyone gets their money and manages it in a straightforward way.

## 3 Governance: Enhancing Transparency and Accountability

The findings show that Bangladesh's SSN programs are affected by digital cash transfers. According to the World Bank's Good Governance Framework (1992), the findings demonstrate that digitising services has increased their effectiveness, accountability, and clarity. For example, 98% of users chaptered that digital solutions eliminated middleman fees, and 97% noted a decrease in travel and paperwork costs ("Measuring Success: Evaluating the Effectiveness of Digital Cash Transfers in Bangladesh's Social Safety Net Programs" chapter, Sect. 4.1). This aligns with the idea that transparency and responsiveness are essential for effective governance. Digitising cash transfers has helped the government lower its fraud risk, limit the power of middlemen, and make administrative tasks easier. These changes have made it easier for people to access services and have increased trust in the system. The open sharing of transaction statuses and real-time payment tracking have further clarified the situation. People who receive money can now hold the system accountable for how they spend it and find out where it went.

On the other hand, the study indicated that putting government systems into place is not always straightforward, especially in rural areas. For instance, 10% of Union Parishad (UP) officials chaptered that network or technology issues occasionally caused delays ("Enablers and Challenges: Key Determinants Shaping Digital Cash Transfers in Bangladesh's Social Safety Net Programs" chapter, Sect. 2.2). This study shows how important strong institutional skills and infrastructure are for making sure that digital government systems work well. Digital platforms may become less effective as internet connections and technology problems happen more often. This concern is especially true in rural and remote places where infrastructure is often not adequate enough. These issues demonstrate how crucial it is to keep spending money on technological infrastructure and helping people learn new skills so that digital systems operate for everyone. Ignoring these factors could lead to an unfair distribution of technological benefits, making it harder for businesses that are doing well in areas that are not doing well to receive their money back.

The findings are in line with a study that looked into how digital technology might make things more open and less crooked. Muralidharan et al. (2016) state that fingerprint smartcards in India cut down on leaks and made social programs more effective by removing middlemen and increasing transparency. GSMA (2020) suggests that mobile money services can enhance government transparency and simplify the monitoring of financial activities. However, the challenges this study identified, including inconsistent connectivity and technical difficulties, point to more significant problems related to the digital divide in low-income nations. Due to these problems, it appears that digital cash transfers might improve government efficiency, but only if fundamental issues like limited technology and poor infrastructure are addressed. Without constant digital platforms and dependable internet access, digitisation may not yield all its benefits, especially for people living in rural or impoverished areas.

Policymakers should prioritise several key steps to enhance governance in digital cash transfer systems. First, the internet infrastructure needs to improve, especially in rural and remote areas, so that connections are stable and reliable. This includes making networks more reliable, expanding broadband networks, and addressing connection issues in areas that are currently underserved. Only a strong internet link enables the use of digital tools. Rural families may still have problems getting their payment on time if they do not have a reliable internet connection. The second most important thing to do to assist local governments in adopting digital technology is to teach them how to use it. Local administrators must possess the necessary skills to resolve technical difficulties and address enquiries from recipients in order for digital cash transfer systems to function well. In this way, we can be certain that everything is functioning properly. Skills in problem-solving, expertise in one's field, and the encouragement of administrative accountability should all be part of any quality training program.

Enhancing the methods through which individuals submit complaints is crucial to reducing wait times and ensuring prompt resolution of issues. Things are still imperfect, especially in areas with little infrastructure, even if digital technologies have greatly reduced shadowy dealings and made everything much more transparent. A strong feedback management system lets people identify problems, which makes sure they are fixed quickly. These things might happen if there are feedback hotlines and websites, if local governments learn how to solve problems well, and if additional steps are taken. If lawmakers could fix these problems, digital cash transfer systems would be more dependable and useful, and everyone, no matter where they are, would be able to make payments.

Besides these actions, legislators should consider how policy support helps improve government control. Strong legislative frameworks are necessary for digital cash transfers, but their operational efficiency hinges on their usage. To achieve this, operational difficulties need to be solved, regulations need to be created to match the present circumstances, and people need to be given the tools they need to use digital technology well. Policies that foster the public and private sectors to work together could make it simpler to employ the private sector's tools and knowledge to address infrastructure problems and improve services. Laws that protect equal rights for men and women can help women, who typically have problems utilising digital services, participate in designing and using digital money transfer systems.

The findings indicate how digital cash transfers are transforming the way Bangladesh's Social Safety Net (SSN) initiatives improve government services. By cutting down on theft, getting rid of intermediaries, and accelerating regular procedures, digital technologies have made everything much more open, accountable, and effective. Problems with technology and connection, especially in remote places, show how important it is to keep investing in infrastructure and helping people get better at using digital systems. Policymakers can improve oversight of digital cash transfer systems and ensure that everyone has equal access to payments by putting more money into internet infrastructure, teaching local governments, and setting up reliable ways for people to file complaints. These rules are in line with the idea that fairness and efficiency are important parts of beneficial government. They will make the social safety system work better and be easier for people to enter.

## 4 Digital Adoption: Overcoming Barriers to Technology Uptake

The devices displayed varying levels of digital usage. Their ability to use technology, their perception of its usefulness, and their social and cultural beliefs all contributed to this. Based on Davis's Technology Adoption Model (TAM) and Rogers' Diffusion of Innovations Theory (2003), the findings indicate that users' adoption of digital cash transfers was influenced by their perception of the platforms' usability and ease of use. As an example of how user-friendly design can enhance usability, 100% beneficiaries who benefited from the digital platform described it as "easy" or "very easy" to use. This high level of ease is crucial for driving technology adoption because it makes digital platforms appear less complicated and encourages people to use them. The system's simple layout, clear instructions, and wide range of functions have all contributed to building trust and confidence, especially among users who may not have been initially comfortable with digital technologies.

The study identified significant issues with the digital transition, particularly among older individuals and women. For instance, 52% of recipients stated that their digital skills were "very poor," indicating a need for specialised training classes ("Enablers and Challenges: Key Determinants Shaping Digital Cash Transfers in Bangladesh's Social Safety Net Programs" chapter, Sect. 3.1). This finding supports Rogers's idea that complexity and the ability to try something new are the primary factors that lead people to adopt new ideas. Many recipients, particularly women and older adults, have trouble with basic digital skills like navigating transaction screens, entering their PIN, or logging into the system. These issues are frequently worsened by social norms that make it harder for older people to adopt new technology and for women to use digital tools. For instance, women frequently depend on male family members to make a living in many rural areas, which reduces their independence and hinders their ability to effectively use digital systems. For the same reason, older people may be nervous about digital platforms and need extra help to learn more and feel more confident.

The findings back up a study that has shown over and over that infrastructure and digital literacy are important factors in determining how people use technology. Ahmed and Islam (2019) found that people in rural Bangladesh, especially women and the old, do not use digital banking services as much as they could because they do not understand how they work. The World Bank (2018) stressed how important digital knowledge is for helping more people gain access to banking services. They discovered that people who are not good at technology might make digital assistance programs less useful. These comparisons show how important it is to close the digital knowledge gap so that people of all ages, genders, and income levels can use digital tools effectively. Ignoring these problems will only help people who are already proficient at using technology, leaving those who are not as lucky behind.

To encourage more people to use technology, policymakers need to put many important projects at the top of their priority lists. It is critical to have digital literacy programs to help people feel more comfortable using technology, especially women and older people. Different types of people should be able to benefit from these programs, which should include hands-on lessons, real-life examples, and ongoing support to make sure that participants can use the skills they have acquired in the real world. Local governments in rural areas could set up community-based training programs so that people can learn how to use digital tools in a fun and helpful environment. Specialised training programs for women can help them overcome traditional hurdles and learn the skills they need to handle their own money.

Simplifying the layouts of digital tools will make them easier to use and understand. Despite the simplicity of this method, there is still room for improvement. Support in multiple languages, visual aids, and audio guidance would make the app easier for people who have trouble with computers or reading to use. Making the signup and authentication steps easier could improve the user experience and bring more people to the website. People need to receive hands-on training to use their computer skills successfully in the real world. Some people, especially older adults, may need to keep using digital platforms to learn new things and boost their confidence. Practical training can narrow this gap. We could dispatch mobile training units to faraway places to help people and resolve tech problems as they come up.

Lawmakers should also think about how cultural norms impact how individuals use technology. How people interact and what they think about their culture may affect their readiness to use digital platforms. Because of conventional gender norms, women in some rural regions may have problems acquiring cell phones or going online. These issues demand technological solutions, community engagement, and initiatives to raise awareness and understanding in order to shift cultural attitudes and promote gender equality. Policymakers can make sure that everyone who benefits from buying digital currency can get the most out of it by encouraging people to use technology, no matter their socioeconomic or cultural background.

The findings show that Bangladesh's SSN plans need to address problems with digital use in order for digital cash transfers to work properly. Digital platforms, despite their ease of use, still pose certain challenges, particularly for women and the elderly. Consumers may believe in digital platforms and be more comfortable with them if policymakers put more emphasis on digital literacy programs, improve user interfaces, and give them hands-on training. These actions would support the idea that people accept new technology primarily due to its flexibility and observability. A more transparent and effective digital cash transfer method would benefit everyone.

## 5 Synthesis: Integrating Financial Inclusion, Governance, and Digital Adoption

The study's findings show that digital development, good governance, and financial inclusion are all linked to and affected by how well cash transfers work in Bangladesh's SSN programs. The findings show that automation has greatly improved government services and made it easier for more people to use banking services. In addition, they show that it is challenging to encourage people to use technology, especially those who do not have much money. The findings are in line with the theory, which stresses how important it is to contemplate user approval, accessibility, and transparency when judging the success of digital actions. By looking at three main areas, the study gives a full picture of how digital cash transfers affect SSN in low-income areas. Bangladesh's SSN programs have significantly advanced due to the digitisation of cash payments. The government can now remain in touch with millions of people more easily and in public.

The findings demonstrate how digital systems have accelerated the administrative process, removed middleman fees, and greatly facilitated information access. Governance and financial inclusion have improved as a finding. For instance, 98% of users said they no longer had to pay middle-level fees, and 97% said that digital systems made it simpler for them to obtain information ("Measuring Success: Evaluating the Effectiveness of Digital Cash Transfers in Bangladesh's Social Safety Net Programs" chapter, Sects. 2.3 and 4.1). The latest advancements show how digital technology can help with persistent problems like inefficiency, corruption, and exclusion. The study highlights how crucial it is to use technology to guarantee that these advantages are shared equitably among individuals. Digital platforms cannot reach their full potential until they are widely adopted and used, particularly by adults, women, people from rural areas, and other under-represented groups.

The study contributes to the body of theoretical literature by demonstrating how digital cash transfers can make the concepts of financial inclusion, governance, and digital adoption tangible in low-income contexts. By providing people with direct and fast access to financial resources, the findings indicate that digital treatments can enhance individuals' capabilities, as outlined in Sen's Capability Approach. Similarly, the World Bank's Sustainable Governance Framework demonstrates how technology can enhance service delivery by making it more efficient, accountable, and transparent. Lastly, Davis's Technology Adoption Model and Rogers's Diffusion of Innovations Theory help us understand the factors, such as ease of use, perceived utility, and sociocultural norms, that affect people's decisions to adopt and use digital platforms.

The study provides a comprehensive framework for examining the effects of digital cash transfers and identifying ways to improve their effectiveness by applying these theoretical perspectives. The findings indicate that digital interventions can alter SSNs, but only if fundamental issues such as poor infrastructure, low computer literacy, and societal and cultural norms are addressed. For example, only 33% of survey respondents use cell phones, and 52% feel "very poor" at using technology ("Enablers and Challenges: Key Determinants Shaping Digital Cash Transfers in Bangladesh's Social Safety Net Programs" chapter, Sects. 2.1 and 3.1). These problems hurt poor people, especially women and people who live in rural areas, who have a harder time using and getting to digital tools. To address these issues, we require a comprehensive plan that incorporates new technologies, projects that enhance people's skills, and targeted actions to ensure that the most disadvantaged groups benefit from digitalisation.

The findings are important for both practitioners and lawmakers. To reap the most out of the benefits of digital currency deals, people should focus on three main areas. First, digital tools are vital for everyone to optimise digital systems, but especially for women and low-income families. This could be done by supporting cheap cell phones, offering rewards to buy mobile devices, and funding facilities in remote areas to make the internet easier to connect to. Second, there is a need to enhance control methods to guarantee the transparent and honest distribution of SSN payments. These initiatives make it easier for people to file complaints about problems with technology and delays. Additionally, they construct internet infrastructure and impart new skills to local leaders. Third, the implementation of user-friendly platforms and the provision of digital skills training are indispensable strategies for promoting the widespread adoption of technology. If people are provided with specialised training, digital platforms are simplified, and they are provided with hands-on assistance, they may experience increased confidence and proficiency in digital technologies.

These steps are very important, but the government should also look at the possible benefits of gender-sensitive laws for making people better at using technology. Women in Bangladesh have a harder time using computers and the internet because of cultural and financial limitations. For example, many women cannot manage their money and become financially independent since they have to rely on male relatives to send money home. To address these issues, it is essential to establish community outreach programs, specific training for women, and policies that promote women's access to mobile phones and digital services. By removing these structural and social barriers, governments may ensure that digital cash transfers benefit everyone, regardless of their gender or socioeconomic background.

The findings of this study demonstrate the interplay among financial inclusion, good governance, and digital development in enhancing the effectiveness of digital cash transfers inside Bangladesh's social safety net programs. Access has grown a lot, services are easier to use, and transparency has improved. There is a need to fix issues like poor infrastructure, a lack of digital skills, and social and cultural barriers so that the most vulnerable groups can benefit from digitisation. Policymakers can develop a better digital cash transfer system that involves more people by looking at systems as a whole. The solution includes tailored treatments, attempts to improve skills, and new technologies. Thereby, all recipients can safely view and manage their funds on their own.

## 6 Conclusion

This chapter goes into extensive detail about how well digital cash transfers work in SSN systems. It looks at what the study found about digital equality, government, and adoption. The findings indicate that digital cash transfers are changing how people receive money, making deals more open and accountable, and speeding up the delivery of services. Still, they stress the ongoing problems that make it difficult to fully enjoy these perks, especially for women, the old, and people who live in rural or resource-poor areas. This study combines the data with the theoretical framework to present us with additional information about how digital solutions might be able to improve social safety systems in places with low incomes.

As cash transfers have become more electronic, the process for sending out SSN payments has changed a lot. These changes support Sen's ideas about financial inclusion based on his capacity method. Digital technologies have made it easier for people to gain access to financial resources. This has made them more capable and less reliant on middlemen. According to research, some people cannot fully use these platforms because of problems in society, such as not knowing enough about technology, not having access to cell phones, and differences in income. Providing targeted solutions, like subsidising mobile devices, improving digital education programs, and funding national infrastructure, can help solve these problems and ensure that everyone has equal access to technology.

The World Bank's Good Governance Framework states that digital cash transfers have improved governance by making things more accessible, accountable, and of higher quality. People feel better about the system now that there are no more agency fees, travel and paperwork costs are cheaper, and they can see where their money is going in real time. The challenges and failures of internet connectivity, especially in rural areas, make it really important to continue investing in infrastructure and educating people. Digital cash transfer networks need improved government institutions to perform well and reliably. For example, local governments should receive training, and it should be easier for people to file complaints.

The study emphasises the need for digital usage to assess the effectiveness of digital cash exchanges. The research indicates that an individual's assessment of the platform's utility, its perceived user-friendliness, and their social and cultural values significantly influence their engagement with digital platforms. The Diffusion of Innovations Theory by Rogers and the Technology Adoption Model by Davis both support this claim. More people are using digital platforms since they are easy to utilise. Adoption, on the other hand, is still a problem, especially for older women and those with impairments. To fix these problems, we must take real steps, like creating digital literacy programs, making it easier to use the system, and giving people hands-on training so that everyone can use digital platforms effectively.

These numbers show how important it is for everyone to have access to financial services, how technology is always becoming better, and how the government supports digital currency transactions. The research shows that a thorough strategy that deals with problems in technology, society, and government is very important, even if there have been many triumphs. To make sure that everyone can benefit from digitisation, there is a need to take a multi-faceted approach that includes helping marginalised groups use digital technology, making government more efficient, and giving people the tech skills they need. Politicians might use this method to make digital money transfers work better and be easier to use. This would give everyone a safe way to manage and access their money.

The book argues that digital cash transfers are changing Bangladesh's SSN systems, which shows how important it is to fix these ongoing problems. If governments make a complete strategy that includes new technology, skill-building programs, and targeted interventions, digitisation might help the most vulnerable communities. Digital cash transfers will work if the internet is made more open and fairer and solve faults that are built into the system. This is because everyone will trust each other when they pay.

# Bridging the Gap: Key Findings, Challenges, Recommendations, and Conclusion

**Abstract** The conclusion puts together the study findings and stresses how powerful digital cash transfers are in Bangladesh's Social Safety Net (SSN) programs. It shows how important targeted actions are for solving long-lasting problems. The research shows that digitisation has greatly improved financial inclusion, government, and service delivery by making it easier for people to receive cash quickly and easily, being more open about how things work, and reducing leakages. Not having enough internet access, not knowing how to use technology well, and social and cultural barriers make it hard for some groups, like women, the elderly, and people living in rural areas, to fully capitalise these benefits. Policymakers who take a broad view and employ new technology, initiatives that teach people new skills, and tailored solutions might establish a digital cash transfer system that is more open and works better. The latter section of the chapter includes helpful recommendations, focusing on how to make digital tools simpler to get to, teach people how to use them, strengthen government processes, and deal with social and cultural concerns. The book helps achieve sustainable development goals by ensuring that the advantages of digitisation extend to the most disadvantaged populations. This makes society more fair and welcoming to everyone.


P. K. Panday, A. H. M. K. Ahsan, *Digital Revolution for the Vulnerable*, https://doi.org/10.1007/978-981-95-7980-8_7

**Keywords** Digital cash transfers • Social Safety Net programs • Bangladesh • Financial inclusion • Digital literacy • Vulnerable populations

## 1 Introduction

This chapter examines digital cash transfers inside Bangladesh's Social Safety Net (SSN) programs by synthesising the primary research findings, challenges, and policy recommendations. It compiles data on the impact of digitisation on financial inclusion, governance, and beneficiary involvement, drawing from the theoretical and empirical findings of the study. It also takes a critical look at ongoing differences in access, equality, and performance. The discussion carefully describes the structural, governmental, and sociocultural problems that stop digital SSN systems from changing things, especially for disadvantaged groups. With these ideas in mind, the chapter offers specific suggestions on how to make programs better, hold people more accountable, and encourage acceptance by everyone. Emphasising the necessity to combine technical innovation with systematic interventions addressing underlying reasons for exclusion, it ends by considering the broader consequences of the findings of digital welfare reforms in low-resource environments. This last chapter provides a road map for policymakers to maximise the advantages of digitisation by connecting research, theory, and practice, hence minimising its hazards in social protection systems.

## 2 Key Findings

The study's main findings emphasise the transforming power of digital cash transfers in SSN programs in Bangladesh, therefore fulfilling the research goals of assessing the present state of digital systems, investigating beneficiary experiences, evaluating the impact of digitisation, identifying challenges, and offering policy recommendations. These findings are structured around these goals to offer complete knowledge of the effectiveness of digital cash transfers.

### 2.1 *Current State and Effectiveness of Digitalised Cash Transfer Systems*

The findings demonstrate how digital cash transfer systems have significantly improved SSN payment transfers in Bangladesh. Cash transfer digitisation has improved the general system of efficiency, cut transaction costs, and simplified administrative tasks. For instance, 97% of recipients said digital technologies lessened their access issues, while 64% said they were "totally" removed. Digital solutions can give people more power by giving them quick and easy access to cash. Digital platforms have also cut down on the need for middlemen, which makes it harder for people to be crooked and makes sure that cash gets to the right people. Even more trustworthiness and transparency have been added to the system by letting people see and talk about payment progress in real time. These changes show how well digital cash transfers solve long-standing issues like waste, fraud, and leaving out groups that are not included. But the study shows that digital systems are not perfect right now, especially when it comes to being accessible and welcoming. For instance, only 33% of recipients have cell phones, and none of them have computers, which makes it impossible for them to use any digital platforms at all. This shows how important it is to keep investing in facilities and resources so that everyone, no matter their income, can receive and benefit from digital cash transfers. The findings show that digital cash transfer methods in Bangladesh have made it much easier to send and receive SSN payments.

### 2.2 *Beneficiaries' Experiences and Perceptions*

The study provides a deep look into how users feel about and have used the digital cash transfer system. People who received the feedback liked how easy it was to use, rely on, and access digital platforms. All recipients said the digital tool was either "easy" or "very easy" to use, which shows that user-friendly design works to get people to use it. For 98% of those who benefitted, digital solutions cut down on agent fees, and for 97%, they said they spent less on travel, which made their overall experience much better. The study does, however, bring to light other areas that also need research. For instance, 23% of users, especially those who did not know much about computers or technology, said the system was "unfriendly." Beneficiaries in rural areas also said that they had trouble getting their payments because of random technology issues and uneven internet connection. These findings show how important it is to address problems with ease and make sure that all users, even those with different levels of digital understanding, can access digital platforms.

### 2.3 *Impact of Digitisation on Efficiency, Transparency, and Accountability*

Findings like this show how automation has changed how effective, clear, and accountable cash transfer systems are in SSN programs. By getting rid of middlemen and making routine tasks easier, digital systems have greatly dropped transaction costs and increased the speed and reliability of payments. For example, 98% of those who benefited said that digital methods got rid of middleman fees, and 97% said that their travel costs went down. Tracking payments in real time and being open about the state of payments have helped to make things even more accountable and clear. Beneficiaries can now keep track of their payments and check transactions, which give them faith in the system. This is especially important in places where social safety systems have been less successful for a long time because of cheating and lack of skill. Digital systems have made it less likely for corruption to happen and made sure that cash gets to the right people by letting users see their payouts right away and cutting out middlemen. The study, on the other hand, shows that it can be hard to keep digital systems reliable and efficient, especially in rural areas. For example, 10% of UP officials said that late payments were caused by random network issues or technical issues, which could affect the distribution of payments and annoy consumers. To address these problems, continued investments in infrastructure and capacity-building are needed to make sure that digital systems work well everywhere.

## 3 Challenges in Digitising Cash Transfer Systems

The study finds several problems that keep Bangladesh's SSN programs from fully benefiting from digital cash transfers, even though digitisation has brought about a lot of progress. Several technical, social, and cultural problems need to be fixed before digital cash transfer systems can be used by everyone, work well, and last for a long time. The following is a full breakdown of these problems:

## 3.1 *Limited Access to Digital Tools*

Not having access to digital tools by the people live in remote areas is one of the significant problems. The study found that only 33% of those who were surveyed have cell phones, and none of them have computers. This low ownership rate makes digital inclusion much harder because people who do not have cell phones cannot use digital cash transfer methods right away. Most people who have cell phones use feature phones, which are not as powerful as computers. Beneficiaries cannot fully use digital services like mobile banking apps or internet platforms because they only have feature phones. This makes it harder for them to be independent and take charge of their funds. It is clear that people in rural places, where supplies and infrastructure are usually not well developed, do not have access to modern technologies. Many users in these places use borrowed or shared phones, which makes it harder for them to use digital services on their own. Beneficiaries might not want to share private financial information with other people. Because of this, using shared gadgets also raises security and privacy concerns. To solve this problem, specific steps need to be taken, such as providing low-cost smartphones to families and supporting more affordable smartphone options so that everyone can get the tools they need to use digital systems.

## 3.2 *Low Digital Literacy*

Another significant problem is that some groups, like older people and women, do not know how to use technology well. The survey found that 52% of respondents thought their digital skills were "very poor", which is a significant problem for digital inclusion. Many users have trouble with simple tasks like logging in, entering their PIN, or moving through transaction choices. They cannot access and manage their bills on their own because they do not know how to use computers, so they have to rely on local agents or family members for help. This dependence slows down payments, hurts the system's effectiveness, and makes receivers feel less in control. Women and older people have a huge digital literacy gap since they already have problems accessing digital tools and services. Cultural conventions that make it hard for women in rural places to gain an education or utilise technology may mean that they do not have many chances to develop digital skills. Also, elderly folks could be hesitant to utilise digital platforms and require more guidance to be sure of themselves and learn new things. We need specific training programs that are created for the requirements of diverse groups in order to overcome this challenge. To make sure that individuals can implement what they've learnt in real life, these programs should involve hands-on training, practical discussions, and continuous assistance.

### 3.3 *Inconsistent Internet Connectivity*

Another huge concern is that the internet connection is not always consistent, especially in rural and distant places. Most of the people who worked for or received help from the Union Parishad (UP) reported they had access to the internet all the time. But 10% of UP officials claimed that network problems or technological challenges occasionally made things take longer. These issues can make payments late and make people angry, especially when the weather is poor or the network connectivity is terrible. Connectivity problems also make digital systems less reliable, which means that recipients cannot get their funds quickly. The problems with internet connection are made worse in places that do not have enough infrastructure. Coverage for mobile networks is not always the same or reliable, and many rural parts of Bangladesh do not have access to reliable internet networks. This digital gap between cities and rural areas shows how important it is to focus infrastructure spending so that everyone, no matter where they live, has equal access to digital services. To make digital payment systems more reliable, internet connections need to be made stronger, especially in rural areas, and network stability needs to be ensured when things go wrong.

### 3.4 *Technical Glitches and Platform Instability*

The finding also shows that platform instability and technical issues are significant problems that make it hard to use digital cash transfer systems. Most of the people who received the platforms said they were reliable and consistent, but 10% of UP officials said they were "unstable" or "very unstable," especially when they were being used a lot. These technology related issues can make people lose faith in the system, lead to delays, and obstruct the handling of payments. Beneficiaries may have trouble signing in to the site, finishing transactions, or seeing their payment records if the system goes down or there are technical issues. People who are poor and depend on digital cash transfers to meet their basic needs are especially worried about technical problems. Even small changes could have a significant impact on these users, which could make it take longer for them to get the cash they need and make them lose faith in the system. To make sure that the digital platform always works well, especially when there are a lot of transactions, this problem needs to be constantly watched and improved. Giving people more ways to get help, like community-based booths or helplines, can also help lessen the effects of technology problems.

### 3.5 *Socio-Cultural Norms and Gender Dynamics*

Gender roles and social rules make it harder for some people to use technology, especially women. The findings show that 32% of those who received the cash think gender patterns have a significant impact on their ability to use digital systems. This is because many women count on male family members to get paid. Women lose their freedom and control over their cash when they have to rely on male middlemen. This makes digital cash transfers less useful for them. Women's limited access to cell phones and other digital services is made even worse by cultural norms. This is especially true in rural areas where traditional gender roles are more common. In many rural areas, women may not be able to move around freely or use technology because of cultural beliefs and societal standards. Women have a harder time using digital systems because of these problems, which make it even harder for them to get cash. To solve these problems, targeted actions such as training programs just for women, community information campaigns, and laws that make it easier for women to use digital services and cell phones are needed. Making it easier for people to use technology will help women get the most out of digital cash transfers and gain more financial freedom, which is a certainty.

### 3.6 *Affordability and Financial Constraints*

Another significant problem is that it is not always affordable or possible, especially for families with low incomes. Only 8% of those who were denied entry said it was because of cash issues, but 67% said their family income was not enough to pay for digital services. The cost of cell phones, the internet, and transaction fees can be very hard for low-income families, especially in rural areas where poverty is higher. For example, many users would find it hard to pay for the original cost of a cell phone or the ongoing costs of an internet link, which would make it harder for them to use digital systems. More often than not, women and older people have fewer ways to make cash and can see these cash problems more clearly. Focused efforts are needed to deal with this problem, such as giving low-income families free cell phones and internet access so that everyone can afford to use digital systems. Providing cheap digital services and lowering the costs of transactions will also help make digital cash transfers easier for people who need them.

### 3.7 *Regional Disparities*

Finally, differences between regions in infrastructure and supplies make things even harder for people who live in poor areas. According to the survey, 40% of UP officials said that differences in geography affected how digital cash transfers were carried out, especially in places where networks were weak or digital tools were hard to get to. It is harder for people in rural and remote areas to use digital tools when they do not have a good internet link, the right infrastructure, or enough resources. These differences show how important it is to spend on the right facilities and resources to make sure that everyone has fair access to digital services, no matter where they live.

## 4 Policy Recommendations for Strengthening Digitisation

The recommendations below are meant to help with the problems listed above and get the most out of digital cash transfers in Bangladesh's SSN programs. These suggestions are meant to be reasonable, doable, and fit the needs of many people, such as lawmakers, program managers, and people who receive the cash.

### 4.1 *Expand Access to Digital Tools*

The fact that cell phones and computers are hard to come by is a significant problem for digital inclusion, especially in rural and remote areas. Only 33% of the recipients have cell phones, and none of them have computers. This makes it harder for them to fully use digital platforms. Many users depend on borrowed or shared electronics, which limits their freedom and raises concerns about privacy and security.

**Recommendations:**

1. **Subsidise Mobile Devices for Low-Income Households:** Families with low incomes should be able to get low-cost or free cell phones through government programs that work with cell phone companies. This could be based on projects that have worked well in other countries, like India's plan to support smartphones. The digital gap hurts women and people in rural areas the most, so they should get extra help.
2. **Promote Affordable Smartphone Options:** Policymakers and phone companies should work together to make affordable smartphone models, especially for people with low incomes. Even though they are still not too expensive, these devices should have basic features like internet access and mobile banking apps that are needed for digital cash transfers.
3. **Establish Community-Based Access Points:** The government should set up community-based entry places, like digital stalls or service centres, so that people who cannot afford their own cell phones can still use digital platforms. With trained staff, these centres should have internet access to help people finish their deals.
4. **Invest in Rural Infrastructure:** Making sure everyone has equal access to digital services relies on connecting more rural and faraway places to the internet. The government should put most of its cash into building cell towers and internet networks in places that need them. Public-private agreements may speed up the building of infrastructure.

### 4.2 *Promote Digital Literacy*

Low digital literacy skills among elderly persons, women, and rural communities erode their ability to access and control their payments autonomously. The finding shows that 52% of recipients consider their digital abilities "very poor," stressing the demand for focused training courses. Many beneficiaries postpone payments and lose trust in utilising digital systems by finding even simple activities like connecting to platforms or entering their PIN difficult.

**Recommendations:**

1. **Launch Targeted Training Programs:** Digital literacy initiatives suited to the requirements of various groups should be created and carried out by the government working with NGOs and community organisations. Such as:

   - **Women-Only Training Sessions:** Women-only training courses should be planned in rural areas to overcome cultural challenges. These lessons should emphasise fundamental digital abilities such as platform logins, PIN entry, and transaction completion.
   - **Older Adult-Friendly Programs:** Programs for older people should provide practical examples, easy-to-understand directions, and continuous assistance to help them gain confidence in utilising digital tools.

2. **Incorporate Digital Literacy into Existing Programs:** Digital literacy training should be included in current SSN programs and community projects. For instance, local officials may organise digital literacy seminars during monthly payment distribution gatherings.
3. **Leverage Community Volunteers:** Train "digital champions" or local volunteers to give clients one-on-one assistance, especially in remote areas. These volunteers can help recipients negotiate digital platforms and fix typical problems.
4. **Develop Multilingual and Visual Training Materials:** Training materials should be developed in local languages, and visual aids—such as diagrams and videos—should be used to clarify important ideas for recipients with low literacy.

### *4.3 Strengthen Governance Mechanisms*

Digital systems' dependability is compromised by inconsistent internet connection and sporadic technological problems, especially in remote locations. Network problems or technological faults cause 10% of UP officials to experience delays, possibly postponing payments and frustrating beneficiaries occasionally. The absence of strong complaint redressal systems further hinders the system's responsiveness to beneficiary issues.

**Recommendations:**

1. **Invest in Internet Infrastructure:** To guarantee consistent connection, the government should prioritise Internet infrastructure improvements, especially in rural and distant locations. This includes guaranteeing network reliability during lousy weather, enhancing mobile network coverage, and extending broadband networks.
2. **Train Local Administrators:** Implementing digital cash transfer systems depends much on local authorities. Training courses should improve their technical knowledge, problem-solving capabilities, and awareness of digital platforms. This will help them to handle technological problems and offer improved beneficiary assistance quickly.
3. **Strengthen Grievance Redressal Mechanisms:** An intense grievance redressal procedure best handles delays and technical problems. Beneficiaries should be allowed to notify of problems and get quick fixes through government-run mobile-based feedback systems, online complaint portals, and specific helplines.
4. **Monitor and Evaluate System Performance:** Regular monitoring and assessment of digital platforms should be done to identify and fix technological issues, particularly during peak usage times. Real-time data analysis can assist in finding system weaknesses and enhance general performance.

### 4.4 *Simplify User Interfaces*

Many users find internet platforms challenging, especially those with little literacy or technological knowledge, as 23% called them "unfriendly," stressing the need for design and functionality enhancements. Completing transactions can be more difficult for older people and women, compromising their autonomy.

**Recommendations:**

1. **Simplify Platform Design:** Digital platforms should be rethought to be more natural and user-friendly. This means utilising simple, understandable language, streamlining the registration and authentication procedures, and lowering the number of transaction stages needed.

2. **Incorporate Visual and Voice-Based Features:** Digital platforms should provide visual aids—e.g., symbols, pictures—and voice-based instructions in local languages to serve individuals with low literacy. Users will find utilising the platform more straightforward and carrying out transactions independently.
3. **Provide Multilingual Support:** To guarantee that users from all linguistic origins can utilise the system efficiently, digital platforms should promote several local languages.
4. **Conduct Usability Testing:** Regular usability testing should be done with beneficiaries—especially those with little digital literacy—to find problematic areas and enhance the site's design. User input should guide continuous upgrades and changes.

### *4.5 Address Socio-Cultural Barriers*

Women, who usually depend on male family members to reach their payments, are further hampered by socio-cultural norms and gender dynamics. Because of cultural standards, many women have limited access to mobile phones or digital services. Hence, 32% of beneficiaries believe that gender dynamics greatly influence their capacity to use digital systems. These challenges restrict women's autonomy and control over their financial resources.

**Recommendations:**

1. **Promote Gender-Sensitive Policies:** The government should implement gender-sensitive policies to guarantee that women have equal access to digital tools and services. These covers encouraging women's ownership of mobile phones and offering financial incentives for women to engage in digital literacy initiatives.
2. **Launch Community Awareness Campaigns:** Cultural attitudes should be changed, and the advantages of digital participation for women should be promoted through community-based awareness initiatives. To guarantee widespread acceptability, these initiatives should include local leaders, religious leaders, and community leaders.
3. **Establish Women-Only Access Points:** The government should provide women-only access points, including digital booths or service centres, where cultural norms limit women's access to digital

tools so that women may use digital platforms in a secure and encouraging setting.
4. **Engage Male Family Members:** Awareness campaigns should also aim at male family members so they may help women obtain digital tools and financial independence by addressing cultural challenges.

### 4.6 *Address Affordability and Financial Constraints*

For low-income families, the price of mobile phones, internet access, and transaction fees creates notable challenges. Though 8% have financial limitations restricting access, 67% of recipients said they have enough cash to pay for digital services. Rural regions with greater poverty rates see a particularly noticeable affordability disparity.

**Recommendations:**

1. **Subsidise Internet Access:** In rural regions, the government should cooperate with mobile network providers to offer subsidised or free Internet access for low-income families. This can be free access to vital digital services or subsidised data contracts.
2. **Reduce Transaction Fees:** To lessen the financial load on recipients, transaction costs for digital cash transfers should be minimised or abolished. Government subsidies or alliances with financial service firms might help to this end.
3. **Promote Low-Cost Digital Services:** For low-income families to be able to use digital cash transfers more easily, lawmakers should back the creation of free digital services, such as mobile banking apps.

### 4.7 *Address Regional Disparities*

Infrastructure and financial gaps between regions make things harder for people who live in poor areas. Forty per cent of UP members said that regional differences affect how digital financial moves are carried out, especially in places where networks are not very strong or where digital tools are hard to get to. Some people in rural areas and faraway places find it harder to use digital platforms because they do not have access to good internet connections or the right tools.

**Recommendations:**

1. **Targeted Investments in Underserved Regions:** The government should give top importance to investing in digital infrastructure in rural and remote places. This could mean building cell towers, improving internet access, and setting up community-based access points.
2. **Public-Private Partnerships:** The facilities of underdeveloped places can grow faster with the help of public-private partnerships. For example, tax breaks or grants could encourage cell network providers to expand their service to more rural areas.
3. **Mobile Training Units:** Mobile training units could be sent to help people on the ground and teach them how to use technology, which would help places that do not have many resources.

## 5 Contribution to the Existing Body of Literature

This study adds important new information to what is already known about digital cash transfers, financial equality, digital adoption, and government. The study carefully explains how digital interventions could make low-income social safety networks better by using both theories and real-world data from Bangladesh's SSN programs. The study's contributions are looked at in more detail below:

### *5.1 Operationalising Financial Inclusion, Governance, and Digital Adoption*

By putting the ideas of financial inclusion, government, and digital adoption into practice, this study provides a solid framework for looking into the effects of digital cash transfers. According to Sen's Capability Approach, the study shows that digital cash transfers may help people do more by giving them quick and easy access to cash. Together, these ideas support Sen's claim that poverty is a loss of wealth and abilities. Because of this, digital tools can help close this gap. Digital cash transfers make it easier for people to get cash, which gives them more control over their cash and improves their overall health. The study uses the Good Governance Framework from the World Bank to look at how technology makes service delivery more efficient, accountable, and clear. The findings show that digital technologies have made things much less crooked, cut down on the need for middlemen, and made routine tasks easier. This adds to the body of literature on governance by showing how digital technology could fix problems from the past, like the fact that social security systems were often inefficient and bribed. Finally, this study blends Rogers's Diffusion of Innovations Theory with Davis's Technology Acceptance Model (TAM) to look into the factors that affect how beneficiaries accept and use digital platforms. The findings show that to get people to use technology, it needs to be easy to use, useful, and fit in with their culture. Adding real facts about the problems and helpers of adopting technology in low-income areas to the study of digital adoption is helpful.

## 5.2 *Highlighting the Interconnectedness of Financial Inclusion, Governance, and Digital Adoption*

One of the study's most notable achievements is that it looked at the links between digital adoption, government, and financial inclusion. The findings reveal that digital cash transfers need to fix significant flaws with the system, such as bad infrastructure, low digital literacy, and social and cultural norms, if they want to operate. For instance, problems with Internet access, not knowing how to use technology efficiently, and the way men and women talk to each other may all make it tougher for digital systems to make governance and cash more equitable. This comprehensive approach will impart significant knowledge to policymakers and practitioners on the creation and implementation of efficient digital cash transfer systems in low-income regions. The study also highlights how crucial it is to have a strategy that involves a lot of people in order to cope with these issues. For example, mobile phone companies, the government, and neighbourhood organisations need to work together to get more people to adopt digital technologies. On the other hand, promoting digital literacy and altering social and cultural norms need focused initiatives that include local lawmakers, community leaders, and those who will benefit. The research enhances the understanding of digital financial systems by providing a comprehensive framework for examining their impacts and identifying methods to optimise their functionality with an emphasis on interdependencies among various components.

### 5.3 *Contributing to the Global Evidence on Digital Cash Transfers*

This study contributes to the expanding corpus of research examining the effectiveness of digital tools in enhancing governmental operations and mitigating financial disparities. The findings corroborate those of other global academics regarding the transformative effects of digital cash transfers, such as diminishing fraud, eliminating intermediaries, and enhancing service delivery. For instance, studies conducted in India (Muralidharan et al. 2016) and Sub-Saharan Africa (GSMA 2020) have demonstrated that digital aid programs may enhance transparency and accountability. This book builds on previous work by providing concrete examples from Bangladesh, where digital cash transfers have been used extensively. The research concentrates on issues that are specific to the context and require resolution to guarantee equity and inclusivity. It is crucial to bridge the digital divide since many of the people who need help do not have cell phones or computers, especially those who live in rural regions. The study's findings about the influence of gender roles and sociocultural norms on digital acceptability contribute to our understanding of digital inclusion by emphasising the necessity of addressing cultural challenges in low-income regions.

### 5.4 *Providing a Framework for Future Research*

The study provides a robust basis for future research on digital cash transfers and SSN programs. The study presents significant challenges that require further investigation using both empirical data and other theoretical perspectives. For instance, researchers may examine how digital cash transfers affect individuals' spending behaviours, health, and income-generating capacity over time. Moreover, cross-contextual comparative study might help identify best practices and lessons learnt for implementing digital cash transfer systems across diverse settings. The study also underlines the importance of research on new technologies, such as blockchain and artificial intelligence, in improving digital cash transfers' efficiency, transparency, and inclusiveness. Though their application calls for close attention to ethical, legal, and technological concerns, these technologies might help lower transaction costs even more, strengthen data security, and improve the user experience.

## 5.5 *Informing Policy and Practice*

Finally, the study adds to what is already been done by giving professionals and lawmakers useful ideas. The findings make it clear that we need to deal with systemic problems like poor infrastructure, low digital literacy, and social and cultural norms to make sure that digital cash transfers work. Recommendations of the study—such as subsidising mobile devices, encouraging digital literacy, and improving governance mechanisms—offer a road map for policymakers trying to improve the effectiveness of SSN programs. The study presents a comprehensive framework for establishing and managing digital cash transfer systems, emphasising the interconnectedness of financial inclusion, governance, and digital adoption. This strategy makes sure that the benefits of digitisation are shared properly and reach the most impoverished groups. This helps reach the larger goal of sustainable development.

## 5.6 *Limitations and Future Research*

This study has some limitations, even though it does provide some useful information. The cross-sectional approach makes it harder to look at long-term effects, and the fact that people had to do their own study for the data could lead to bias, for example. Longitudinal studies that track changes in recipients' access, use, and happiness over time could help solve these problems in the future. Comparative research in various settings and the investigation of developing technologies like blockchain and artificial intelligence will also help better understand the scalability and sustainability of digital cash transfer systems. This research adds notable contribution to the current body of literature by operationalising the concepts of financial inclusion, governance, and digital adoption, stressing their interdependence and offering context-specific insights from Bangladesh. Policymakers, practitioners, and academics trying to improve the influence of digital cash transfers in low-income settings will find great value in the findings and recommendations of the study. The research aims to lower poverty, support sustainable development through an inclusive and fair digital environment, and tackle systematic challenges.

## 6 Conclusion

This study focuses on how the power of digital cash transfers is changing in Bangladesh's SSN programs. It brings attention to the problems that still need to be fixed to make sure that everyone is treated fairly and includes everyone. The findings show that even though problems like limited access to technology, a lack of digital knowledge, and social and cultural norms still make it hard to fully enjoy these benefits, digitisation has made financial inclusion, government, and service delivery much better. Policymakers can establish a more inclusive and successful digital cash transfer system that offers everyone more power by making a whole strategy that incorporates new technology, tries to increase people's abilities, and focuses on specific problems. The SSN payment service has improved a lot since cash transfers went digital. Digital solutions have made them less reliant on intermediaries and helped them keep track of their cash by making it simple for them to get to cash resources. This goes along with Sen's capacity approach, which says that we should assist individuals in realising their maximum potential for happiness. It also makes things more transparent and accountable by getting rid of middlemen fees, lowering the cost of travel and study, and putting in place real-time payment tracking that follows the World Bank's Good Governance Framework. People who get services now have more faith in the system because of these changes, which have made the delivery of services better.

The study finds several problems that need to be fixed to make sure that the most vulnerable groups get the benefits of digitisation. A significant problem is that not everyone has easy access to digital tools. This is especially true in rural and remote areas. Only 33% of the recipients have cell phones, and none of them have computers. This makes it harder for them to fully use digital platforms. Unreliable internet connections and random technical issues make these problems even worse, especially in places that are not well off. Some groups, such as elderly persons and women who do not know how to utilise technology properly, also have a tougher time managing and getting to their own cash. For instance, 52% of those who answered indicated their computer abilities were "very poor," which shows how important it is to have specialised training programs. More problems are caused by gender roles and societal norms. For example, many women count on male family to get their cash, which limits their freedom and control over cash.

To deal with these problems, the study offers a complete plan that includes new technologies, projects that build people's skills, and targeted interventions. We need to make more digital tools available, especially for women and families with modest budgets, so that everyone who benefits may utilise them. This may involve paying for internet connection in remote locations, pushing affordable smartphones, or giving people cash when they acquire mobile devices. To help people feel more confident and able to use digital platforms, they require focused training sessions that teach digital skills. These programs should be able to benefit different populations, such as women and older persons. They should give participants hands-on training and ongoing support to make sure they can use their skills.

One of the main objectives is to make government processes stronger. Investing in internet infrastructure, training classes for local officials, and strong ways to file complaints are all important for making digital systems reliable and fast. Digital platforms would be easier for people who do not know much about technology or reading to use if they had less of an interface and more features like voice-based directions, visual tools, and multilingual help. To promote gender equality in digital participation, we also need to address sociocultural concerns through community-based policies and programs. Women may obtain their payments and influence how people think about it by taking part in training programs and awareness initiatives that are only for women. By fixing these structural issues, Bangladesh might show how to make digital social safety programs operate successfully in low-income communities. Digital cash transfers function best when everyone who gets them can use digital services, no matter where they live, how much cash they make, or what gender they are. The government, businesses, non-governmental organisations (NGOs), and community organisations all need to work together to make this happen. The study's findings and recommendations can assist practitioners and legislators in enhancing the effectiveness of digital cash transfers and ensuring that the advantages of digitisation are accessible to the most disadvantaged populations.

Digital cash transfers assist in achieving the objective of sustainable growth in the long run. It can assist the United Nations in meeting its Sustainable Development Goals (SDGs). SDG 1 (No Poverty) and SDG 10 (Reduced Inequalities) may be achieved by eradicating poverty, fostering financial inclusion, and enhancing governmental efficiency. The study's emphasis on equity and inclusion ensures that the most disadvantaged populations receive the advantages of technology. This makes the world a better place for everyone. Policymakers can make social protection programs more efficient and effective by using new technologies, projects that help people learn new skills, and targeted interventions. They can also give recipients the tools they need to become more financially independent and improve their health.

## References

Global System for Mobile Communications (GSMA). (2020). The mobile economy 2020. GSMA.

Muralidharan, K., Niehaus, P., & Sukhtankar, S. (2016). Building state capacity: Evidence from biometric smartcards in India. American Economic Review, 106(10), 2895–2929. https://doi.org/10.1257/aer.20141346

# Index






P. K. Panday, A. Ahsan, *Digital Revolution for the Vulnerable*, https://doi.org/10.1007/978-981-95-7980-8

The manufacturer's authorised representative in the EU is Springer Nature Customer Service Centre GmbH, Europaplatz 3, 69115 Heidelberg, Germany. If you have any concerns regarding our products, please contact ProductSafety@springernature.com

Printed and bound by CPI Group (UK) Ltd, Croydon, CR0 4YY

22/09/2026

02220962-0004